HUMAN RELATIONS AND MODERN MANAGEMENT

STUDIES IN INDUSTRIAL ECONOMICS

EDITED BY

J. L. MEIJ, Professor of Industrial Economics, State University of Groningen, The Netherlands

E. M. HUGH-JONES, Professor of Economics, University College of N. Staffordshire, England

JOHN PERRY MILLER, Professor of Economics, Yale University, U.S.A.

QUADRANGLE BOOKS/CHICAGO

HUMAN RELATIONS
AND
MODERN MANAGEMENT

EDITED BY

E. M. HUGH-JONES

QUADRANGLE BOOKS/CHICAGO

First published in The Netherlands 1958 by
North-Holland Publishing Company, Amsterdam

First published in the United States 1959
QUADRANGLE BOOKS, INC., CHICAGO 1

Library of Congress Catalog Card No. 59-15786

Printed in the Netherlands
Dijkstra's Drukkerij N.V., voorheen Boekdrukkerij Gebrs. Hoitsema, Groningen

INTRODUCTION TO THE SERIES

As business life becomes more complex, so the field of industrial economics grows increasingly important. Though the problems in the micro-world of the firm and the influence of its behaviour on society as a whole are studied extensively there still exists a lack of that collaboration between students of different nationalities which has proved to be so fruitful in other sciences and even in other parts of economics.

Another obstacle to the development of this field of our science is the relatively few contacts in many countries between economists and business men.

The principal aim of this present series is to stimulate study and research in this part of economics and to further an interchange of ideas and results on an international basis. In general it is expected that contributors will not only give the present state of informed opinion in their respective countries on the subjects treated but also include the results of their own study and research. Although this may sometimes lead to some overlapping the editors feel that this may not be undesirable, in so far as it serves to link together the parts of the subject.

As the reader will see, the level of treatment is that appropriate to an audience of graduate academic standard. Nevertheless, the volumes are not addressed to academic scholars only but also to those engaged in management. A knowledge of basic economic principles is assumed.

If the publishing of this series gives an impulse to the fostering of international collaboration in this important section of economics and focuses attention on the necessity for further development of industrial economics and on the mutual benefit economics as well as practical business life may derive from it, the goal of the editors will be achieved.

THE EDITORS

BIOGRAPHICAL NOTES

DR. J. L. MEIJ: Professor of Industrial Economics, State University of Groningen, The Netherlands.
Author of: *Weerstandsvermogen en Financiële Reorganisatie van Ondernemingen* (Financial Stability and Financial Reconstruction of Enterprises); *Leerboek der Bedrijfshuishoudkunde I en II* (Principles of Industrial Economics, Vols I & II).

W. H. SCOTT, B. A., Ph. D.: Reader in Industrial Sociology, University of Liverpool, England.
Author of: *Industrial Leadership and Joint Consultation; Industrial Democracy-a Revaluation;* (with J. A. Banks et al.) *Technical Change and Industrial Relations.*

ROBERT L. KAHN, Ph. D.: Program Director of the Survey Research Center and Associate Professor of Psychology, University of Michigan, Ann Arbor, Michigan, U.S.A.

EDWIN YOUNG, M.A., Ph.D.: Professor of Economics and Chairman of the Economics Department, University of Wisconsin, Madison, Wis., U.S.A. Sec-Treasurer, Industrial Relations Research Association.
Editor (with M. Derber) of: *Labor and the New Deal.*

N. S. ROSS, M.A., Ph.D.: Senior Lecturer in Employer-Employee Relations, Faculty of Commerce and Social Science, University of Birmingham, England. Sometime convener of shop stewards, trade union branch secretary and director of a retail co-operative society.

E. F. L. BRECH, B.A., B.Sc(Econ), M.B.I.M.: Senior Partner, Urwick, Orr & Partners Ltd., Consultant specialists in organization and management.
Author of: *Management, its Nature & Significance;* (with L. Urwick) *The Making of Scientific Management; Organisation, the Framework of Management.*
Editor and part-Author of *The Principles & Practice of Management.*

R. W. REVANS, B.Sc., Ph.D. M.I.M.E.: Professor of Industrial Administration, University of Manchester, England. Formerly Research Fellow of Emmanuel College, Cambridge. Director of Education, National Coal Board. Research consultant on management structure of British coal mines.

E. WIGHT BAKKE, B.A., Ph.D.: Sterling Professor of Economics, Director of Yale Labor & Management Center, Yale University, New Haven, Conn., U.S.A.
Author of: *The Unemployed Man; Unions Management and the Public; The Fusion Process; Structure and Dynamics of Organization; Bonds of Organization.*

CONTENTS

PREFACE

It is very proper that a Series on Industrial Economics should begin with a study of Human Relations and Modern Management. For it is being increasingly realized that the ultimate concern of industrial management is with human beings, that no amount of technical expertise in devising mechanical instruments, whether of production or of administration, is of any avail if the human factor be ignored.

The plan, such as it is, of this volume is designed to explore these relations and their implications for management in three situations, among workers on the shop floor, when labour is organized, and at the highest level of management itself. In two preliminary chapters are given first an esquisse of a general theory of management and secondly an analysis of the particular setting — the factory — in which this pattern of relations is woven. A later chapter considers the relevance to the problem of the particular dimension of size, and in a final chapter the function of management is discussed.

I have not sought to impose any particular point of view on the various authors. It may well be that the careful reader will find some overlaps and repetitions; I hope he will agree that these are helpful in linking together the various parts of the volume. He may also find divergencies of view and even disagreement: I would ask him to reflect that the study of human relations and the study of management are a like in their infancy, and it is early yet to expect a completely agreed canon of doctrine.

Yet agreement is probably more extensive than might appear. It is not, I think, desirable that an editor of a volume such as this should try to draw all its lessons — far better that the reader should do this for himself. But I may be allowed to indicate briefly some of the more obvious points of agreement that seem to emerge.

First and foremost is the importance of the human factor in industry — a point that has already been made. As was said by a well-known publicity officer in one of the British Wartime Ministries, "People matter". But this factor is not a simple homogeneous one. Not only are people infinitely various as individuals, they also form groups both formal, as trade unions, and informal. The pattern of human relations thus resembles that of a highly intricate tapestry, involving not only relations between individual and individuals, but those between individuals and groups (formal and informal, the group to which he belongs or those to which he does not belong) and between groups and groups. In all these there is likely to be exhibited a mutual tension, a clash of interests or goals, quite apart from any conflict with the particular interest or goal of management, whether this be defined as maximum profit, maximum output, or just survival. Thus any theory of management must be prepared to operate as it were on two levels, or in two dimensions. Analytically it can be usefully developed in a framework of control, and worked out with the aid of such concepts as "span" and "depth". Operationally it must seek to relieve these tensions, reconcile interests, harmonize goals and thus provide the maximum of self-realization both for individuals and for groups. This will be made more difficult as the size of groups increases, and unless a sound pattern of relations exists within management itself. But the degree of success in achieving this object is the ultimate test of management and, even, the condition of its material success.

The index was compiled by Dr. W. H. Scott and I am most grateful to him for undertaking this laborious task.

One point of arrangement must be mentioned. All references that are primarily concerned with sources are indicated by small numerals and have been grouped at the end of the various chapters. Only notes explanatory of the text have been put at the foot of the page. This was my own idea because I thought it more convenient for the reader. But if I was wrong, and it is in fact less convenient, then I alone am to be blamed, as indeed for other demerits the reader may find in this book. Its merits must be attributed to the various authors whose collaboration I have been so fortunate as to obtain.

E. M. HUGH-JONES

December, 1957

Chapter 1

HUMAN RELATIONS AND FUNDAMENTAL PRINCIPLES OF MANAGEMENT[1]

J. L. MEIJ

Institute of Industrial Economics, State University of Groningen

The aim of this chapter is to attempt to outline a theory of management and to show the central position of human relations in such a theory.

Though we must acknowledge that there are as many definitions of management as there are authors in this field, there is, nevertheless, a growing agreement that the concept has a twofold character. First, and in this we are considering the concept dynamically, we can define management as a process of exerting leadership over followers. Secondly, it consists in the creation of an organization devised to allocate authority, responsibility and accountability within a group.[2]

If we want to treat the different subjects in this field against a more general background, we must be aware of the fact that a general theory of management is still lacking. Usually management problems have been treated descriptively instead of analytically and also more as an art than as a science. Nevertheless, we are convinced that a theory of management is not only necessary but must also be possible. The heart of all management-problems lies in the fact that management in its essence always is control. Business activities are economic activities; that means that they must be planned and, above all, controlled activities.

In my opinion this might be at least an acceptable starting-point for developing a general theory of management.

Therefore the basic principle underlying all organization patterns and all kinds of management-technique is to be found in what we might call the scope of control, that is the sphere in which control is effective.[3]

First we can distinguish the span of control defined as the number of immediate subordinates for whom one leader can be responsible.

In this definition control is only considered in its width, or, as we may say, in a horizontal direction. We can nevertheless see the scope of control also in a second dimension, in its depth, the effectiveness of leadership from top to bottom. This may be called the vertical dimension of control.

In accordance with these two aspects or dimensions of the scope of control we can speak by analogy with the practice of business-cycle theorists of the widening and the deepening of the scope of control. Widening then is the process of giving the leader the ability to control more workers on the level just below his own, in other words the process of enlarging the span of control; deepening that of improving the quality of reception of the leader's commands at the lower levels and finally at the bottom of the pyramid.

As we will show in what follows the organization structure as well as the technical means used to exert leadership can be brought within the same description, the extending of the scope of control in the sense of widening as well as in the sense of deepening.

Moreover, because managerial control is control of men, this starting-point seems particularly apt to serve as the background for a treatise on human relations in business. Even when not explicitly stated, it may be considered implicit in all discussions of the subject.

In a growing enterprise it will soon appear that the leader's scope of control is limited. His span of control has limitations to be found in the leader's knowledge, in his capacity to watch the performance of a number of subordinates, in his available time and in his personality. Limitations are also inherent in the degree of difficulty of the work to be performed and finally in the knowledge of the workers and their willingness to collaborate with each other and with the leader. The limitation of the span of control gives rise to stratification, the formation of management levels, so that as the span of control is limited, more levels come into existence.

If we call the number of leaders L, that of subordinates A and r the span of control (being the same on all levels 1 to n) we find the following formula for the total number of leaders:

$$L = \frac{1}{r}A + \frac{1}{r^2}A + \ldots + \frac{1}{r^n}A = \frac{1}{r^n}A\frac{r^n - 1}{r - 1}$$

As L represents the total number of leaders at all levels, we have expressed this number in our formula as a function of r and n.

The items r and n not being independent variables, we can express n in terms of r, or r in terms of n, as the case may be.

If we may suppose that the top is formed by one leader, president or general manager and therefore $\frac{1}{r^n} A = 1$, we can write for r:

$$r = \sqrt[n]{A}$$

The span of control is presented here as a function of the stratification, the number of levels. As already said, we can conversely express the stratification as a function of the span of control:

$$n = \frac{\log \cdot A}{\log \cdot r}$$

As log. A is constant, A being given, n and log. r have a constant product; therefore we can say n is inversely proportionate to log. r. An increase of the span of control therefore causes a diminution of the number of levels proportionate to the increase of the logarithm of the span of control.

The number of leaders can be represented as a function of the span of control in this case by:

$$L = \frac{A-1}{r-1}$$

With this formula the total number of leaders can be derived —A being given—from the span of control.*

Our formulae, though based on somewhat unrealistically simplified conditions, nevertheless demonstrate the great influence of the span of control on the number of leaders, and the number of management-levels i.e. on the functional distance between the leaders at the top and the subordinates at the bottom.

Enlarging the span of control, or, as we may say, widening its scope, does not mean only a diminution of the number of subordinate leaders but also of management-levels and therefore a diminution of the functional distance from top to bottom.

However, this distance still exists and therefore we have to find means to deepen control as well as to widen it. Thus we can say that all problems of management are concerned with widening and deepening the scope of control.[4]

* The above functions hold true for every finite number of top-managers. If we suppose two, three or more leaders at the top, we find:

$$L = \frac{A-2}{r-1} \quad L = \frac{A-3}{r-1} \quad \ldots.$$

In accordance with the twofold character of management we can divide those problems into two groups, one concerned with the organization structure and the other with the means of exerting leadership. As will be shown, both have their human relations aspect.

First we will focus our attention on the organization structure. It can be defined as the system according to which the work to be done, the whole activity of the business, is grouped together in functions and how these functions, and therewith the different functionaries, relate to each other.

With the functions an adequate authority ought also to be distributed. This necessity is often forgotten. Many leaders will voluntarily share a part of their functions and delegate something of their work to lower levels, but want to hold the same authority as they did before. Here we come to an inadequacy in organization structure which often gives rise to unpleasant conditions of work for the leaders on lower levels as well as for the labourers they control.

Before discussing the question how to enlarge the leader's scope of control by an adequate organization structure we may ask: why do not we try to adapt the size of the business to the leader's scope of control instead of looking for measures to enlarge it. Indeed, if we fear that the scope of control will be exceeded, we can split up the business into a certain number of units, each with its own leader.*

This form of decentralization in management and managerial control can often be seen applied in large concerns. Nevertheless, it is easy to understand that this solution is only a partial one. It is applicable on the higher levels of management, but not on the lower. We cannot organize every department or every shift in an enterprise as an independent unit, e.g. splitting up a dock-yard into drilling, transporting, machining and other enterprises. We should never forget that an enterprise in respect of its constitution and structure is a unity in itself. Just as the organs of the human body cannot exist on their own, so it is impossible for the departments of a business unit to have an independent life. We, therefore, cannot see those departments as if they were autonomous units. In our opinion this process of decentralization is suitable only if such departments have their own buying and selling markets and if their connecting

* As may be easily seen, the scope of control has a decisive significance in this device—sometimes called substantive decentralization, — for it indicates how far we have to extend this decentralization.

link is to be found only in finance or research. Even in these cases the problem of the scope of control still exists for the management of the whole concern and also for the lower levels of management in each independent part of the concern.

Nevertheless, we have seen that in practice these splitting-up processes are often introduced, but without successfully eliminating the consequences of the limitation of the scope of control while at the same time introducing the dangers of competition within the concern itself. A department of a concern will never be the same as an independent shop. For this reason splitting up a growing business into a series of independent units can never give an allround satisfactory solution to the management problem.[5]

This kind of splitting-up process may be called decentralization in management.[6] It is, however, a process of eliminating management of the concern as a whole, until in the end some financial ties between the several parts of the business alone remain. Nevertheless, even financial control has its limitation of span.*

In this process the size of the business unit is adapted to the capacity of the leader. We do not try to enlarge the scope of control but going the other way round try to contract the size of the business unit.

There is, however, another way of adaptation to the leader's capacity, viz. managing by boards. The formation of boards can be considered as a means of subdividing the task of managing and distributing it over a number of managers. In lieu of splitting up the unit, the task is subdivided.

Like the former process this one is also limited to the top rank of management and is not applicable to the lower. It has the advantage that the size of the unit does not depend on the capacity of the leader alone. His limited capacity forms no hindrance to large-scale production with all its advantages. Meanwhile, however, this form of adaptation to the capacity of the leader has its own disadvantages. It leads to management by the majority and thus it is a form of decentralization of authority and responsibility. Here the danger exists that the members of the board may not act as a unity. Each of them may have his own objectives and as a consequence management is weakened.

There are two main ways of subdividing the task of managing, viz.

* There may be other ties holding a concern together, e. g. the experience or wisdom of a central laboratory.

along product lines or along functional lines. The latter is the preferable one, since the unit of activity can be preserved better than in the first way. In large concerns, moreover, where the business is already split up into several units, the functionally organized board can be a means of tying those units together. The managing board becomes more and more similar to the board of directors in smaller companies. In my opinion here lies a reason for a different structure of top management in large concerns as compared with that in smaller companies. In the large ones we will often find a board of managing directors acting under the supervision of an advisory council that represents the interests of stockholders.* The latter then has taken over the trustee-ship function of the board of directors of a smaller company. Only the management-function remains in the hands of such a board of managing directors.

Though we must concede that in large concerns individual leadership must be replaced by government by boards, we cannot say that this gives a solution of the problems arising from the limitations of men's scope of control. It is clear that we cannot replace every leader whose scope of control tends to be exceeded by that of a board.

However, there are means to enlarge the leader's scope of control in the way the organization is built up.

We may divide the leader's work into two categories, viz. constitutional work and directing work.

It is rather difficult to draw a sharp line of demarcation between the two. We can only say that all work that can be repeated, all work remaining the same in the leader's task for a shorter or a longer time, can be made constitutional. It can be done according to a previously prepared pattern or directive. The directive once prepared can be used for a whole range of orders of similar character. We can therefore try to divide the work of the leader between two sorts of men: those who make the general directives and those who are only giving particular orders; the latter are the leaders in the most strict sense. The span of control can be widened substantially by doing this. For constitutional work the span is practically unlimited. Perhaps, one could better say that constitutional work, as it is not "leading" work at all, has no span of control. The

* Compare for example the management structure of Unilever and other large concerns.

drawing up of an instruction or directive can be done for one labourer, for ten or for a thousand; the amount of work needed remains practically the same.

By splitting off this constitutional work a lot of weight is lifted from the shoulders of the leader of a group. Now he has only to give his particular orders and to supervise their performance. Sometimes he has to modify the prepared orders as circumstances change but he has never to prepare the directives himself. As constitutional work requires specialist knowledge we can say that splitting it off diminishes the limitation of the span of control caused by the need for such knowledge. In other words: it widens the span of knowledge.

It is obvious that all leadership work is simplified if it can be done according to schemes prepared previously and moreover it is obvious that by simplifying the work of the leader his span of control is widened. Moreover, we have good reason to expect that the total number of persons involved in management will diminish. As constitutional work has no limitations as to the number of persons it can affect nor the period of time over which its results can be applied, provided the operations to be performed remain the same, it will be clear that the decrease of the number of leaders due to the widening of the span of control will not be offset by an increase in the number of men now needed to do constitutional work.

Meanwhile, this splitting off has some other advantages, particularly in relation to the human relations aspect of the problem of designing workable patterns of organization.

First we might state that the qualities making a man a good commander are not the same as those that are necessary for a good organizer. It will seldom be the case that one man fulfills both conditions in the same degree for we have to do here with two different types of men. In this respect splitting off constitutional work serves as a means of widening the span of control in its relation to the capacity of the leader. Here we can say that the limitations due to personality are diminished.

The constitutional work becomes the task of specialized staff-employees. The splitting off of constitutional work gives rise to the so-called line-and-staff organization. Almost all modern organization schemes are built upon this line-and-staff principle.

Moreover, such splitting off has still another human relations aspect. It enables the desire of workers to have a say in management to be fulfilled in a more practical way than by means of works councils of any type, because this splitting off enables management to consult groups of labourers, directly interested, on measures of a constitutional character. Works councils on the contrary can have but a very limited significance in business life. We can hardly expect it to give great satisfaction to the workers just to have the possibility of electing their representatives on a council. The questions brought to such councils are for the most part of minor importance. Leadership is not a subject for councils but for individuals. The forms of democracy developed in local and central government cannot be introduced into business life. That they can is the fallacious belief upon which all the ideas of works councils have been based. Members of parliament or of county councils are elected to give effect to the principles of the parties they represent. We cannot run a business along the various principles represented by the different members of a works council.

The splitting off of constitutional work is a means for widening control.* The deepening of control might be furthered by other means and institutions.

First we will mention the function of the controller. As the number of levels increases because of the limitation of the span of control and the distance grows from top-management to ultimate labourer we are confronted with several disadvantage. First of all there is the danger of distortion of an order on its way from the top to the bottom. On the other side there exists a still greater danger, the mutilation of reports on their way from the bottom to the top. Here we need a cross-section showing the facts as they are at a certain moment. The controller and his staff, who are not in charge of the performance of the production processes as such, are better able to give the required information than the bosses under whose supervision the work has been completed. It must be the task of the controller to bring out all deviations from the leader's requirements or at least their consequences.

Meanwhile control can be made simpler and more effective if we are able to distribute tasks in such a way that performances control one another to a greater or less extent; in other words, if we are able to set up internal checks. Therefore, adequate distribution of functions can be considered in this respect as a method of enlarging the span of control. Some functions are to be regarded as real

* It is certainly not the only one as is shown on p. 11 *et sqq*. Several means of deepening control also enlarge it.

incompatibilities. The performance of the one cannot be combined with that of the other. A bookkeeper for instance cannot be put in charge as a cashier, nor in general can he have proxies. In general we cannot combine functions of registering and store-keeping, nor can we give decisive management power to registrars. Though these principles are familiar to auditors and accountants, they are often set at naught in business life and not only in smaller units. Nevertheless, they are very important, and not only in the administrative section but for the business as a whole.

If these rules are infringed, effective control is hardly possible, even with the utmost endeavour. Therefore it seems to be the task of good organization not only to avoid these incompatibilities but also to create effective internal checks. Making an organization adequate in this respect means not only widening but also and even in the first place deepening the scope of control. Where internal checks are lacking, control becomes more and more difficult and, of course, its span as well as its depth limited.

The structure of the organization, however, must provide to employees and workers opportunities for action both as individuals and as groups. This seems necessary, for otherwise the limits of the span of control will soon be exceeded, as the theories of Davis and Graicunas have shown.[7] From the fact stated by Graicunas, that if more labourers are employed a fast-growing number of group-relationships and cross-relationships comes into existence, these authors have concluded that the span of control must be strictly limited.

According to more modern views and experience, those relationships need not be formed or conducted by the leader. It even seems much better when they function without action by the leader. Within the group an intensive coordination must be assured so that it acts as a single person. The relationships within the group are controlled by the group itself. Thus the span of control may be widened substantially by group-formation. However, we cannot have those groups acting as if they were more or less autonomous bodies. As to the groups on lower levels of management, we must state that they are not created to realize the objectives of the business. The possibility exists that those group-activities at lower levels work against the penetration of the will of the leaders in the lower levels of the business. Therefore those group-formations, granted that they are widening the span of control, call at the same time for deepening control.

We might make use of group-relationships and group-activities, but only after the group accepts the objectives of the business as its own. This is not possible without giving directives to the group and its members. Much can be done by the group itself, but the activities of the group always must be coordinated with and directed to the final objectives of the enterprise. This can only be done by the leader who derives his authority from delegation by top management.

Moreover, we must not exaggerate the importance of group-relations at the level of performance. If, as in many cases, labourers often change their positions there cannot be a development of strong group-relationships. On the other hand, if those relationships do in fact produce a body acting as an individual, we lose the mutual check of the members on each other. Thus as the coordinating task of the leader diminishes, his controlling activities will increase.

We now turn to consider particular management techniques, the means the manager might use in action. It seems neither possible nor necessary to sum up the whole arsenal of techniques management can apply. We will limit ourselves for the most part to standardizing and budgeting.

Standards are means of widening the span of control as they enable the leader to give his commands a simpler form. Moreover, the setting up of standards can be considered as constitutional work and be split off.

Nevertheless, standards are also means of deepening the scope of control. As far as the performance of commands at the higher level is based on standards, there can be no doubt about the leader's will. Standards of performance, once fixed, are decisive for the use of raw material, labour and other factors of production, for to each method of performance there corresponds a certain amount of labour, raw material and other means of production. It is an economic problem to find the right method of performance out of several that are technically possible. Therefore, the fixing of standards is neither in the first place, nor only, a technical question, but also, and still more, an economic one.

The standard of performance may vary with the scale of production, with the size of the series of products and with the values of the different factors of production. As a consequence the amounts of labour and of the other factors used in the process of production vary too. Therefore the optimum method of performance and the standards deduced from it are relative items.* However, we cannot always pursue the optimum method of performance. If, e.g. the equipment cannot be altered, we are obliged to choose the best method within the limits given by the actual equipment. These standards can be described as "building blocks" for making instructions with respect to planning, budgeting, routing and scheduling as well.[8]

In large concerns it becomes impossible for the managers at the top to direct their leaders in lower ranks by immediate command even if standards for the ultimate performance are in use. Budgeting and budgetary control then become necessary. This necessity is a consequence of geographical or functional distance. We first saw the development of the budgeting system in business life in our country in the companies operating in our former colonies, especially in the East Indies. The top managers of those companies for various reasons remained in Europe, near the markets where their products were sold. This was rational in a certain respect, but on the other hand they could not give any direct command to their employees overseas. Hence the budget system was introduced to meet the difficulties.[9]

Nowadays the functional distances arising in large concerns are producing the same difficulties. Here, just as in the case of geographical dispersion, the will of the leader can hardly reach the lower levels of management, nor the level of performance. The budget system has therefore been chosen to solve the problem. The budget system once applied becomes a method of distributing authority and responsibility over the lower ranks of management. Therefore, with this system the scope of control can be enlarged in depth or deepened to a substantial degree. Here, as in the case of standards, the work of preparing the budget can be split off from the leaders and shifted to specialists.

Thus those means are apt to widen as well as to deepen control, though we would prefer to see budgeting, arising from the functional distance between top and bottom, as a means for deepening.

However, we can handle those means not only as commands or even directives but at the same time as devices for interesting the workers in the problems of management and giving them a say therein. We can use their knowledge of the tasks to be performed in

* This conclusion is in accordance with those reached by Ragnar Frisch, Kenneth E. Boulding, Sune Carlson and others in their theory of production.

setting up standards and making preparations for the budget. In this way we can stimulate their interest in the business, and can hope to make labourers feel themselves to be important and responsible links in the process of realizing its objectives. Therefore, it seems to be of great value to set up the standards in agreement with, and after discussion with, the workers. This produces a far better condition for the realization of standards and budgets, for now the labourers are responsible for things they agreed to beforehand. We may therefore conclude that both widening and deepening the scope of control opens large possibilities of giving labourers a say in management.

The application of modern principles of management, therefore, gives us the possibility of offering opportunities to labourers and leaders on lower levels to participate in managerial decisions in cases which have a real meaning for them, i.e. in questions relating to their own daily work. The "new look" of standards and budgets, therefore, is that they are no longer commands but agreements between management and workers.

The participation of workers in management in this way has still another advantage. As we have shown, the possibility exists of widening and deepening the scope of control of the leaders as business grows. It is clear that there is not only a necessity to expand the scope of control; it is necessary also to enlarge the possibility of the leader being responsible for a larger group of men. In accordance with our definition of the scope of control, we may call the total number of workers for whom the leader can be held responsible his scope of responsibility.

We now may ask: is it equally possible to expand the scope of responsibility? In my opinion the means at present in use to enlarge the scope of control do not automatically widen or deepen the scope of responsibility.

With task- or function-delegation authority-delegation is necessarily connected. One cannot fulfill his task without the authority to make the necessary decisions and issue the commands required.

However, there is not such a complete similarity between the distribution of authority and that of responsibility. It is quite true that everyone invested with authority has to bear the responsibility for the way he makes use of it, but only in a certain respect can we say that with the authority responsibility is delegated.

In spite of the fact that authority-delegation also means a

delegation of responsibility, the total responsibility of the delegator is not diminished. Here we have a fundamental difference as compared with task- and authority-delegation. We might even say that for those who have delegated part of their tasks, their responsibility still exists and is even increased in a certain respect.

Before the delegation they were responsible for the task now delegated. After the delegation the delegate, of course, is responsible for the fulfillment of the delegated task and thus must get the authority to do what is required. For the delegator—we are only speaking of delegation within the enterprise—the original responsibility for the performance of the delegated part of his task remains the same. Moreover in a certain respect he has got more responsibility. He is responsible now for the delegation as such and also for the delegate.

The delegator has to accept responsibility for the delegation. He must be able to justify, if required, his decision to delegate. He has also to take over responsibility for the man to whom he delegated a part of his task.[10]

Now we are able to state a remarkable difference between the effects of expanding business on control and on responsibility. If there is a danger of exceeding the leader's span of control, a part of his task and the corresponding authority can be delegated. New levels of management then come into existence. Thus the task of the leader is adapted to his span of control. In order to prevent a too rapid increase in the number of levels, with its consequent necessity of deepening control, we can try to widen the span of control by means partly lying in the organization structure, partly concerned with the management-process.

However there is, as we have already stated, also a span or scope of responsibility[11] which might be called the degree to which the leader is able to bear responsibility.* As we have seen, responsibility cannot be diminished by delegation, every delegation rather increasing the responsibility than diminishing it. Thus the problem arises: how can we enlarge the scope of responsibility? Though this is a problem quite different from that of widening and deepening control, it also has its human relations aspect. Moreover, we might say that it is concerned with human relations more directly because

* Though we have to distinguish, after delegation, between different categories of responsibility there is no need to distinguish—as in the case of control—between two or more dimensions of responsibility.

responsibility regards not only the outcome of the processes of production but also is a responsibility for men.*

To meet the problem of enlarging the scope of responsibility in privately owned companies, there are available, as far as I see, some of the means also used in adapting the scope of control to the requirements of the expanding business. Three devices particularly need to be considered in this respect:

1. the formation of boards to replace the single leader at the top;
2. the deepening of control;
3. giving the leaders on lower levels and even the labourers a say in the formulation of their task and in fixing their authority and responsibility.

Studying these means from the angle of extending responsibility, we state that the formation of boards seems inevitable when a business has grown into a large concern. Even if there is a president having the decisive word in the board meetings, the others must be willing to accept the responsibility for the decision taken. Government by boards might therefore be defended, rather with regard to the bearing of responsibility than to adapting control to the capacities of the leaders. Nevertheless, if concerns are very large, we may doubt whether it would be possible even for a board to bear the enormous responsibility for their policy.

Deepening control enables the leader to see sooner and better what is happening on the levels below him. He must know of course what is going on if he is obliged to bear responsibility for it. Therefore, not only a system of task-setting and budgeting is necessary but also a system of fast and frequent signalling of what is actually happening.

Though sub-leaders and workers are always responsible for their tasks, even if they are only communicated by a bare command, it seems more desirable that their responsibilities should be fixed by themselves. Therefore, the leaders on lower levels as well as the performers must accept their task not as a command but, as already said, as an agreement between themselves and the managers at the top or on the higher levels.

We may distinguish—but only for top management—between internal and external responsibility. External responsibility may be

* Perhaps we might formulate the difference mentioned as follows; we control men in order to promote the result of the processes of production; we bear responsibility for the latter as well as for the men we control.

defined as responsibility for the course the enterprise follows in order to reach its goals, the responsibility for the enterprise as such. The internal responsibility concerns the maintenance of the enterprise as a source of income for all those that are collaborating within it, the capital-owners as well as the labourers. By the procedure mentioned in the preceding paragraph we can make the internal responsibility more bearable for the leader. The decisions made and the commands given are no longer solely the leader's decisions and commands, but can be considered as coming from the whole community or group within the enterprise. Externally, top management alone is responsible, not only to shareholders but also to the society as a whole. In our society in this respect there is no way out. Even if we make out of a larger concern a number of more or less independent smaller companies, the responsibility for the conduct of the whole concern remains unaltered, concentrated as it is at the top.*

Perhaps we might say that in respect of the problem of responsibility-bearing in our modern society, things have developed in a wrong direction. In order to get the advantages of large-scale production it is not necessary for the single company to be big. These advantages are commonly connected only with but one or a few specific functions. Small companies may combine for those functions only and remain small for the others.

That is the aim of the cooperative movement. Small plants cooperate only in those functions in which there are real advantages in executing them on a larger scale. In such cases responsibility is not concentrated as in the case of larger concerns, for it remains in the original small units. From the viewpoint of preventing the accumulation of responsibility we might prefer the cooperative activity of small plants, if this can produce the same results, to the concentration of business in large concerns. Nevertheless the large company, created by a man of rare gifts, is probably inevitable.

The theoretical note given in the preceeding pages is still based on the span of control concept. Although it has been criticized, the concept can be used, as we have already stated, as a jumping off point[12] for a theory of management. However it must be understood,

* Total independence cannot be reached before the concern is liquidated.

as we have proposed, in a broader sense than was usual hitherto, viz., in the sense of scope of control. So interpreted, the concept has the advantage that it brings several management devices onto one common denominator, thus making them comparable.

In a theory based on the scope of control the human relations problems can find their place without difficulty. Furthermore, it focuses our attention on the significance of the formal structure of the organization. Its pattern must be designed and handled in such a way that informal group-formation as well as individual initiatives may develop in it without friction. For that reason there need not be a contradiction between formal and informal organization as is so often suggested. The organization as it actually exists, the real organization, must be in accordance with the aims and objectives of the enterprise, and at the same time coincide with the interest of all those engaged in it. The formal structure must leave open opportunities for the real organization to develop in such a way. As William Foote Whyte has correctly stated: the organization pattern most appropriate for a particular business will depend on what it produces[13].

The way the formal organization is built has great influence on its pattern of human relations. We need not, however, follow this author and several others and reject the span of control theory.

References

1. In my contribution to the *Journal of Industrial Economics* vol. IV nr. 1 I have tried to develop "Some Fundamental Principles of a General Theory of Management". I have made use of this paper by permission of Basil Blackwell, as well as of the discussion of W. W. Suojanen and myself on the same subject in *Advanced Management* vol. 22 nr. 2.
2. Petersen E. & Plowman E. G., *Business Organization and Management*, Chicago 1949, p. 3
3. In his reference to my paper in the *Journal of Industrial Economics* mentioned above Suojanen also agrees that a theory of management can be developed by using the span of control limitation as a jumping-off point *op. cit.* p. 20. In my opinion, however, in this respect it is better to speak of the scope of control than of the span of control.
4. Brech, E. F. L., *Organisation, the Framework of Management*, London Longmans Green & Co 1957, p. 77. I cannot agree fully with the position taken in this book (which reached me while this chapter was going through the press) that the concept of the span of control has nothing to do with the authority over subordinate operatives. This is true only if all they need is supervision. If they are required to collaborate and their work needs to be coordinated, then a span of control also exists for the foreman which is, in principle, of the same character as that for leaders at higher levels.

5. I must state this, notwithstanding the fact that particularly in large concerns there seems to be a growing enthusiasm for this substantive decentralization. When judging the process of decentralization we must carefully distinguish between splitting-up a large concern into a number of independent smaller companies and the delegation of functions and authority to lower levels. The latter can be heads of divisions, departments etc.
What Suojanen *op. cit.* p. 19 quotes from the *National Petroleum News,* Febr. 1954: "Decentralization—key to better marketing" seems to be only a delegation of functions on the well-known principle that all those questions which can be solved by a smaller group need not be treated by a larger one. Compare: *Quadragesimo Anno; on the restoration of the social order* (1931).
6. Sometimes, in order to make the splitting-up as realistic as possible, the divisions can buy and sell from each other what they need at competitive prices. If different processes of production, commonly executed in independent companies, are integrated in one concern, this practice seems reasonable. Then there are prices and markets for the goods and the services produced in different parts of the concern. If this is not true, as for instance in the case of the dock-yard mentioned above, we must create interplant markets and a mechanism for the formation of interplant prices. All this becomes very unrealistic. Moreover, it seems to be not without danger, particularly in smaller companies.
This we must keep in mind when speaking about such substantive decentralization as practised by the Ford Motor Company, Bata and other concerns. Comp. T. O. Yntema, "Establishing More Effective Management", *Management Review,* October 1954. This decentralization movement in large concerns might be seen as a mean to diminish responsibility at the top.
7. Graicunas, A.V., "Relationships in Organization", *Bulletin of the International Management Institute,* March 1933. Davis, R. A., *The Fundamentals of Top-Management,* New York 1951. Though Graicunas' theory cannot be accepted in its stringent form, it has had its value in showing the influence of the limitations of the span of control on organization structure.
8. Billy Goetz refers to standards as "building flocks" for management. *Management Planning and Control,* New York/London: McGraw-Hill Book Co., 1949, p. 92 *et sqq.*
9. Kruisinga, H. J., *Vraagstukken van directie-voering in geografisch gedecentraliseerde bedrijven* (Problems of management in geographically decentralized businesses) Leiden 1956.
10. Though I have stressed this aspect of the delegation problem it has had, as far as I can see, but little attention in the literature of the subject. See however: John M. Pfiffner, "How to delegate authority", *Public Management,* Dec. 1953 and A. de Jong, "Taakdelegatie en taakverantwoordelijkheid" (Task delegation and task responsibility), *Maandblad voor Accountancy en Bedrijfshuishoudkunde,* 1955, nr. 5.
11. Brech *op. cit.* p. 54 *et sqq.*
12. Suojanen, W. W. *op. cit.* p. 20.
13. Whyte, W. F., Human Relations Theory—A Progress Report, *Harvard Business Review,* 1956, nr. 5. Comp. also: H. J. Kruisinga, "De spanwijdte van de leiding als concrete norm, fabel of werkelijkheid?" (The span of control, as *a concrete standard, fable or reality?), Maandblad voor Accountancy en Bedrijfshuishoudkunde,* 1957, nr. 7.

Chapter 2

THE FACTORY AS A SOCIAL SYSTEM

W. H. SCOTT

Department of Social Science, University of Liverpool

I Introduction

Only a limited amount of systematic research into behaviour in factories has been completed, and the frame of reference of much of this work has been very different from the one suggested by the title of this chapter.

The earlier studies undertaken in the first two decades of this century regarded man primarily as a physiological mechanism. In England, for example, a number of studies were sponsored by the Industrial Fatigue Research Board (later the Industrial Health Research Board) into the relations between such factors as lighting, ventilation, humidity and hours of work and the reactions and fatigue of employees; similarly, Rowntree sought to ascertain the minimum material needs that had to be satisfied if workers were to be maintained as efficient producers.[1] After the First World War, the emphasis changed to a view of man as the possessor of certain identifiable psychological traits or manipulative skills, such as intelligence, arithmetical ability or sociability in the first case, or dexterity in the latter. Later, and stemming in particular from the well-known Hawthorne investigations[2], industrial researchers were preoccupied with the analysis of the relations of employees in small work groups, and this remains characteristic of much current research. Although each of these approaches has produced useful contributions to the development of a systematic body of knowledge, they are nevertheless inadequate. The famous Hawthorne "illumination"—the discovery that although production and satisfaction increased as lighting was improved, they also continued to do so when it deteriorated again—made the approach of the physiological school appear naive. When it was demonstrated that behaviour and performance on the job were influenced far more by factors in the work situation than by the supposed attributes of the individual, as ascertained by prior tests, the limitations of the traditional school of individual psychology were exposed. Similarly, although small group analysis is still popular and is making a more valid contribution than earlier approaches, it is clear that an exclusive preoccupation with analysis at this level is inadequate. The reasons for this will be apparent later, but at this point we may note that to regard employees simply as members of small face-to-face groups is to ignore the importance of their other affiliations and particularly those, such as trade union membership, which derive from the fact that a work force is divided into a number of occupational categories.

If we criticize the shortcomings of these approaches to the study of behaviour in industry, we must emphasize at once that all systematic study gives only an incomplete description of the external world. Study involves selection, or at least should involve it, if we are to obtain meaningful results; we abstract, as it were, certain elements from the totality, we concentrate our attention on those selected, and we seek to ascertain the nature of the relations between them. The choice of significant elements is, therefore, a crucial question, and our ability to make this choice should improve as systematic work develops and our knowledge and understanding increases. Profiting from earlier approaches, some sociologists (alas, as yet few) have more recently focused attention on the social system of the factory viewed as a whole. This orientation is open to criticism, since, as we have said, the field of study must be delimited. Nevertheless, it has become increasingly apparent that many specific problems can be understood only in terms of the social structure of the plant[3], and in this connection it should be emphasized that it is not so much the *area* of study, as the *selection of elements within it*, that must be limited. This realization stems from a growing appreciation of the complexity of social situations; in studying them, we are usually dealing with a cluster of interdependent elements, from which it is not easy to isolate one or two for analysis, even if this course were deemed likely to lead to significant conclusions. Moreover, though it is essential to restrict our observations, it is clearly unwise to delimit them unduly until the elements which are more significant in relation to behaviour have been identified and defined.

What do we mean by a "social system"? Social, of course, refers to the relations between people, and system implies an ordered relationship of the parts to the whole. The psychologist primarily views individuals as the parts; to the sociologist the parts consist, in the first place at least, of groups. A social system then is a network or pattern of interrelated groups and persons, which is characterized by a measure of stability and persistence. It tends, in other words, to have a definite structure, and we speak, therefore, of *social structure*. The full connotation of these terms will become more apparent as we proceed, but a few words should also be added at this point about the implications of the term "group". A group consists of persons whose interrelations are structured, and who share common characteristics, such as attitudes, values and forms of behaviour, which differentiate them from the members of other groups; they will also evince, to some extent, a common awareness of group membership. Thus a group necessarily implies more than a simple aggregate of individuals, although groups differ considerably in the degree to which they are structured or cohesive.

We are concerned then with the analysis of the social structure of the factory. This, however, is a broad conception, and we require an analytical framework, or a definition of those elements or facets of social structure which we deem most likely to influence behaviour. As stated earlier, only a very limited amount of work of this kind has been undertaken, and this makes it difficult, and indeed unwise, to adopt too rigid or delimited a framework. Nevertheless it should be definite, and be followed consistently throughout a research project, if the collection of information is to be systematic and if comparability of the results of different researches, which is essential to the development of a body of knowledge, is to be achieved. In the present state of knowledge, the categories of an analytical framework for the study of the social structure of the factory should, therefore, be limited in number but fairly broad; and we should use methods of research which will not exclude the possibility of eliciting other information which may be significant in the process of obtaining the data called for by our framework.

II Analysis

The industrial sociologist has been concerned almost exclusively with behaviour in the workplace, and this emphasis is legitimate and understandable; if it is important to limit the field of study, he is wise to stick to his last, particularly in the early stages of development of his subject. Nevertheless, relationships within factories influence, and are influenced by, the social structure and values of the wider society, and recently industrial sociologists have become more aware of the desirability of taking this connection into account if a fuller understanding of behaviour in factories is to be achieved. We cannot undertake a systematic exploration of the relations between the social structure of industrial institutions and of society at large here, but some of the more important and particular links will be indicated as we proceed with the analysis of the social system of the factory. A similar consideration applies to the problem of the basic formative influences on the social structure of the plant which arise within the industrial situation itself. The technical organization, the size and the nature of the ownership and control of a factory, for example, all have an important influence on social relations. We will discuss, as we go along, some particular examples of these influences, but a systematic assessment of their significance will be deferred, as to attempt this at the outset would involve the use of terms and concepts which are to be described in the following analysis.

The factory then is an institution existing within a wider society, and, more specifically, within a framework of legal, economic and collective bargaining arrangements. The plant itself may be regarded as consisting of varying numbers of persons of different occupational categories who are brought together within, and whose activities are defined and coordinated to some extent by, a formal organization; the latter will normally lay down, *inter alia*, a system of authority and responsibility, the duties to be performed, and the conditions of employment. These last will form part, but part only, of a system of rewards, which may be defined as the differential benefits which accrue to groups and to individuals by virtue of the roles they play in the factory. As time passes, relations will develop between groups and individuals which are additional to those based on the occupational and formal structures, and these will be described as the informal structure of the plant. Finally, the importance of values, ideas and beliefs must not be overlooked. Some of these will derive from the structure of the wider society, others will be related closely to the social system of the factory, and certain elements in both these categories may be traditional, in the sense that they have persisted despite changes in social structure. We shall speak, therefore, of the occupational structure, the formal structure, the system of rewards and the informal structure of the factory, and in connection with each we shall examine the values which appear to be related closely to the existing structure, leaving the question of traditional values for separate treatment. Each of these elements will now be described and discussed, and we may then pass to a tentative examination of the relations between them.

Occupational Structure

Occupational structure is the division of a labour force into categories and groups on the basis of differences of function and skill. A highly specialized division of labour is one of the most important characteristics of an advanced industrial society; the number of distinct occupations today far exceeds that of the early years of industrialism, and that of pre-industrial times to an even greater extent. This phenomenon was the theme of a classic work by Durkheim[4], who argued that the increasing division of labour and the expanding scale of social organization must lead to a greater differentiation of values and interests, which would threaten the maintenance of social cohesion and solidarity. We shall return to this point later. Meanwhile, whilst recognizing the importance of advancing occupational differentiation, we must not overlook the common characteristics of particular groupings of occupations which are based on similarities in the type of activity or of function performed, and in the type and level of skill and qualification required. The broad conventional distinction between management and workers, although too crude for many purposes, is of course very important. It is based on manifest differences of functions, interests and objectives. The manager's task is to plan, to organize and to control, the operative's to carry out a particular job of work; similarly, management's first concern must be the efficient operation of a factory, or at least to keep it in business, whilst the employee's primary aim is to secure an adequate reward for his services. A more refined occupational analysis is, however, necessary for a fuller understanding of behaviour in the factory, and the following division of a labour force into seven categories has often been made and has proved useful: 1. directors, 2. managers, 3. supervisors and technicians, 4. clerical workers, 5. skilled manual workers, 6. semi-skilled manual workers, 7. unskilled workers. This, nevertheless, is only a general system of classification, and often must be refined further when applied to the larger factory which is becoming increasingly typical. A brief discussion of each of the categories will serve to clarify both their general and particular relevance.

The directors are, of course, the elected representatives of the shareholders, and are responsible for the formulation of the general policy of the firm, at least in the short run. Modern development, however, has been marked by a growing separation of the functions of ownership and control. The very small business run by an owner-manager, or the small factory managed by a few persons who own most if not all of the shares, is less typical today than in the past, although it is still important. It is still found frequently in the service trades, and to some extent in manufacturing industry, even in the case of large firms, and particularly those which began as small family businesses and have managed to preserve ownership and control predominantly in the hands of one family, despite considerable expansion of operations. With the growing scale of manufacturing enterprise, however, ownership and control have been increasingly separated.[5] When ownership is divided amongst a large number of shareholders, the directors, some of whom will probably also fill the top executive posts in the factory or business, may control both long-term and operating policy, without any direct influence being exercised by the shareholding interest as a whole or by any substantial portion of it. There are, of course, many gradations between the two extremes of owner-manager and "independent" directorate, but the emphasis in particular cases may have an important bearing on policy and relations within the factory.

The management group as a whole has also become enlarged and differentiated with increasing scale, the extent to which this has occurred varying again with the size of an enterprise and with the technical complexity of its processes. This trend has developed in relation to both the "vertical" and the "horizontal" division of functions, that is, as regards the various levels of responsibility and the division of labour between those at a similar level. In a large plant there will normally be a clear distinction between top, senior and middle management. The top management will comprise working directors and other executives at works level who have responsibilities in connection with the coordination and control of the activities of the factory as a whole; senior managers will be responsible for the oversight of a particular department or function;

middle managers will work within departments and have duties connected with some particular aspect of their activities. These three levels are, therefore, distinguished by differences of function; they will also vary in status and rewards. The mode of recruitment to these positions, and the qualifications favoured, may differ; middle managers may continue to be recruited predominantly from the lower ranks, whereas senior posts may be filled increasingly by persons with formal qualifications who have been "imported" from outside the firm.[6, 7] It is, however, the "horizontal" differentiation of functions which is perhaps the most striking characteristic of modern management in the larger plant. Increasing scale makes a more refined division of labour economical and desirable, and this trend has been reinforced by the growing complexity of technical organization. The various branches of engineering, production scheduling and control, quality control, costing and employee relations, to mention only some of the more important examples, have been organized increasingly as separate functions. This progressive differentiation of "staff" or "service" functions has accelerated changes in managerial recruitment, since these activities in particular demand persons with special qualifications.[7] These changes have led to the emergence of complex managerial organizations which, whilst providing the benefits of specialization, have undoubtedly aggravated the problem of achieving overall coordination.

Some managers express surprise when supervisors and foremen are enumerated as a separate occupational category. It is clear, however, that they should be so regarded today. Traditionally, the functions and loyalty of the foreman have been managerial, but this is changing rapidly. Many managements have recognized this during the post-war years; some have made zealous, but somewhat misguided, efforts to restore the foreman's lost position by re-integrating him into the ranks of management; others have adjusted to the changed situation, perhaps more wisely, by seeking to develop the supervisor as a group leader. What, of course, has happened is that the changes in management outlined above have reduced both the authority and the functions of the foreman, so that today he is often little more than a petty administrator and a disciplinarian. As his chances of promotion are also diminishing rapidly with changes in managerial recruitment, and as his earnings are often less than those of senior operatives, it is not surprising that his undivided allegiance to management is changing. Evidence of the latter has emerged in several studies[8, 9, 10, 11], and the development of an independent group consciousness amongst foremen is witnessed by the extension of unionization amongst them. Finally, technicians have been included in this category, and there is much to support this course, although it is important to recognize the differences between foremen and technicians. With increasing specialization and technical complexity, the number of technicians, such as draughtsmen, laboratory staff and instrument mechanics, has expanded rapidly. They are similar to supervisors, in that they are not of managerial status, but their rank and conditions are superior to those of routine office and clerical staff. Their function, however, is different, although they are often responsible for the supervision of a small number of junior "staff" persons.

Clerical workers in the past often constituted the bulk of the "white-collar" group which enjoyed "staff" status, and also conditions of employment which were superior to those of most manual workers. Foremen normally receive "staff" conditions, and, as already indicated, technical and administrative personnel are a growing proportion of this group as a whole. With the expansion of supervisory and technical staff, the mechanization of many office jobs, the spread of literacy throughout the general population, and the growing power of organized manual workers, the status and rewards of clerical workers have tended to decline. Nevertheless, tradition still accords them a higher status than most manual workers, and since their function, and the skill required for its execution, is different from that of supervisors, technicians, or manual workers, their recognition as a distinct occupational category is necessary and useful. Moreover, clerical staff have traditionally identified themselves with management, but, as in the case of foremen, it is probable that their changing position is leading to modifications in their outlook and loyalties today.

The skilled manual workers consist predominantly of craftsmen who have served an apprenticeship to a trade. They were long regarded as the "aristocracy" amongst workers, and still enjoy a relatively high status, although the position of craftsmen as a whole has undergone marked changes during the past 50 years. For many years they were the leading operatives amongst production workers in most industries, and in a few, such as printing and certain branches of engineering, they still retain this position. Increasingly, however, during the present century, they have been confined to a maintenance and constructional role, as mechanization has proceeded and skilled jobs have been broken down into their component parts. This trend has had a serious impact on their position and conditions[12, 3], but more recently the very complexity of mechanical equipment has steadily increased the importance of their newer "servicing" role, and it appears that the wheel may now come full circle as the proportion of craftsmen employed expands.[7] In certain industries there is also a small group of senior operatives on the process who, although they have not served a formal apprenticeship, have developed a high degree of skill by long experience. In the steel industry, for example, the keeper on a blast furnace, the first-hand melter in a melting shop, or the roller in a rolling mill, come within this category. Their position and problems, however, are more akin to those of semi-skilled operatives than of craftsmen.

The semi-skilled category includes two elements in nearly all factories. The largest and most important comprises the production workers who man and operate the processes, with the exceptions already noted. Mechanization has greatly simplified many production jobs, with the result that often a short period of on-the-job training is all that is necessary for effective performance, and it may thus be easy to transfer production workers from one operation to another. The second and smaller element in this category consists of the semi-skilled maintenance men, who either assist the craftsmen as "mates" or perform semi-skilled operations in maintenance workshops.

Finally, the unskilled workers are those who are employed almost exclusively as labourers, to move or to carry materials. Their work requires little or no training or instruction, and they may, of course, be used either on the process itself or in connection with maintenance or ancillary work.

The various occupational categories which are normally found in the larger factory have been discussed at some length because of their basic importance for an understanding of industrial behaviour. Behaviour is, of course, a function, at least in part, of the values, attitudes, experience and interests of the persons concerned, and divergences in these features are related to differences in occupational position. We have referred to one or two of the more obvious distinctions between management and workers, but just as structure is more complex than this simple division suggests, so there is a further differentiation of values and interests within each of these broad groupings; this has been shown by recent work[7], and will be illustrated in the discussion of the system of rewards below. It has also been suggested by many that occupational differentiation is related, not only to differences in behaviour in the factory, but also to divergent attitudes towards broader economic and political questions. Most of these formulations, of what is usually referred to as interest group theory, stem from the work of Marx; Centers' definition of the kernel of this theory is that "a person's status and role with respect to the economic processes of society imposes upon him certain attitudes, values and interests relating to his role and status in the political and economic sphere . . . and . . . gives rise in him to a consciousness of membership in some social class which shares those attitudes, values and interests."[13] Some formulations of this theory have, of course, been crude and exaggerated, but it is a fact not only of common observation but also of empirical research[13] that there are undoubtedly *tendencies* in the directions indicated. The existence of these tendencies emphasizes both the importance of occupational differentiation in shaping attitudes to general social and economic questions, and the need to take into account other group memberships and influences for a fuller understanding of these phenomena. Moreover, we have spoken so far only of occupational *categories*, in terms of a system of classification imposed by reference to differences of function and skill; these categories within a plant, however, may in some cases constitute, and in others contain, occupational *groups*, in the sociological sense of the term group which was discussed above. An occupational group consists of persons who perform a similar function in relation to the organization of production, have a common awareness of group membership, and who tend to share certain common values, attitudes, interests and patterns of behaviour. The professions provide perhaps the best examples; the common characteristics of their members are well known, and have been the subject of several studies.[14] Craftsmen are the most cohesive of these groups amongst manual workers, but the same tendencies are apparent within other occupational categories, as Caplow's recent study has shown.[15] We have, moreover, referred already to the distinguishing characteristics of managers, supervisors and clerical staff, which are becoming more apparent as their functions are increasingly differentiated. The importance of the development of occupational group consciousness is clear; to the extent that it has grown amongst those in a particular occupation or grouping of occupations, it will reinforce the tendency of common occupation to shape similar attitudes and patterns of behaviour, which will probably be different from those evinced by the members of other groups. Finally, two other important implications of occupational structure must be noted. The specialization typical of industrialism is related to the development of another characteristic structural feature, *associations*. The membership of an association tends to be specialized, and it exists for the pursuit of limited rather than general purposes and interests. Associations are found in most spheres of life in modern society, but they predominate in industry, where the more important of them are trade unions, employers' associations and professional organizations, whose members tend to consist of those in a particular occupational category or group, although there are exceptions. These bodies have of course an important function in expressing the problems and interests of their members, and in influencing their rewards and conditions of employment. There is indeed a close relationship again between occupational structure and the system of rewards, and we pass now to a consideration of this.

The System of Rewards

The system of rewards may be defined as the differential rewards or deprivations which accrue to the members of the various occupational groupings in the factory by virtue of their position in the social system. We are prone to conceive of rewards in purely material terms, and particularly as wealth or income, and contractually they are usually defined in this way. Nevertheless, although earnings are a very important element in the system, others are often valued, such as status, security, job interest, chances of promotion and satisfying relationships. The differential distribution of most of these elements is related closely to the occupational hierarchy. It has been shown that there is a high degree of agreement amongst people in their ranking of occupations according to status[16], which follows, on broad lines and in descending order, the seven-point classification of occupations given earlier. Similarly, the intrinsic interest of jobs is widely considered to increase as one ascends the occupational hierarchy, and opportunities of promotion to manager are often better for "staff" employees than they are for skilled workers, and in turn better for the latter than for production workers.[7, 17] Paradoxically, it is perhaps income, of all the elements in the system of rewards, which today has the lowest degree of association with occupational status; there is, of course, a broad correlation between the two, but there are important exceptions, as in the cases of the lower earnings often received by supervisors, clerical employees and craftsmen in comparison with process workers. Nevertheless, although there are formidable problems in the way of precise assessment, since this would involve an endeavour to aggregate elements which are qualitatively different, it appears, if one considers the total rewards of each occupational category, that there is a close relation between these and occupational status, and that they decline as one descends the hierarchy. Thus, in the estimation of supervisors, for example, if they receive somewhat lower earnings than some of their charges, this may be more than offset by their greater security and status. Some evidence of this has been adduced in a recent study, which has also confirmed that members of different occupational categories differ in the importance which they attach to the various elements in the system of rewards.[7] Manual workers, for example, emphasize wages and security, whereas "staff" employees are often more concerned with promotion chances and with the interest and satisfaction to be derived from a job.

Formal Structure

The purpose of formal structure, as implied earlier, is the coordination and control of activities, which are differentiated but interdependent, for the achievement of the predominant aims of an organization. Durkheim's prediction that advancing differentiation would increase the difficulty of maintaining cooperation for common purposes has proved a valid if rather exaggerated one, as the industrial history of the present century has shown, and it provides one of the reasons for the extension of formal structure. Barnard has defined it, or rather, formal organization, as he calls it, as "the consciously coordinated activities of two or more persons for the achievement of common purposes"[18] and this expresses the basic features of formal structure, provided that the consciousness of it is common to the persons concerned, and that "common purposes" is taken simply to imply defined and recognized, and not necessarily mutually accepted, ones. In most plants of any size, the division of functions, authority and responsibility, and the rank and conditions of service of the various grades of employees, will be formally prescribed, and formal structure may extend to other aspects of relationships. It is not, of course, confined to the formal organization of management; it will embrace important elements in the structure of trade unions associated with the factory, of the external and internal machinery of management-union relations, and, for example, of a works social club or even a departmental sports team.

Significant aspects of formal structure may be recorded in, for example, constitutions, articles of association, organization charts or employee handbooks, but commitment to paper is certainly not essential to its existence. Relations may be structured formally by verbal communication, but, strictly speaking, even this is not necessary. Departmental heads, for example, will recognize their responsibility to a chief executive, the latter will be aware of his authority over them, and both parties will know the purpose of this arrangement, even though no organization charts exist and the arrangement has never been explicitly defined or discussed, just as an operative will perceive the foreman's jurisdiction and the reason for it. Moreover, formal structure has other characteristics in addition to explicit definition and particularity of purpose. It is impersonal, in the sense that it prescribes, for example, certain functions and the relations between them, without reference to the personalities of the particular incumbents who may occupy these positions from time to time, although in practice there may be certain exceptions so far as new appointees to senior posts are concerned. This impersonality derives from the values which influence its nature and purpose; much of formal structure is the outcome of an endeavour to organize relationships "rationally", in order to maintain or improve the "efficiency" of an organization. Whilst deliberate planning does often predominate, it is, however, important to note that formal structure may crystallize out gradually, as it were, from relationships which previously were informal and spontaneous, and both its extent and the manner of its emergence may be related to the age and history of a plant. Thus a factory which is established from the outset as a large unit will require a considerable degree of formal structure based on planning and prescription; in another factory, which has grown gradually from a small unit, the formal structure may be minimal and derive for the most part from traditional arrangements, although it will certainly tend to increase as a plant becomes larger and more complex. Finally, formal structure reflects the distribution of power in an organization. Some elements at least will be prescribed by top management initially, but as time passes the distribution of power may change, and this will lead to modifications. Thus, for example, the development of trade union organization amongst employees may achieve a limitation of the authority of junior managers, or the transfer of responsibility for certain decisions to joint bodies.

Informal Structure

The informal structure of the plant consists of those elements in face-to-face relations which are not regarded by the participants as, nor preconceived for the purpose of, achieving simply a specific objective or objectives. As suggested earlier, previous studies, and particularly those of the Mayo school, have been preoccupied with this aspect of social structure, particularly amongst rank and file employees, to the neglect of others, but it is nevertheless important. Small face-to-face groups tend to arise at every level of a factory, and are based primarily on congeniality and affinity. They supplement the formal structure, and may modify its operation appreciably. Their emergence stems basically from the need of most persons to establish fairly close and satisfying relations with some of their fellows, and is facilitated by the close proximity of people at work. Thus they invariably arise on the shop floor, even though cooperation amongst operatives for work purposes is not required by the formal structure or by the nature of techniques; amongst managers too they derive frequently from similarity of function or of professional and social background. Although they arise in connection with work, they will, however, often extend to, and be consolidated by, other activities such as eating and recreation. Moreover, the influence of occupational structure on social differentiation is exemplified by the fact that membership of face-to-face groups tends to be confined to those within a particular occupational category. Informal structure is important in several ways. It has a significant influence in establishing and maintaining norms and patterns of behaviour, as several studies have shown; it is the "grapevine" which often functions as a far more effective channel of communication than any formal media; and, when it does not conflict seriously with the demands of formal structure, it may promote stability and satisfaction in work, but where such a conflict exists, it may exacerbate cleavages between groups. Finally, the informal structure of the community may also, of course, influence relations within the factory. With the growth of large industrial areas, a high degree of overlap between the informal structure of factory and community, in the sense that those who associate together in leisure time are also colleagues at work, is less frequent today, but is still found in many instances. Where it does obtain, kinship may be particularly important. A high proportion of the labour force of a plant may be related in this sense, and recruitment to the factory may be effected to a large extent through kin connections. A high degree of overlap will reinforce the influence of the internal informal structure; given intelligent managerial policies and an effective formal structure, it will promote stability and identification with the firm; on the other hand, in the face of adversity or arbitrary decisions, it will sustain employee solidarity and resistance.

Traditional Values

In the foregoing analysis we have suggested that occupational structure and the system of rewards, formal structure and informal structure are the more important aspects of the social system of the factory. Some of the ways in which social structure influences values and attitudes, and hence behaviour, have also been indicated. There are, however, values which do not derive from existing structure, although this may assist in maintaining their vitality; these values are of older origin and have persisted despite intervening structural changes. These traditional values, as we may call them, are of considerable importance in maintaining cooperation and integration in a society in which roles and interests are highly differentiated. There are many of them in society at large, expressed in such phrases as "live and let live", "fair play", and "a fair deal", or embodied in abstract terms like "justice", "compromise" and "reasonable". Certain elements in political and religious ideologies provide other examples, although these are almost certainly less important within factories in Britain than they are in a number of Continental countries. Similarly, some of the beliefs of early capitalism, such as in the desirability of a free market, unrestricted competition, and non-interference by the State, still command adherents despite their incompatibility with existing structure.

Many traditional values are more specific in their application to conditions in the factory itself. An exaggerated belief in the value of "experience" may persist despite the development of technologies, and the craftsman has retained his relatively high status although mechanization has advanced and his role as a production worker has declined. Another traditional element, which is found in many firms, consists of a complex of values which may be termed a "family ideology". Most firms began as small family businesses, but over the years many of them have grown to be large public companies. Some still retain ownership and control predominantly in the hands of a founding family, but in the majority ownership has been widely distributed and control is exercised by professional managers, although a member of the founding family may survive on the Board of Directors. They cannot, therefore, be regarded in any real sense as "extended families", but values nevertheless tend to persist from the time when they could. Some of the more important of these may be the emphasis placed on the maintenance of the "family spirit", on informality in relationships, on paternalism in management-employee relations, on the centralization of managerial authority and on the desirability of a stable labour force with preference in recruitment given to the relatives or nominees of present employees. Any or all of these characteristics may persist despite the consolidation of trade union organization, the growth of a large plant and management cadre with a consequent need for the extension of formal structure, and changing technical demands which call for more persons with specialized qualifications.

Interrelations

We must now relate the categories we have discussed, and it is essential that our model should be dynamic. Indeed, the importance of an historical approach to industrial situations has been implied throughout the discussion of each of the structural elements. As was said at the outset, however, in the present state of knowledge it is possible to relate the categories only in fairly general terms; the definition and testing of many more specific hypotheses within the general framework is necessary, both for a fuller understanding of behaviour and for the refinement of the framework itself. We shall refer now to studies of three groups—managers, supervisors, and craftsmen—and will suggest that an approach to the understanding of their behaviour can be made by regarding it as the outcome of the interplay of the influences deriving from the various elements of social structure. It must of course be borne in mind that we are generalizing about larger firms, and that particular situations may diverge significantly from these general characterizations; nevertheless, we would suggest that these divergencies may be understood by analysing the structural elements, and their interrelations, as they obtain in particular situations.

A recent study in the steel industry exemplifies some of the trends and problems that are often found within a management organization today.[7] Managers are uncertain and insecure concerning the limits of their authority and responsibilities. Rapid functional differentiation has occurred, and this has produced a more diversified occupational structure of the management group. This tendency—allied to the fact that patterns of recruitment are changing, as more managers with formal qualifications are recruited from outside whilst some continue to be promoted from the ranks—is making the informal structure more complex. Thus face-to-face groups may develop on the basis of differences of function, as, for example, between "production" and "service" managers, or derive from differences of background and outlook between "professionals" and those who have "come up the hard way". Cleavages can readily arise between these groups, and these may prove serious, since managerial functions are normally interdependent, and cleavages may reduce the individual manager's capacity to make particular decisions relating to his own function in the light of the needs of the organization as a whole. Functional differentiation and the development of cleavages complicate the problem of achieving effective coordination of the activities of managers, and a solution of this problem, and a clarification of the authority and responsibilities of individuals, may be impeded by formal structure and traditional values. The formal structure of management in British industry is often minimal, and consists of a simple "line" organization which stresses the centralization of authority, and this is related to traditional values which emphasize informality and the importance of a close link between operating and general managers. These may clearly be incompatible with the needs of an enlarged and differentiated structure, which will require considerable decentralization of authority, and the development of effective "horizontal" relations between the proliferating functions at each level. In the absence of these adjustments, uncertainty and insecurity will arise amongst managers.

We referred earlier to several studies that have been made of the position and attitudes of the foreman and of the changing characteristics of foremen as a group.[7, 8, 9, 10] In general terms, we may say that the formal structure defines the foreman as the lowest rung of management, and that the traditional evaluation of his status has accorded with this. His position in the occupational structure has, however, changed; his function is not to take decisions but to apply them—in other words, his function is neither that of a manager nor that of an operative—and his possibility of further promotion into the ranks of management has been severely curtailed. Indeed, promotion to foreman is seen today by the rank and file employee as the limit of aspiration. As regards informal structure our information is less systematic. Nevertheless, it seems clear that the personal associates of foremen are other foremen and often operatives, rather than managers. Moreover, we must also bear in mind in this connection that the foreman himself has invariably risen from the ranks, and that in order "to get the work out" under the changed balance of power in post-war industry, he must rely increasingly on a close and effective relationship with the operative rather than on respect for formal authority. In the case of the foreman, therefore, we again have a situation in which formal structure and traditional values on the one hand, and occupational and informal structure on the other, may make conflicting demands. It is against this background that we can understand Roethlisberger's characterization of the foreman as "the master and victim of double talk."[8]

As the craftsman, in many industries, has become increasingly a maintenance and constructional worker, the formal structure has accordingly defined him as an "ancillary"; indeed, in some plants he feels that he is regarded by both management and production workers as "a necessary evil", and at best as "just another employee". Despite his changed position in the occupational structure of factories, however, his occupational group consciousness has remained strong; this has been maintained by the transferability of his skill, his consequent ability to move from firm to firm if he so desires, and his identification with the craft rather than the workplace. These factors have been reinforced by the traditional status accorded to craftsmanship and craft skill, which has not been affected materially by the change in his function. Once again, therefore, there is a discrepancy between the formal definition of his role and status and the influences deriving from occupational position and traditional values, and the resulting problems have been exacerbated by the decline in his rewards relative to those of production workers as his role has changed. Thus the craftsman has often been on the defensive, and the position we have summarized goes far to explain his spasmodic militancy. There are now signs, however, that the wheel is coming full circle. As mechanical equipment becomes more complex and semi-automatic, the importance of the craftsman's servicing function increases, as does the proportion of craftsmen to production workers. This will undoubtedly lead to more demands for an adjustment of their material rewards to a level more consonant with their skill and traditional status, which will probably create problems of industrial relations vis-a-vis both managements and the trade unions of production workers.[7]

These three examples serve to demonstrate that behaviour must be considered in terms of the relations between the various elements of social structure, as these change over time. At many points in our analysis it has also been obvious that the immediate cause of change in social structure has been a modification of techniques themselves or of the technical organization of production. This is not, of course, to suggest that technical organization is a rigid determinant of the social structure of the factory. The role of traditional values, or the influence of the structure of the wider society, would preclude this in any case. Techniques of production nevertheless set certain limits to the possible variation of social structure, and these limits are wide for some aspects and narrower for others. A mechanical process, for example, requires a minimum number of persons for its effective operations, and a further number to repair and to service it. These numbers may, however, be exceeded, due to the power of organized workers or managerial inefficiency, for example. Occupational structure is, however, the aspect of social structure which is probably influenced most closely by techniques, although comparison of plants of similar technical organization shows that quite wide variations can nevertheless occur.[19] Informal structure is also affected directly, since the types of workers employed, and their spatial distribution throughout the factory, will be related closely to the nature of the processes. Formal structure, for reasons that have been discussed, is linked less closely to technical organization, but its extent and degree will bear a broad relationship to the size and technical complexity of plants. Technical changes, therefore, will tend to lead to changes in social structure, but other factors must be taken into account if we wish to understand the nature of a particular structure. This is not the place to attempt to state a theory of social change, but one concluding consideration must be noted. Technical organization and social structure are interdependent, and in reality they interact. Thus whilst technical change does lead to social change, technical change is itself conditioned by the social structure, both of the factory and of the wider society. A "family" firm, for example, may hesitate to undertake a major technical change, since this might involve capital recruitment beyond the means of the family, and thus a threat to the continuance of family control. Similarly, the introduction of a technical change may be delayed by the resistance of an organized employee group whose interests would be threatened by it. Finally, it is clear that the structure of the society, and in particular such factors as the degree of monopoly or competition in an industry, or the extent to which economic acquisitiveness *per se* is valued, will influence the rate of technical change in factories.

III Implications

We have suggested that, from the sociologist's point of view, an industrial plant may be regarded as consisting of the members of a number of occupational categories and groups, which perform different functions and are characterized by differential attitudes and interests, brought together within an organizational structure for the achievement of specific purposes, the predominant one being, of course, the provision of goods or services. Top management is the initiator of this process, and its overall function clearly is to promote cooperation and coordination for the realization of the objectives of the organization.

The successful performance of this function today cannot be accomplished by those who possess just technical knowledge or the intuitive ability born of experience, any more than a simple maximization of profit motive—if it ever did operate—can guarantee success in the market. Even if industrial organization had not grown to its present scale and complexity, the changed balance of power in industry since the War and the onward march of humanism and social welfare would have demanded a new approach of management. These trends have created a situation in which people in industry expect that the improvement of their material standards shall proceed simultaneously with the satisfaction of other basic human needs, and this presents a challenge to the leadership ability of management at a time when the growing complexity of industrial organization demands greater administrative skill in its ranks.

Barnard has distinguished between the "effective" and the "efficient" organization.[18] The "effective" one pursues, and may achieve, organizational goals; the "efficient" firm does this, *and* seeks to satisfy the needs of its members. Indeed, recent research has suggested that there are limits to the effectiveness of an organization, at least in the long run, unless it also succeeds in being "efficient". A firm may achieve its economic objectives at the expense of the morale and quality of its labour force, but this, even if possible under the conditions of today, is likely to be a transient success, since its effect on employees, and their inevitable reaction, will undermine its ability to continue to do so. There has, therefore, been a growing recognition that the satisfaction of human needs is not only a goal whose attainment is desirable in itself, or which has been demanded increasingly as the power of organized labour has developed, but is also "good business", or a condition of the successful economic operation of the enterprise in the long run.

Increasing attention has been given, therefore, to the problem of industrial morale. Unfortunately, the term has often been used loosely, and in some cases no endeavour has been made to define it at all. Frequently it has been equated with "satisfaction in work", in a rather nebulous and compendious sense; at the other extreme, there have been detailed studies of the supposed components of morale, based on an elaborate factor analysis, in which sufficient prior attention has been given neither to the identification of the crucial variables nor to the need for an adequate measure of morale itself. Basically, morale refers to the attitude of persons to the activity in which they are involved, in the sense of their degree of attachment to it, and hence the strength of their desire and willingness to continue to pursue it. In terms of our analysis of differential occupational attitudes and interests, we should expect the level of morale to be related to the extent to which these interests, and other needs of employees, are met. Moreover, our brief discussion of the system of rewards should have made it clear that these interests and needs are not confined to the material conditions of employment which are usually defined contractually. Indeed, wages and welfare provisions can be of a high standard, yet morale can be low. As Roethlisberger has pointed out, the evaluation of material rewards tends to be a function of the quality of relationships in an organization; where, for example, relationships are approved, the introduction of a reasonable wage incentive scheme may be interpreted as further evidence of the justice of management; where, on the other hand, there is considerable suspicion and hostility, it may be seen as one more attempt to "drive" the workers.[20] The failure to recognize the importance of non-material needs has been the main shortcoming of paternalism in industry; the benevolent autocrat, who tends, however unconsciously, to regard employees as children, whose every material need must be anticipated and catered for, is pursuing a misguided policy. It generates a latent strain in relationships which will grow progressively, until an explosion may occur, since each improvement in material conditions will serve to draw more attention to deficiencies in other directions. Assuming, then, that acceptable material conditions are desirable but are inadequate of themselves, what other needs are most important and how can both these and material desiderata be satisfied?

At the present time, it seems probable that security and participation are the basic conditions of high morale in an industrial organization. Although the degree to which people in industry feel secure is partly determined by the external situation, the two conditions mentioned are closely related within the factory; for whilst the decisions of an authoritarian leadership may be predictable, they are likely to be arbitrary and dictated by sectional interest. Reasonable security is thus dependent to a large extent on participation, or an ability on the part of the constituent groups and individuals in the factory to influence directly the decisions and acts of leaders. This ability is essential if the needs of people are to be met within an institution in which, as we have suggested, interests and values differ; it is also a condition which has been demanded increasingly as the power of organized labour has grown, and as people in industry have come to expect rights analogous to those which they enjoy in the political sphere.

There must, therefore, be adequate opportunities for the discussion of policy between top management and representatives of the various groupings of employees in a factory. This requires, in the first place, a full recognition by management of the legitimacy of the role of trade unions and of collective bargaining. This may sound trite today, but it must be appreciated that although this now obtains in most industries at the national or industrial level, it is often ill-developed within factories. I have suggested in a recent publication[21] that the main need today is for a fuller development of the role of union representatives at plant level, and for the extension of management-union discussions within plants beyond the rather narrow limits of conventional collective bargaining. This is essential, because the determination of basic conditions of employment has now been removed to higher levels, and many of the newer problems of today, such as the need for higher productivity, work satisfaction and effective relationships, arise in individual factories and cannot be resolved satisfactorily elsewhere. If it is to be achieved, it requires not only a continuing initiative on the part of management, but also the delegation by the unions of a real measure of responsibility and authority to lay officials in plants; it demands, in fact, a division of responsibility between national and local officials analogous to that found in the International-Local pattern of organization prevalent in American unions.

Adequate procedures for the joint discussion of policy are essential; they are, however, of limited value unless consultation for the elaboration and execution of policy becomes part of the administrative routines of a factory at every level. It is only in this way that a feeling of participation can be engendered amongst a work force as a whole, and in any case many matters concern only particular groupings or even individuals, and should if possible be settled at, or near to, their point of origin. This requires the development of what I have termed "consultative leadership"[21], which implies a continuous ability on the part of a leader to take decisions in the light of the facts, the latter including, and due weight being given to, the views and needs of the led. It also presupposes a sensitivity to the subtleties of human relations, rather than a preoccupation with the technical aspects of situations, a matter which Dr. Kahn will no doubt enlarge upon in Chapter 3. This does not of course mean that decisions will be taken by a show of hands; although a manager is charged with the oversight of a particular activity or function, his primary task must be to take decisions relating to that activity which are consonant with the needs and policies of the organization as a whole, and his formal responsibility must therefore be "upwards" to a superior, and ultimately to the policy-making body. It does mean, however, that he will endeavour to make due allowance for the needs and views of his subordinates, and that he will consult them, or their representatives, when, for example, changes are to be made, or doubt exists as to the most appropriate interpretation of policy, or they wish to make suggestions. It should moreover be re-emphasized that "consultative leadership" is not only a necessary condition for satisfying the subordinate's need to participate; it is also, as implied earlier, a prerequisite of effective coordination and cooperation within the management organization itself. As the scale of plants has grown, the functions within management have become more specialized, with the result that they are necessarily more interdependent; thus the coordination of activities and the formulation of general policy require more consultation within the management structure. The development of committees within management, and the growth and diversification of works management to coordinate the work of departments, reflect this need. Moreover, the practice of consultation within management is a condition of effective consultation between management and employees. When, for example, regular discussions take place between top management and employee representatives, without prior consultation within the management organization, other managers, and particularly junior managers, are likely to feel "by-passed", and to be reluctant themselves to practise consultation when dealing with employees. If, on the other hand, consultation is seen by top management not simply as an activity in which they engage periodically with representatives, but as a continuous day-to-day process within management itself, this will encourage junior managers to follow the same pattern. In other words, a "chain-reaction" will develop down the "line". The development of administrative procedures of this kind is essential to the success of other measures designed to improve the quality of management or supervision. In their absence, measures such as supervisory training programmes may "boomerang", since the supervisor who has assimilated new ideas may be frustrated upon his return to an environment which precludes their expression. Similarly, although in recent years managerial selection schemes have placed increased emphasis on the possession of appropriate personality and social skills, the individuals selected will be unable to develop their potentialities to the full in an inadequate structure.

In short, effective relations within management are a condition, not only of satisfactory management-union and management-employee relations, but also of the success of measures undertaken at any level which are designed to improve efficiency.

References

1. Rowntree, B. S., *The Human Needs of Labour*, London: Nelson, 1918.
2. Roethlisberger, F. J., and Dickson, W. J., *Management and the Worker*, Harvard University Press, 1940.
3. Scott, W. H., *Industrial Leadership and Joint Consultation*, Liverpool University Press, 1952.
4. Durkheim, Emile, *The Division of Labour*, Glencoe, Illinois: The Free Press, 1933.
5. Florence, P. S., *The Logic of British and American Industry*, London: Routledge and Kegan Paul, 1953.
6. Acton Society Trust, *Management Succession*, Acton Society, London, 1956.
7. Scott, W. H. et al, *Technical Change and Industrial Relations*, Liverpool University Press, 1956.
8. Roethlisberger, F. J., "The Foreman—Master and Victim of Double Talk", *Harvard Business Review*, XXIII, 1945.
9. Scott W. H., and McGivering, I., "Some Impressions of Human Relations Training for Supervisors", *Occupational Psychology*, **27**, 1953.
10. National Institute of Industrial Psychology, *The Foreman*, September 1951.
11. Segerstedt T. T. and Lundquist, A., *Man in Industrialised Society*, S. N. S., Stockholm, 1956.
12. Cole, G. D. H., *Workshop Organisation*, Oxford University Press, 1923.
13. Centers, R., *The Psychology of Social Classes*, Princeton University Press, 1949.
14. Carr-Saunders A. M., and Wilson, P. A., *The Professions*, Oxford University Press, 1933.
    Parsons, T., "The Professions and Social Structure", *Social Forces*, **17**, 1939.
15. Caplow, T., *The Sociology of Work*, Minnesota University Press, 1954.
16. Hall, J., and Caradog Jones, D.,"Social Grading of Occupations", *British Journal of Sociology*, **1**, 1950.
17. Warner W. L., and Abegglen, J. G., *Occupational Mobility in American Business and Industry*, Minnesota University Press, 1955.
18. Barnard, C., *The Functions of the Executive*, Harvard University Press, 1938.
19. Harbison, F. H., "Steel Management on Two Continents: a Comparative Study", *Industrial Relations*, **10**, 1955.
20. Roethlisberger, F. J., *Management and Morale*, Harvard University Press, 1946.
21. Scott, W. H., *Industrial Democracy—a Revaluation*, Liverpool University Press, 1955.

CHAPTER 3

HUMAN RELATIONS ON THE SHOP FLOOR[1]

ROBERT L. KAHN

Survey Research Center, University of Michigan

Bertrand Russell once summed up the purpose of formal work organization by stating that "mankind decided that it would submit to monotony and tedium in order to diminish the risk of starvation."[2] Without pausing to question the costly exchange which Russell's statement asserts, let us consider the important organizational truth implied in his phrase "to diminish the risk of starvation." Organization is above all purposeful. The formal, large-scale work organization is a social invention which is eminently rational in its fitting together of component parts, and in its carefully planned pattern of related functions serving an overall organizational goal. That the goal in some cases be trivial, or evil, is for the moment irrelevant. An organization exists for the achievement of some goal—the creation of a product, the rendering of a service, or the edification of its members—and one of the criteria by which it may properly be judged is its success and efficiency in achieving that goal. In this sense the concept of organizational productivity has great social and theoretical importance, and cannot be dismissed as the sole concern of leaders in industrial management or in government.

This aspect of organizational rationality, which is so clearly observable in the industries of highly developed nations throughout the world, has not grown haphazardly. On the contrary, it reflects strenuous and self-conscious efforts, beginning almost a century ago, to create industrial organizations which would make the most of the technological innovations begun with the Industrial Revolution.[3] We will use the term "scientific management" to refer to this entire movement. Generally speaking, it includes the work of Frederick W. Taylor and others on job methods and the layout of work, the development of time-and-motion study, and the standardization of parts and processes. It includes the development of such auxiliary tools as cost accounting and such recent enthusiasms as work simplification. It includes such organizational theories as those of Fayol, Urwick and Gulick.[4]

These various theories and processes, while spanning a wide range of content and many decades of time, have certain essential features in common. They are all machine-derived; that is, they aim to create an organizational form which is maximally compatible with the technological requirements of machine production. But they are machine-derived in another sense, as James Worthy has pointed out.[5] They regard the organization itself as a machine to turn out a collective product; by extension, the parts and human units of the organization must meet the same standard specifications as the parts of a machine and must bear the same interdependent relationships.

The analogy is an attractive one, and it has the advantage of concentrating attention on the technology of production, and on the desirability of evolving organizational forms which conform to the needs and make the most of the potential of that technology. The great improvements in productivity which have been brought about by scientific management have resulted from changes consistent with this machine theory of industrial organization —from reduction in waste and spoilage of material, from improved planning and coordination of work units, and from the constant simplification of work-cycles (not infrequently to the happy point of complete mechanization at which the substitution of a machine for a man finally eliminates a job which has grown steadily more robot-like in its requirements). Standardization, meticulous attention to the movement of materials and completed parts, detailed prescription of work methods have eliminated much waste motion and physical effort. They have reduced the skill requirements for much industrial work, thus shortening the period of learning or apprenticeship and rendering individual workers more nearly interchangeable in fact as well as theory. There can be little question that the relatively high economic standards which have come since the turn of the century owe much, directly and indirectly, to the machine theory of organization and the many ramifications of scientific management.

There are, however, great flaws in this approach to organization, and these flaws have become increasingly apparent. The theories of scientific management are essentially non-psychological. They purport to specify the manner in which human activities shall be organized, without taking into account the nature of human beings. They assume that for any function which is to be performed in an organization, there is one best method which can be prescribed and that it is the business of a management expert or a time-and-motion engineer to discover that method. It remains only to procure a worker, teach him the simplified motions of the best-of-all-possible methods, and then arrange for him to repeat those motions each hour of the day at the pace which time study sets as "normal" in physiological terms.

These assumptions, which seem so harsh and over-drawn when stated explicitly, are easily found, for example, in Taylor's classic description of his approach to Schmidt, the laborer whose increase from 12½ to 47 tons of pig iron carried daily from stock-pile to flat-car, launched the scientific management movement in the United States. After establishing Schmidt's interest in "becoming a high-priced man," i.e., earning more money, Taylor proceeded to educate him in the requirements of scientific management, which were for the worker to do "just what he's told to do, and no back-talk".[6]

Taylor's approach to Schmidt illustrates the non-psychological character of scientific management. It is non-psychological in its disregard for the feelings and needs, the satisfactions and frustrations of men in the work situation. Indeed, it is almost a non-motivational system, in that only the motive to earn money is taken into account. Even the economic motivation is inadequately treated; it is merely the bait which brings the worker into the orbit of scientific management and perhaps keeps him from leaving. His acceptance of the wage presumably constitutes a kind of psychological contract, by which he agrees to do as he is told, relinquishing any aspirations and suppressing any conflicting feelings of his own. One other implication of this approach to management must be made explicit: that work is drudgery, intrinsically unrewarding and offering no important social satisfactions except through the spending of one's wages.

On the face of it, scientific management appears to epitomize Lord Russell's assertion that mankind had decided on submission to monotony and tedium in the production of goods for the sake of increasing their availability. But is the bargain kept? How well does such a system work? There is reason to think that the unpadded grip of scientific management provokes strong resistance, and is endured by workers only when they find at hand neither the means of resistance nor more desirable kinds of employment. It is not coincidental that such procedures were more easily established at a time when jobs were chronically scarce, and before the emergence of strong labor unions. As these conditions gave way to labor shortages, union-influenced conditions of work, and an extension of democratic values beyond the area of politics, the weaknesses of scientific management became more obvious.. Resentment and dissatisfaction which under earlier conditions had remained covert or found expression in oblique ways, came to be reflected in absence rates, turnover, and grievances.

As a result, there has developed a trend, both in industry and social science, which is critical of the psychological foundations of scientific management and emphasizes the social-psychological aspects of work and work organization. It would be difficult to date exactly the beginning of this concern about human relations. There were men who spoke in such terms from the earliest days of large scale industry, and after World War I they became a significant minority. More general attention to the human problems of industry has come about during the past twenty years. During this period the experience of management has demanded such attention; during this period also there has begun to develop a body of research findings which is gradually replacing assumptions and opinions with empirical evidence.

Most famous of the studies of human relations in industry is the research of Mayo, Roethlisberger, and their colleagues at the Hawthorne plant of the Western Electric Company.[7] Their work showed beyond question that in an apparently well-managed, "efficient" plant, productivity was systematically restricted by workers, incentive pay did not have the intended motivational effects, and supervisors were regarded with marked hostility. Moreover, the attitudes and values of the workers, which were so different from the assumptions of scientific management, were developed into a coherent system of norms and values which were enforced through what amounted to a second organization. An informal organization had been created to meet needs which the formal organization either ignored or directly frustrated. Through this informal organization the workers were able to regulate the pace at which they would work, could work (in part) under the jurisdiction of leaders of their own choosing, and on occasion neutralize the vast apparatus of the formal organization. Finally, the Western Electric researches made it clear that, under certain conditions, the informal organization could reinforce rather than oppose the formal organization. The work norms of the informal organization need not be low, but could be very high. Under such circumstances, the ingenuity of group members would be devoted to increasing productivity, and the workers show as much creativity and derive as much satisfaction from the attainment of such goals as formerly from opposing them.

The Hawthorne experiments did not, however, provide a comprehensive explanation of the conditions which would be required to attain so high a state of worker motivation and satisfaction, nor did they specify the structure and leadership practices which would facilitate such a development. It is perhaps ironical that the high satisfaction-high productivity pattern which the researchers created inadvertently in their first experimental groups could not be extended to the rest of the Hawthorne plant or to industry at large. The great significance of the Hawthorne experiments was in their demonstration of the resistances and human waste which characterized a "scientifically managed" plant, and in their suggestion that the next great gains might be made through a better understanding of the human factors in organization.

Since World War II, there has been a great increase in the number of studies which bring the techniques of quantitative social science to problems of industrial organization. Among them is a series of studies conducted by the Survey Research Center of the University of Michigan. The objectives and point of view which characterize this program are contained in the following quotations, taken from the proposal with which the program was launched in 1947:

> "The capacity of a nation to survive depends in no small part upon its skill in organizing industrial, governmental and military activity. The effectiveness of the political, economic and military activity of any society is determined in large measure by the nature of that society's social organization and by its knowledge and skill in organizing human activity.
>
> For purposes of research, the dynamics of group behavior can be broken down into six fundamental phases which can be stated in question form:

1. What are the forces which determine the objectives and goals that a group has at any particular time? That is, how do groups establish and accept their objectives and goals?

2. What factors influence the success or failure achieved by a group in reaching its goal? What qualities of leadership, participation, membership and interaction bring success or failure?

3. What forms of social structure work best in a given situation?

4. What forces determine the kinds and numbers of members that a group attracts and holds? What makes members more or less active and partisan with regard to any group?

5. What influences the satisfactions that members derive from membership and activity in any given group? How does this vary with different kinds of groups?

6. What causes a group to assume a relationship of cooperation or of conflict with other groups? What principles are involved?"

During the past ten years we have sought the answers to these questions by means of a series of quantitative research projects in large scale organizations of various kinds—business and industry, government, labor unions, and voluntary groups. In many of these studies we have concentrated on the criteria of productivity and satisfaction, i.e., the ability of an organization to achieve its formal goals and also to offer high psychological return to its members. These organizational abilities and effects we have attempted to understand in terms of leadership patterns, organizational structure, peer relations, and to a lesser extent, in terms of individual attributes of personality and background. It is in terms of these research aims and with the findings of perhaps two dozen major projects now in hand that we turn to a more specific discussion of "Human Relations on the Shop Floor." In this discussion we will attempt to describe and understand human relations, worker attitudes and motives as they are revealed by empirical research in industry, not as the machine model of organization might have predicted them. This we will do by considering first, the meaning of work to the worker himself; second, the worker's goals on the job and his views of how they may be attained with particular reference to criteria of productivity and satisfaction; and third, the different patterns of leadership which we have found to be characteristic of high-performing and low-performing groups in industry.

The Meaning of Work[8]

We have said that the conception of work inherent in the theories of scientific management makes the job entirely an instrumental thing. Work is valued, presumably, neither for itself nor for the social environment in which it is carried on; it is valued only for what it can bring in exchange. It would be interesting to speculate on the persistence and viability of this idea, in the face of mountainous evidence to the contrary. Perhaps some managements persist in thinking of labor merely as something exchanged for money because the employer's role leads him to define the laborer's work in precisely these terms: it is something which the employer buys for money; therefore, by extension, something which the worker gives only in exchange for money. Whatever the reason, people at each hierarchical level in industry seem quick to perceive

Table 1

FACTORS RATED OF MAJOR IMPORTANCE ON THE JOB

Per cent who give a rank of 1, 2, or 3 to:	Men[1]	Foremen's[2] Perception of Men	Foremen[1]	General[2] Foremen's Perception of Foremen	General[1] Foremen
Steady work and steady wages	61 %	79 %	62 %	86 %	52 %
High wages	28	61	17	58	11
Pensions and other old age security benefits	13	17	12	29	15
Not having to work too hard	13	30	4	25	2
Getting along well with the people I work with	36	17	39	22	43
Getting along well with my supervisor	28	14	28	15	24
Good chance to turn out good quality work	16	11	18	13	27
Good chance to do interesting work	22	12	38	14	43
Good chances for promotion	25	23	42	24	47
Good physical working conditions	21	19	18	4	11
Total	*	*	*	*	*
No. of cases	2499	196	196	45	45

* Percentages total over 100 because they include three rankings for each person.

[1] Question: Different people want different things out of a job. What are the things you yourself feel are *most important* in a job?

[2] Question: Different people want different things out of a job. What are the things you think most of the people you supervise feel are *most important* in a job?

the importance of non-financial factors in their own work, but equally swift to assume that people at lower levels of responsibility are motivated first of all by the dollar. The preceding table illustrates this point with data taken from approximately 4,000 workers and supervisors in a company manufacturing household appliances in the midwestern United States.

With respect to the importance of high wages, for example, 61 per cent of the foremen expect the men to rank them of major importance, but only 28 per cent of the men do so. Similarly, 58 per cent of the general foremen expect the foremen to rate high wages of major importance, but only 17 per cent of the foremen conform to these expectations. The results show the same pattern for steady work and steady wages, and for pensions and other old-age security benefits.

Conversely, the foremen and general foremen tend to underestimate the importance of non-monetary, social-psychological factors to their subordinates. Thus, 36 per cent of the men consider getting along with the people they work with to be one of the three most important factors on the list, but only 17 per cent of the foremen expected the men to rate this factor so high. General foremen similarly underestimated the importance of this factor to the foremen. Differences of the same sort are observable for such factors as having a good chance to do interesting work and having a good chance to turn out work of good quality.

If we think of the first four items in the table as representing goals of money, economic security, and avoidance of undue physical effort, we find that the foremen overestimate grossly the men's emphasis on such goals. The average difference between the men's actual responses (column 1) and foremen's perceptions of the men (column 2) is 18 percentage points for these items. For the items which reflect needs for social approval and self-expression—getting on well with one's supervisor and fellow workers, and having a chance to do work of high quality and interesting content—the pattern is reversed; foremen underestimate by an average of 17 percentage points the proportion of men who consider these factors to be among the most important.

The perceptions of the foremen have some base in reality, of course. The foremen do differ from the men in their greater emphasis on factors of job content, and in their less frequent mention of high wages as a requirement. But the actual differences between foremen and men are modest, in comparison with the differences as the foremen perceive them to be. The rank order correlation between the responses of foremen and men on factors of major importance in a job (columns 1 and 3 in Table 1) is .76, but the correlation between the responses of the foremen and their perception of the men's opinions is only .05. Such misperception may be useful for the foremen, in that it helps them maintain a sense of superiority to those they supervise, but it can hardly be useful for the organization. The organizational effects of management's inability to assess correctly the needs and motives of workers have yet to be traced out in detail. We would expect, however, that such misperceptions would lead inevitably to unintended offenses on the part of supervisors, and to the choice of ineffective devices for motivating employees. Foreman and worker, in such circumstances, fail to communicate in a way which has the intended effect. It becomes impossible to establish a pattern of reciprocal influence and accommodation, and in spite of their physical proximity they become, in Rogers' phrase, two people "missing each other in psychological space."

Some evidence for this assertion comes from a study of worker productivity in a tractor factory. All employees who worked on jobs for which time-study had established a rate were asked to estimate what they considered to be "reasonable productivity" on their job. The foremen of these workers were then asked to estimate what *the men* would consider to be reasonable productivity. A comparison of the responses of foremen and men revealed that the foremen consistently overestimated the men's productivity standards. Moreover, the foremen who were least accurate in estimating the standards of their men also were least successful in achieving high productivity. For example, foremen whose work groups had average productivity of 68–77 per cent of the time-study norm overestimated the men's standards by 16 percentage points; foremen whose work groups averaged above 90 in actual productivity were able to estimate the men's standards within 3–6 percentage points.

There are problems of interpretation with these findings. We cannot be certain that the foreman's inability to estimate the standards of his subordinates is a cause of his failure to achieve high productivity. This conclusion is consistent with the data, however. We cannot lead well people whose motives we misunderstand. That the needs and goals of foremen and men should be so similar in fact lends a special irony to the misunderstanding.

Some union leaders, like some managements, have tended to deprecate the non-economic aspects of the job, perhaps because they viewed with suspicion any efforts of management to improve the social or "human relations" aspects of work. An ounce of energy bought at the going wage rate was an open transaction, but management efforts to deal with the less tangible aspects of work seemed like a kind of psychological legerdemain designed to motivate the worker to unpaid effort or to develop in him loyalties and gratitude more appropriately directed to the union. Some years ago, the CIO publication *Ammunition* provided an example of this point of view in an article which classified human relations in industry as a kind of "milk-cow sociology," intended to develop a kind of spurious placidity among workers.[9] It must be admitted that many a "fringe benefit" and many a program of research or training in "human relations" has been sponsored by management in the hope that productivity might be increased or union organization avoided, but these facts should not lead to the under-evaluation of the psychological aspects of the job.

One way of getting insight into the importance of any object or experience is to observe the effects on the individual when he is deprived of it. It is difficult, however, to observe the effects of losing the intrinsic and social rewards of work, because the effects of these losses cannot easily be separated from the loss of livelihood which typically accompanies them. Thus, Jahoda's pioneering study of the unemployed of Marienthal, which documents vividly the personal disintegration of the men who were long without jobs, describes the effects of economic deprivation as well as the other losses which were involved.[10] More recently, the emotional problems of retired workers, even those who are free of economic difficulties, have provided additional evidence that men do not work only for money.

In a study conducted by the Survey Research Center in 1954, an attempt was made to measure directly the extent to which work served other than the instrumental purpose of making a living, and to determine some of the other functions which work served for people in different occupations. The study involved personal interviews with a nation-wide sample of employed men, employed women, and housewives. All the employed persons in the sample, of whom 401 were men, were asked the following questions:

"If by some chance you inherited enough money to live comfortably without working, do you think that you would work anyway or not?"

And, for those who answered that they would continue working:

"Why do you feel that you would work?"

Finally, for the same group:

"Suppose you didn't work; what would you miss most?"

The responses to these questions illustrate clearly the extent to which workers depend upon their jobs for self-expression, for social relationships, and to give meaning to life. Only one man in five said that he would stop working if he had no need for the money which the job paid him; four out of five said that they would continue to work.

People found it easier to reach this hypothetical decision than to explain their reasons for doing so. A variety of reasons were given by those who would continue working, but the answer given most frequently was "to keep occupied." About one-third of the respondents gave this explanation for their wish to continue work, and another third gave answers which make the same point in a negative fashion; they explained that without work they would "feel lost," "go crazy," feel useless or bored, or "not know what to do with my time." The thought which comes through strongly in these interviews is that the pattern of life, for the employed man, has been built around the job and that a state of "no job" sounds to him frighteningly like a state of "no life."

This interpretation is strengthened by the answers of men to the question of what they would miss most if they did not work. The answers, in roughly comparable numbers, point toward the two things which are at the center of life for the individual—activity and contact with other human beings. The latter was mentioned spontaneously by almost one-third of the men as the thing they would miss most if they did not work.

In this research on the meaning of work in the life of the individual, there is no implication that the job serves the same functions for all workers, or that it has equal importance for all. There is a general tendency for the proportion of men who would stop working if they could, to increase with age. Of the men between 21 and 34 years of age interviewed in the Survey Research Center's study,

Table 2

PERCEPTIONS OF THINGS MISSED BY NOT WORKING[8]

	Number	Per cent
General feeling		
Feeling of living, belonging, being part of something	6	3
Feeling of doing something important, worth-while, feeling of self-respect	23	9
Feeling of interest, being interested	12	5
Feeling of doing something, would be restless	62	25
Total expressing general feeling	103	42
Specific things missed		
The kind of work I do	29	12
The people I know through or at work, the friends, contacts	77	31
Regular routine	16	6
Money	5	2
Other	2	1
Total mentioning specific things missed	129	52
Nothing missed	15	6
Total responding	247	100
Not ascertained	67	
Total would work	314	
Total would not work	79	
Not ascertained	8	
Total sample	401	

Question: Suppose you didn't work; what would you miss most?

only 10 per cent said that they would stop working if they were economically able to do so. This proportion shows regular increases in each succeeding age group, until it reaches 39 per cent among those between the ages of 55 and 64 years. Thereafter, it drops again, probably because many men over 65 have a real choice between work and retirement, and the sample of respondents was drawn only from employed men.

More striking differences appeared when the meaning of work was examined for men in different occupations. Professional men most frequently explained their wish to continue working in terms of their interest in their professional field, or the sense of accomplishment which they gained from exercising their professional skills. Managers and sales people were no more likely to speak in such positive terms than to emphasize the job as a way of keeping occupied and active. As we descend the hierarchy of skill, status, and rewards, fewer men think of continuing work for reasons of interest or self-expression, and the importance of the job as mere activity is correspondingly greater.

For the vast majority of men of all ages and in all occupations, however, the work role meets many needs. By fulfilling its requirements he is able to provide for himself and his family, but on it he depends also for many other satisfactions—for self-expression, for new experience, for the esteem and appreciation of others. On the extent to which his work meets all these needs, we may hypothesize, depends his involvement in it, his wish to continue in it, and his willingness to invest energy in it.

Paths and Goals[11]

The attempt to find empirical answers to the ancient question of why men work has provided rich data, data of great complexity and vitality, data much closer to life than the neat and simplified theories which propose to explain behavior on the job in terms of economic self-interest or any other single motive. The responses of workers reveal instead an array of needs which employees attempt to satisfy on the job. Money is important because of its marvellous versatility in our culture as a means to the satisfaction of more basic needs. But in addition there is the need for interaction, acceptance, and approval by others—without which self-esteem becomes impossible of attainment. And in addition to these needs, which depend for their satisfaction on the social circumstances of the job, there are needs still more closely dependent for their satisfaction on the intrinsic content of the job—among them self-expression, desire for new experience, and self-determination.

If these are the needs which men attempt to fulfill in the work situation, they should enable us to understand more fully and to predict more accurately the behavior of workers. We would expect that certain things in the work situation would come to be valued because they were seen as satisfying these needs, and that these things would become *goals*, especially for those workers who felt most strongly the corresponding needs. Thus, making a high wage or gaining the friendship of men in the work group are examples of specific goals, the achievement of which might, in the former case, guarantee the satisfaction of such basic biological needs as hunger, and in the latter the need for acceptance and approval. At this point, we can speak of the worker as *motivated* to obtain a high wage or to make friends. The word *motive*, as Newcomb says[12], points in two directions—to the *need* within the individual and to the *goal*, an object in his environment, which he sees as a potential source of need satisfaction.

We are not yet ready, however, to attempt a prediction of worker behavior, even if we are able to ascertain the relevant needs and goals. A certain worker has as a goal the attainment of a high wage, but we cannot predict from this fact alone what behavior he will manifest in an attempt to reach this goal. He may begin taking night-school courses; he may cultivate more amiable relations with his foreman; he may become active in his trade union, or he may improve his performance on the job. Which of these things he will attempt will depend upon his perceptions—upon what he sees as a *path* to his goal.

With the concepts of *need*, *goal*, and *path*, we have the major elements for attempting to predict behavior in the work situation. We have not, however, taken account of the barriers which may prevent the worker from taking the path which he perceives to lead to the attainment of his goals. For example, the worker who is convinced that high productivity will lead to increased wages may still be prevented by the flow of materials, or the pace of the assembly line, or his dependence upon other workers, from actually increasing his own productivity. This possibility requires the addition of *freedom* or opportunity for the employee to take the path or engage in the behavior which he sees as leading to his goal.

The prediction of productivity in terms of these concepts might be stated as follows: if a worker sees high productivity as a path leading to the attainment of one or more of his personal goals, he will tend to be a high producer, provided that he is free to do so. Conversely, if he sees low productivity as a path to the achievement of his goals, he will tend to be a low producer.

This prediction, called the "path-goal hypothesis," rests upon a number of postulates or assumptions: that people have in common a number of needs; that, placed in a common environment, people will seek out goals by which these needs may be satisfied; that their choice of behavior will be (in part) determined by their perception of what behaviors are most likely to lead to the attainment of their goals. Such an approach to the prediction of productivity is no less rationalistic than the approach of scientific management. It asserts that productivity behavior is the implementation of a rational decision, but emphasizes that the decision may have been made to serve goals other than money, and that the worker may perceive low productivity as a means of achieving his goals under certain circumstances. Finally, the concept of freedom reminds us that productivity is not solely a function of the worker's motivation to produce, but depends also upon non-psychological factors which may enable him to give or restrain him from giving, expression to his motives.

The path-goal hypothesis was formulated and given a first test in a recent study of factory workers in light industry. The study included the incentive workers in the two plants of a company manufacturing household appliances. These workers were asked to rank according to their importance a number of goals which might be attained on a job. Among them were "making more money in the long run," "getting promoted to a job with a higher base rate," and "getting along well with the work group." Workers who ranked a goal-item 1, 2, or 3 on a scale ranging from 1 to 10 were considered to have a high level of need for which this goal represented a potential source of satisfaction. The others formed the low-need group for that item.

For each goal-item, workers were then asked to appraise the instrumentality of high productivity and of low productivity. They did this by rating high productivity on a five point scale, from "helping" to "hurting" the attainment of the goal in question. Low productivity was rated in the same fashion.

Finally, the level of freedom was determined on the basis of the worker's perception, his experience on the job, and his age. Experience was assumed to reflect a degree of expertness necessary to vary one's own pace, and age was assumed to reflect the physiological ability to produce at high levels. Workers who said that they were able to set their own pace on the job, who had more than six months' experience on the job, and who were between 20 and 59 years of age were classified as free. The remainder were put in the not-free group.

The findings from this analysis confirm clearly the basic hypothesis that the behavior of high productivity will occur more frequently among those workers who see it as a path to some goal which they value. As Table 3 shows, a larger proportion of workers who have a "positive perception" of productivity (high productivity helps or low productivity hurts) are higher producers. Workers whose perceptions are "negative" or "neutral" (high productivity hurts or is irrelevant; low productivity helps or is irrelevant) are more often low producers. Of the six comparisons which test this hypothesis, five are in the predicted direction and four are statistically significant. The magnitude of the differences does not follow any clear pattern, but the largest difference occurs between those workers who perceive productivity as a path to the goal of making more money in the long run, and those who do not.

Table 3

Path-Goal Perception in Relation to Productivity Level for the Individual Incentive Group with Respect to Selected Goal-Items*

	Per cent of High Producers**					
	Instrumentality of High Productivity			Instrumentality of Low Productivity		
Goal Item	Positive Perception (High Productivity "Helps")		Negative and/or Neutral Perception (High Productivity "Hurts" or is irrelevant)	Positive Perception (Low Productivity "Hurts")		Negative and/or Neutral Perception (Low Productivity "Helps" or is irrelevant)
(1) More money in the long run	38 % (234)	>	21 % (376)	30 % (380)	>	22 % (215)
(2) Promotion to a higher base rate	26 % (236)	<	30 % (368)	32 % (298)	>	23 % (292)
(3) Getting along well with work group	30 % (416)	>	23 % (195)	33 % (189)	>	24 % (398)

* In all cases, "neutral" perception is combined with "negative" perception except for goal item (3), instrumentality of high productivity, where it is combined with the "positive" perception group.

** Percentages are based on the number in the corresponding parentheses. The complement of each percentage, not appearing in the table, would indicate the percentage of low producers in each case.

The rationale for the hypothesis involves more than the perception of instrumentality, however. To bear out our original prediction we should be able to demonstrate that the kinds of differences observed in Table 3 are sharper when the additional variables of freedom and level-of-need are introduced. Specifically, the differences in productivity between workers who perceive it positively

Table 4

PATH-GOAL PERCEPTION IN RELATION TO PRODUCTIVITY LEVEL, FOR THE INDIVIDUAL INCENTIVE GROUP WITH RESPECT TO SELECTED GOAL-ITEMS, WHEN CONTROLLING FOR LEVELS OF NEED AND FREEDOM

	Per cent of High Producers*							
	Free				Not-Free			
	High Need		Low Need		High Need		Low Need	
Goal-Item	Positive Perception (1)	Negative and/or Neutral Perception (2)	Positive Perception (3)	Negative and/or Neutral Perception (4)	Positive Perception (5)	Negative and/or Neutral Perception (6)	Positive Perception (7)	Negative and/or Neutral Perception (8)
Instrumentality of High Productivity								
(1) More money in the long run	66 % (38) >	22 % (37)	40 % (57) >	39 % (79)	17 % (48) >	11 % (82)	33 % (72) >	17 % (146)
(2) Promotion to a higher base rate .	46 % (35) >	44 % (39)	42 % (48) >	39 % (87)	15 % (52) >	13 % (78)	17 % (89) <	27 % (126)
(3) Getting along well with work group	46 % (48) >	29 % (28)	45 % (94) >	37 % (43)	26 % (85) >	18 % (45)	18 % (156) >	13 % (64)
Instrumentality of Low Productivity								
(1) More money in the long run	49 % (53) >	26 % (19)	40 % (91) <	41 % (41)	11 % (83) <	13 % (47)	27 % (122) >	17 % (87)
(2) Promotion to a higher base rate .	56 % (33) >	31 % (39)	47 % (70) >	33 % (61)	12 % (60) =	12 % (68)	24 % (110) >	20 % (98)
(3) Getting along well with work group	50 % (28) >	32 % (47)	52 % (48) >	38 % (84)	21 % (38) >	23 % (86)	18 % (61) >	15 % (150)

* Percentages are based on the number in the corresponding parentheses. The complement of each percentage, not appearing in the table would indicate the percentage of low producers in each case.

and those who do not should be greatest among workers who have a high level of need for the goal-item in question and who are free to set their own pace on the job. The relevant data are presented in Table 4.

There are, of course, a large number of comparisons which are possible from this table. Those most relevant for the path-goal hypothesis are the comparisons among the differences between columns 1 and 2, in relation to the differences between columns 3 and 4, 5 and 6, 7 and 8. Our theory predicts that, for each goal-item, the difference between columns 1 and 2 should be greater than the difference between any of the other pairs of columns. This is predicted because columns 1 and 2 represent workers whose level of need is high and whose level of freedom to set their own pace is also high. This group, therefore, is highly motivated toward goal achievement and is free of barriers, so far as the "path" of productivity is concerned. For this group, then, productivity behavior should be predictable in terms of the perceived consequences of high and low production.

In general, the results are as predicted. Thus, among "high-need," "free" workers, 66 per cent of those who perceive high productivity as instrumental to the goal of making more money are in fact high producers (column 1). Among workers of equally high need for money and equal freedom, but who do not perceive high productivity as instrumental to their goal, only 22 per cent are high producers. The difference of 44 percentage points should be compared to differences of 1 point between columns 3 and 4, 6 points between columns 5 and 6, and 16 points between columns 7 and 8 —all for the same goal-item. If similar comparisons are made for the other goal-items, and for the perception of low productivity as well as high, we find that 16 of the 18 comparisons are in the predicted direction; one shows no difference, and one shows a difference of one percentage point in the opposite direction.

The results of this approach to understanding industrial productivity are mixed. The predictions were generally borne out, as we have seen, and the concepts of goals, perceived paths, and barriers appear meaningful in this context and related among themselves in a logical way. However, work with some other goal-items yielded findings less clear-cut, and an attempt at multivariate analysis indicated that only a modest fraction of the variance in productivity has been explained in path-goal terms. Nevertheless, the approach has promise, and offers a framework into which fit comfortably the most numerous and consistent of the empirical findings on social-psychological factors related to industrial productivity—those dealing with supervisory and leadership skills.

Patterns of Leadership[13]

Research findings on the meaning of work demonstrate the wide range of needs which man seeks to satisfy on the job. The data on individual productivity which we have just reviewed suggest that this complicated search for need satisfaction can be understood in terms of goals sought, paths perceived for their attainment, and barriers which stand between the goals and the individual who aspires to them. In these terms, we have asserted, may be understood also the specific decisions of workers to produce at top capacity or less, to be present or absent, to remain on a job or to seek a new one. We have yet to consider, however, how the functions of the supervisor or leader fit into this scheme. The evidence of experience and research points to the importance of leadership in determining worker productivity. Indeed, the volume of research data in this area is probably greater than on any other social-psychological aspect of industry. What functions does the supervisor perform? How do they relate to the worker's efforts to achieve his own goals on the job? Why do these functions and the manner of their performance have such great significance for the level of worker motivation and productivity?

Working from the path-goal hypothesis, we can conceptualize the role of the supervisor in terms of four functions:

(1) *Providing direct need satisfaction*

The supervisor may satisfy directly and unconditionally some of the needs of his subordinates. For example, a worker may have a specific need to be approved and accepted by people who have authority over him. To the extent that his supervisor behaves toward this employee in a warm, supportive, accepting fashion, some of the employee's needs are being met directly in the job situation. If such behavior on the part of the supervisor is not conditional upon the behavior of the employee, we have an instance of direct goal attainment and need satisfaction uncomplicated by other factors.

(2) *Structuring the path to goal attainment*

In the preceding discussion of the path-goal approach to productivity, we emphasized the importance of the employee's perception of a means or path by which his own goals may be attained. We need now to consider the supervisor's influence on such perceptions. Suppose that a factory worker wants very much to be promoted to a job of higher skill. From this fact alone we cannot predict what path or course of action the man may take in order to achieve his goal of promotion. He may attempt to increase the quantity or quality of his output on the job. He may attempt to curry favor with his foreman by means of fawning and subservient behavior. He may not change his behavior on the job in any way, but may instead enroll in a night-school for technical training. Which of these varied paths the employee takes will depend upon his perception of which one leads most directly and most surely to his goal of promotion (assuming no conflicting goals or other impediments). But what factors will determine the employee's perception? There may be an infinite number of factors which have some influence on this perception—some of them present in the immediate work situation, some of them a reflection of out-plant relationships, still others remote in time and space from the present job. Among the factors in the work situation which we would expect to be important determinants of the paths which the employee perceives as leading to attainment of his goals is the behavior of his immediate supervisor. The worker is quick to assess whether a supervisor makes recommendations for promotion on the basis of favoritism, special training, performance on the job, or some other set of considerations. What behavioral path the worker chooses then depends in large measure upon the cues which the supervisor has provided. In this fashion the supervisor does much to determine the behaviors by which workers will attempt to achieve their goals on the job.

(3) *Enabling goal achievement*

The path-determining function of supervision which we have just described is largely a motivational process. One supervisor may behave in a way which motivates high productivity as a means to promotion, while another supervisor's behavior motivates flattery and prevarication for the same purpose. But the supervisor does other things which have little to do with employee motivation. Such a function is the enabling aspect of the supervisor's role. When the supervisor improves the planning of the work for his group, eliminates production bottle-necks, or removes some other barrier which prevents workers from following their chosen path to goal attainment, the supervisor is performing the function of enabling goal achievement. Much of the technical planning part of his work would fall in this category.

(4) *Modifying employee goals*

It seems likely that the influence of the first-line industrial supervisor on the goals of his subordinates is not large. We know that many of the important goals for which men strive are laid down very early in their experience and have relatively little chance of being drastically modified by the behavior of a supervisor. If one worker has an acute need to win the approval of his fellows, while another is relatively independent, it is most improbable that the behavior of the supervisor will alter these facts materially. Yet the influence of supervisors is not limited only to paths. The supervisor may have some influence on the actual goals which employees seek to attain. It is possible, for example, that an employee who has never thought of being promoted to a supervisory position may acquire this idea and come to consider it a goal of great importance, as a result of the encouragement and generation of self-confidence which a supervisor is able to provide.

If our derivation of supervisory functions is valid, we should expect that a comparison of successful with unsuccessful supervisors would reveal differences in the extent to which the supervisors perform these functions and in the skill with which they are performed. We would not expect, of course, to find that the pattern of supervisory functions which was optimal for one criterion of organizational effectiveness would necessarily be best in terms of other criteria. For example, it seems likely that, almost by definition the ability of the supervisor to function as a direct satisfier of employee needs would be a major determinant of the level of worker satisfaction. It does not follow, however, that the same behavior by a supervisor would be conducive to a high level of productivity. Indeed if a supervisor were willing and able to provide complete need satisfaction for employees regardless of their productivity, we would predict that employees working under such supervision would not be motivated to a high level of performance. It would be desirable to test our approach to supervisory functions by comparing employee groups and entire organizations which are high and low with respect to a number of criteria—satisfaction, absence, productivity, turnover, and the like. For each criterion of organizational effectiveness, the successful supervisory pattern would be predicted to differ from the unsuccessful, and we would expect that the differences could be understood in terms of the four basic supervisory functions described above.

Let us provide a partial test of this approach by reviewing the relationships which have been discovered between specific supervisory behaviors and the productivity of employees. In doing so we will limit ourselves to the work of the Survey Research Center. These findings are based upon quantitative studies involving the large scale collection of data in industrial situations. The data were collected by means of intensive interviews and paper-and-pencil questionnaires administered to a number of different employee groups—office workers in an insurance company, section hands on a railroad, factory workers in a company manufacturing tractors and earth-moving equipment, and factory workers employed in the manufacture of household appliances. More recently, there have been added to those populations studies of scientists and professional workers, and employees in transportation. In each of these studies the analysis included comparisons of the responses of employees and supervisors in high-producing groups with those in low-producing groups. The findings, categorized in terms of the four supervisory functions described above, are as follows:

(1) *Providing direct need satisfaction*

The needs which appear to be satisfied directly by the supervisor are in the category of ego motives—for example, self-expression, which gives the individual a chance to develop and demonstrate his own abilities and talents; self-determination, the feeling of freedom which comes from choice in decisions which affect oneself; and ego-enhancement, the increase in self-esteem which comes about through the appreciation of the self by others.

There is evidence that the pattern of supervision which meets the worker's need for autonomy tends also to achieve high productivity. Among office workers in an insurance company, low-producing supervisors were found to check up on their employees more frequently, to give them more detailed and more frequent work instructions, and in general to limit their freedom to do the work in their own way. In the company manufacturing tractors and earth-moving equipment, it was the high-producing workers who reported more often that they set their own pace on the job.

Another cluster of research findings reflects the importance of the supervisor as a source of support and ego-enhancement for the employee. Again the supervisors who fulfill this need best have also achieved significantly higher productivity in the work groups under their direction. The specific ways in which the individual supervisor provides a sense of ego-enhancement to the employees in his work group varies from situation to situation, but the resulting supportive personal relationship is generally characteristic of the supervisors with the better production records. Thus, in the railroad study, the workers in high-producing groups more frequently characterized their foremen as taking a personal interest in them and their off-the-job problems. This finding was repeated in a study in heavy industry in which the high-producing employees reported that their foremen took a personal interest in them. It is quite possible that this difference in perception is in part cause and in part effect. The low-producing foreman has a less satisfactory relationship with his employees and he may well be right in thinking that they want no more of the kind of relationship which he offers. At the same time the fact that they wish to minimize the relationship undoubtedly contributes to the psychological distance between him and the work group and reduces the possibility of his satisfying directly the workers' needs for appreciation and ego-enhancement.

Among the workers in heavy industry, there were a number of specific research findings which testified to the greater productive success of those supervisors who made their supervision an ego-enhancing rather than an ego-destructive experience for the employees. In the tractor factory the workers with the highest production records were more likely to report a good overall relationship with their foreman in terms of the quality of his supervision, the way they got along with him personally, and the interest he took in them. In addition, they said that he was approachable and easy to talk to.

Another kind of evidence of the high-producing supervisor's greater concern for meeting employee needs came from the study in the insurance company. In that study the supervisors were asked this question: "Some people feel the job of supervisor is tough because they stand between the workers and management. Do you feel that this is a problem?" Supervisors were encouraged to enlarge on their answers to this question, and to discuss the ways in which they handled their role of mediator between the workers and management. The high-producing supervisors were predominantly employee-identified, according to their own report, and felt that they best fulfilled their supervisory responsibilities by retaining the employee point of view. As one of them put it, ". . . I always try to put myself in their (employees') place because I can remember when I was a clerk and had someone over me and things I was allowed to do and I don't think they feel that I'm above them or anything like that."[14]

The low-producing supervisors were for the most part management-identified, and tended to emphasize their responsibility for carrying management requirements to employees, without the complementary function of communicating workers' needs to higher levels of supervision. Needless to say, this interpretation of the supervisory function generated its own tensions. In the words of one management-identified supervisor, "Yeah, I think it's tough, because when you tell the girls things, I have to tell them that I'm not after the girl personally. It is because someone is always after me. I tell them I dislike things as much as they do, and if we'd all cooperate . . ."

The distinction between employee-identified and management-identified supervisors, and their relative success in achieving high productivity was borne out by the reactions of supervisors to two aspects of company policy which at the time of the study constituted problems in morale or employee motivation. One of these was the dining-room set-up. The company provided lunches to all employees without cost. These lunches were served in a number of different dining-rooms, which differed in furniture, decor, menu, and quality of service. The job title and hierarchical level of each employee determined the dining-room to which he was assigned, and the dining-room to which he was given access thus became a visible indication of his status in the organization. Competition for entree to the "higher" dining-rooms was common and grievances over allegedly improper assignments were equally so. In general, the high-producing supervisors were more aware of this situation as a source of employee disaffection, and were more critical of management for maintaining the graded sequence of dining-rooms. One supervisor of a high-producing group said bluntly, "I don't approve of that. It gives the impression that if their salary is a little higher than someone else's that they're better than the others and that's not so. Certain circumstances have put them there . . ." By contrast, the head of a low-producing section said, "Well, that is all right as far as I'm concerned. After all, our lunch hour is short now and it doesn't matter where you eat."

With respect to the placement policy, similar differences emerged between supervisors of high and low sections. High-producing supervisors were more aware of the adverse effects of placing employees on jobs "where they're needed instead of where they belong." Low-producing supervisors were more likely to feel that the company did well in placing people on the kind of jobs they did best, and that even if people were put on jobs they knew nothing about, "they can always learn the work."

It would be unwise, however, to give the impression that the supervisor can solve the problem of productivity merely by his skills and sensitivity in meeting directly such employee needs as those for autonomy and ego-enhancement. The evidence is strong that directly supportive behavior by the supervisor succeeds best both in terms of satisfaction and productivity when it is combined with equal effectiveness in establishing paths by which employees may attain others of their goals and in enabling the employees to traverse those paths. An analysis reported by Pelz provides one example of such evidence.[15] His data are based on questionnaires and interviews taken with the almost 10,000 supervisory and non-supervisory employees of a public utility in a large metropolitan area. One of his major objectives was to discover the determinants of employee satisfaction, especially those involving the attitudes and behavior of the first-line supervisor. For example, to what extent should the supervisor involve his employees in the decision-making process if employee satisfaction is to be of the highest? Should the supervisor remain dignified and aloof or should he mingle freely with his employees as a social equal? In the case of conflicts between what management wants and what the employees want, does the supervisor go to bat for management or does he go to bat for the employees? These and many other aspects of supervisory behavior toward employees and toward superiors were explored in personal interviews and quantitative measures of them were obtained. An analysis was then conducted which was designed to answer the following single question: "What are the characteristics of effective supervisors—effective, that is, in terms of high employee satisfaction?" The method employed in an attempt to find the answer was a simple one. A measure of overall satisfaction was obtained. Forty high-satisfaction and thirty low-satisfaction groups were identified and their supervisors were compared. We inspected differences between these two sets of supervisors in terms of fifty items of information obtained from interviews with them, expecting to find a number of items which distinguished between them. The items on which they differed might therefore be said to account in part for the high or low satisfaction within their groups.

The fact was that only six out of the fifty items showed differences large enough to be trustworthy. This was hardly more than we should expect solely from chance. Apparently, the ability of the supervisor to provide real need satisfaction to his employees requires more than the superficial evidence of human relations skills. The pat on the back, or even the involvement of the employee in decision-making is not enough in itself.

A subsequent analysis of the same data by Pelz reinforces this point in dramatic fashion. Exploring the effects of the supervisor's power or influence in the larger organization as a factor which might condition the reaction of employees to his intended acts of supportiveness, Pelz found that an apparently identical behavior might have positive effects on employees when performed by a high-influence supervisor and negative effects when performed by a low-influence supervisor. For example, under influential supervisors, an increase in "siding with employees" is accompanied by a general rise in employee satisfaction. But under non-influential supervisors the same behavior produces no rise but a slight drop in employee satisfaction. These findings are best summarized by means of 28 measures of the relationship between a supervisor's behavior and various employee attitudes in different types of situation. Such measures were obtained in identical fashion for high-influence and low-influence supervisors. Under high-influence supervisors in 19 times out of 28 we find that such measures as "siding with the employees" or "social closeness to employees" are accompanied by a rise in employee satisfaction. Under low-influence supervisors, however, these supervisory behaviors are accompanied by a rise in satisfaction only 8 times out of 28.

We may conclude that a supervisor's influence or power outside his own work group conditions the effect which his behavior has upon employee attitudes. Supervisory acts which are directed to providing immediate need satisfaction to employees are more likely to accomplish their purpose if the supervisor also has enough power and influence so that his supportive behaviors have implications for the ability of employees to achieve some of the external goals and benefits for which they strive on the job. In other words, the supervisor is unlikely to function effectively as a direct satisfier of employee needs unless he is able to function also in structuring paths by which employee needs may be satisfied and in enabling the employee to travel those paths more successfully.

(2) *Structuring the path to goal attainment*

The role of the supervisor in structuring or providing paths by which the employee may attain his goals is difficult to measure. Separating this function from the enabling function—the removal of barriers to goal attainment—is especially difficult on the basis of data currently available. Nevertheless, there are a few findings which suggest that supervisors who have actually achieved high levels of productivity have done so in part by making such behavior on the part of the employee a path to supervisory approval and a condition for the exertion of supervisory influence. For example, among employees in a tractor factory, those in the high-producing groups were more likely to say that their foreman considered high productivity one of the most important things on the job. Employees in low-producing groups more often said that other things were equally important or more important to their foreman. The implication of such a finding is that the high-producing supervisor not only wants to attain high productivity but has successfully communicated to his employees that at least one of the paths to supervisory approval is to produce at a high rate.

There is evidence also that establishment of this path to goal attainment does not originate with the first level supervisor, but at higher levels in the organization. When the foremen in the tractor company were asked how *their* supervisors felt about "getting a high performance figure," their responses showed the same pattern as those of their subordinates. Almost three out of four of the foremen with the best production records reported that their supervisors considered high productivity to be one of the most important things on the job; less than half of the foremen of lower producing groups gave the same response.

The emphasis on productivity which characterized these two levels of supervision should not be interpreted as necessarily in conflict with the image of sensitive, employee-centered supervision. The most successful supervisors rate productivity as *one* of the most important things on the job, but not *the* most important. Supervisors who are seen by their subordinates as rating productivity above all other things are as likely to be low as high in actual production. Moreover, the feeling of direct pressure for production is characteristic of the low-producing rather than the high-producing groups. We conclude that the successful supervisor is able to communicate his own reasonable interest in achieving a good production record, and to make clear that he appreciates and rewards productive behavior, without implying that this is his only concern or that pressure and punishment are his major devices for motivation.

Another evidence of the path-determining function of the more successful supervisors came from the study of employees in an insurance company. It was found in that study that the supervisors of the high-producing work groups made on the average *fewer* recommendations for promotion than did supervisors of low-producing groups. This finding, which appeared troublesome at first, was clarified by the further discovery that, despite the smaller number of recommendations made by high-producing supervisors, more of their recommendations were successful. The high-producing supervisor was likely either to make a recommendation which he could support and for which he could get the acceptance of his superiors, or not to make one at all. The high-producing supervisors were more realistic about the situation; they entered the promotion process only when they were willing and able to influence the outcome. We may hypothesize that, from the point of view of the employee in such a high-producing group, high performance was seen as a path to supervisory recommendations, and possible promotion. The employee in the low-producing group, witnessing the frequent failures of supervisory recommendations, could only conclude that the path of high productivity did not lead to promotion for him because his supervisor's efforts or influence in the larger organization were inadequate to establish such a connection.

(3) *Enabling goal achievement*

The functions of the supervisor in enabling goal achievement have to do less with employee motives and perceptions than with the elimination of obstacles. Assume that a goal exists for the employee, and that he sees high productivity as a path to that goal. Many things still may intervene to prevent his taking that path, and some of these barriers his supervisor may be able to eliminate. Moreover, some kinds of supervisory practices might in themselves constitute barriers to high productivity; these practices his supervisor may indulge in or avoid. The following findings are illustrative of the extent to which the performance of the enabling function characterizes those supervisors with the better production records. Foremen of railroad section gangs were found to differ with respect to the amount of time they spent in planning the work and performing special skilled tasks. In general, the foremen with the better production records devoted more time to these aspects of their work according to their own report and they were perceived by their men as possessing superior planning ability. Similarly, in the company manufacturing heavy agricultural and road-building equipment both the foremen and the men of high-producing sections evaluated the quality of planning as superior to that of most other groups. Apparently the foremen in such work groups were acting to facilitate as well as to motivate high productivity.

In the same company, the responses of the foremen themselves gave evidence of consistent attention by the more successful foremen to factors which would facilitate high productivity by removing obstacles. For example, foremen were told that "under its present foreman, a section turns out more and better work than it did under the foreman it had before. What do you think the present foreman does differently from the previous foreman?" The foremen with the best production records were inclined to attribute the difference to improved human relations and to the new foreman's helping the men with technical problems and getting them the tools and materials which they needed. The low-producing foremen were more inclined to attribute the gains to the new man's superior knowledge of the job. The workers corroborated this finding; the majority of those with the best production records reported that their foreman made it part of his supervision to see that they were provided with the required tools.

We may be justified in classifying as facilitative also the findings from the insurance study cited earlier, that high-producing supervisors checked up on their employees less frequently, gave instructions less frequently and in less detail, and permitted workers to do the work in their own way. These findings received corroboration in the research done among employees of the tractor factory, in which the high-producing workers reported more often that they were permitted to set their own pace on the job. To the extent that employees differ in the pacing and methods of work with which they attain their individual peaks of performance, such autonomy is clearly facilitative as well as satisfying in itself.

There is evidence also that a combination of directly need-satisfying and enabling acts is characteristic of the high-producing supervisor. For example, in an appliance factory, workers were more accepting of the incentive system and more productive as well if they perceived their supervisor to be both able and willing to get a time-study rate changed if he thought it was "too tight". In the tractor factory, high-producing employees not only were more likely to feel that their supervisor was easy to talk to, but also that it usually helped to talk over a problem with him and that he took care of things right away. In the same factory the men reported that the high-producing supervisors let them know how they were doing. Here again is a characteristic which might be directly satisfying in relieving anxiety and ambiguity, but which has facilitative implications as well. We can improve our future performance when we have some insight as to how we are presently performing. Without such feedback, learning to improve is difficult.

Finally, there is a behavior found to be more characteristic of high producing supervisors in the railroad study—grooming employees for promotion by teaching them new things. Assuming that the employee has the goal of being promoted and sees the acquisition of new skills as one path to promotion, such teaching by foremen has important facilitative effects.

(4) *Modifying employee goals*

Direct evidence is lacking for the influence of the supervisor on the employee's goals. Of the available findings, the tendency of high-producing supervisors to groom employees for promotion by teaching them new things is most suggestive of a direct influence on the goals of the employee. Workers who considered promotion quite outside their area of aspiration might come to consider themselves promotable and to regard promotion as a goal, as they learned new skills from their supervisor.

Another hint came from the statements of workers in the tractor factory, where it was found that those men in the higher producing groups more often wanted the supervisor to take a personal interest in them. Apparently the most successful supervisors had been able to make the attainment of their interest and approval a goal for their employees, while the low-producing supervisors had been less able to offer a personal relationship that the men would regard as potentially rewarding and therefore actively to be sought.

Summary

We began this chapter with a statement of the classic dilemma of modern large-scale organization—how to reconcile the machine-like rationality of organizational functioning with the human needs of the members of such organizations. The inadequacy of scientific management has been argued and the psychological significance of work for the individual has been examined. Regarding individual behavior as a series of connected efforts at need satisfaction, and viewing the work situation as one of the most important areas in which such satisfactions are sought, we have proposed a framework within which to understand behavior on the job. This schema of needs and goals, paths and barriers, was then utilized to interpret an array of empirical findings on supervisory factors related to industrial productivity.

There is no implication in this approach to employee motivation and behavior nor in the empirical findings that the pattern of supervision which is conducive to high productivity is also best in terms of other criteria. High productivity, in the language of paths and goals, does not necessarily mean maximum attainment of goals and satisfaction of needs. There are situations in which the overall level of need satisfaction may be low, but the only path to any measure of need satisfaction is high productivity. We can predict, however, that an organization characterized by high productivity, and also by a strong wish of members to remain within it despite other choices, would necessarily be one which offered to its members relatively high levels of goal attainment and need satisfaction. To some extent the organizational structure and leadership patterns which best meet these combined criteria of organizational effectiveness can be derived from research on the current practices of supervisors and other leaders. To some extent such solutions must be sought in experiments which create organizational forms and practices not ordinarily encountered in existing organizations. Through research of both kinds we may learn enough of organizations and men so that in time to come we can strike a better bargain with nature than that described by Lord Russell as the surrender of spontaneity and self-expression on the job in exchange for security and its product —assuming the burden of "monotony and tedium" in exchange for "the diminished risk of starvation".

References

1. This chapter draws heavily on the following earlier descriptions of research findings from the Human Relations Program of the University of Michigan Survey Research Center: Katz, Daniel and Kahn, Robert L., "Human Organization and Worker Motivation" in *Industrial Productivity*, Industrial Relations Research Association, 1951. Kahn, Robert L., "The Prediction of Productivity," *Journal of Social Issues*, **12**, 2, 1956.
2. Russell, Bertrand, *The Conquest of Happiness*, New York: Horace Liveright, 1930.
3. The following description is adapted from an unpublished manuscript by Rensis Likert, Institute for Social Research, University of Michigan.
4. See, for example, Fayol, Henri, *Industrial and General Administration*, London: Sir Isaac Pitman & Sons, 1930. Gulick, Luther and Urwick, L., *Papers on the Science of Administration*, New York: Institute of Public Administration, 1937.
5. See, for example, Worthy, James "Organizational Structure and Employee Morale" in *Readings in Industrial and Business Psychology*, Harry W. Karn and B. von Haller Gilmer (Eds.), New York: McGraw Hill Book Company, 1952.
6. Taylor, F. W., *The Principles of Scientific Management*, New York, 1911.
7. Roethlisberger, F. J. and Dickson, W. J., *Management and the Worker*, Harvard University Press, 1940.
8. For a more detailed description of the study on which this presentation is primarily based, see Morse, Nancy C. and Weiss, Robert S., "The Function and Meaning of Work and the Job," *American Sociological Review*, **20**, 2, April 1955.
9. "Deep Therapy on the Assembly Line", *Ammunition*, **7**, 4, 1949, pp. 47-51.
10. Lazarsfeld-Jahoda, Marie, *Die Arbeitslosen von Marienthal*, Leipzig, Germany: S. Hirzel, 1933, Psychologische Monographien, Vol. 5.
11. This section is based on an unpublished manuscript by Basil Georgopoulos, Gerald Mahoney, and Nyle Jones entitled "On a Path-Goal Approach to Productivity", Survey Research Center, University of Michigan, 1956. Tables 3 and 4 are adapted from this study.
12. Newcomb, Theodore M., *Social Psychology*, New York: Dryden Press, 1950.
13. Many of the research findings here discussed have been published in other places by members of the Survey Research Center staff. For an earlier attempt at summarizing them, see, Katz, Daniel and Kahn, Robert L., "Human Organization and Worker Motivation" in *Industrial Productivity*, Industrial Relations Research Association, 1951, pp. 146–171.
14. Quotations are taken from Katz, Daniel, Maccoby, Nathan, and Morse, Nancy C., *Productivity, Supervision and Morale in an Office Situation*, Survey Research Center, University of Michigan, 1950.
15. The description of this analysis is adapted from Pelz, Donald C., "Influence: A Key to Effective Leadership in the First-Line Supervisor", *Personnel*, November 1952.

CHAPTER 4

ORGANIZED LABOUR AND MANAGEMENT

Part 1. The United States

EDWIN YOUNG

Professor of Economics, University of Wisconsin

As early as 1790, workers' organizations for collective dealing with employers were in existence in the United States, but systematic "collective bargaining" with employers culminating in written agreements over the terms of wages and working conditions did not exist until nearly a century later. During that century, unionists experimented with several methods of organization without lasting success until in the 1870's and 1880's workers in a number of crafts and trades joined their local unions together into national unions with relatively large authority vested in the national officers. A number of these national unions, unfortunately miscalled international because of Canadian affiliates, joined in 1886 to form the American Federation of Labor which under the leadership of Samuel Gompers provided a unifying philosophy for the American labor movement. Three basic principles of the American Federation of Labor did much from the very beginning to influence the structure of collective bargaining. The first principle was that each national union should be "autonomous" with complete control over its own internal affairs and its relations with employers. Second, organization was primarily on the basis of craft or trade since the early leaders believed that a worker's lifetime investment in his craft would cause him to join with others to protect the interests of this craft. A third principle was that of exclusive jurisdiction under which each national union staked out a "job territory" for the workers which it claimed.

Samuel Gompers and his fellow leaders guided the young organization along a pragmatic road, ever aware of the realities of the

American scene in which capitalism was so well entrenched. Instead of appealing for class solidarity which would eventually change the basic economic structure of the country, the AFL leaders built their unions on the concern of workers for the security of their jobs and through written agreements with employers developed an industrial government under which workers have a voice in the determination of their wages and working conditions. This view that the task of unionism is not class warfare but rather that of establishing job rights and getting a larger share of the results of production for wage earners continues to be the basic philosophy of American unionism.

At the time it was organized in 1886 the AFL unions had a membership of about 180,000. A decade later, despite a period of depression, the number of national unions had increased and the total membership of affiliates had doubled.

The period from 1898 to 1904 was one of particularly rapid growth in which total American unionists increased to 2,000,000, eighty per cent of whom were affiliated with the AFL. Aroused employers began to combat unionism on a national scale and the ensuing open shop drive is believed to be the principal reason for the failure of unionism to increase in the decade 1904—1914.

During World War I many employers, because of the policies of the government-sponsored War Labor Board and the need for large numbers of employees, relaxed their anti-union attitudes and unionism rapidly expanded. In 1920 there were 5,000,000 union members in the United States.

This wartime toleration by management ended with the war and as a result of the dismantling of war industries and a determined anti-union program of employers the number of union members fell off sharply and during the decade of the twenties total union membership was about three and one half million, nearly three million of whom were in unions affiliated with the AFL. The bulk of this membership was in the building trades and transportation unions. In the depressed coal industry membership fell during the decade from half a million to less than a hundred thousand members. An attempt by twenty-four unions to win an organizing strike against the steel industry in 1919 failed. Unionism had never penetrated many of the new mass production industries such as automobiles, where the craft method of organization ill fitted the needs of the unskilled and semi-skilled workers who made up the bulk of the labor force and where the skills that existed were peculiar to the particular industry.

The inability of the labor movement's structure to evolve in step with the new technology that was rapidly emerging in the nineteen twenties found it ill suited for the organizing opportunity offered by the Roosevelt administration which in 1933, as part of its industrial recovery program encouraged, the formation of unions.

The failure of the dominant craft leadership in the AFL finally caused a minority group of AFL unionists, led by John L. Lewis of the coal miners, David Dubinsky and Sidney Hillman of the clothing industries and others who favored organizations of unions on an industrial basis, to form a Committee for Industrial Organizations in defiance of the craft leadership.

The CIO achieved tremendous successes in organizing automobiles, steel, rubber and other mass production industries in the winter of 1936—37. Its militant organizing and strike tactics aided by the encouragement of the new National Labor Relations Act created the greatest upheaval in American labor history. Union membership both in the CIO affiliated unions and in the AFL, now spurred to new efforts by the new methods of the CIO, rose rapidly. In 1933 the AFL had a membership slightly in excess of two million; by 1939 each organization had four million members. Under the impact of the defense and wartime expansion in employment, union membership continued to rise rapidly to a total of nearly fifteen million by 1945.

The next decade saw a slight growth in union membership so that by 1955 it is estimated that there were 17,000,000 unionists, 15,000,000 of whom were in the newly united AFL-CIO.

From this brief survey it can be seen that collective bargaining as a method of determining wages and working conditions has had a long history in some industries in the United States particularly in construction, transportation, and mining. However, for a majority of employers and workers collective bargaining is a relatively new experience which began with the New Deal or World War II.

Some of the earlier experience on the union side was available to the new unionists because the overall direction of the labor movement remained largely in the hands of leaders drawn from the older AFL unions, but the tremendous expansion meant that the leaders of many unions had to learn about unionism from the experiences which came very thick and fast.

Before examining the nature of the collective bargaining engaged in by these unions, it is necessary to examine briefly the emergence of employers' organizations in the United States which in general followed the coming of unionism. Some early employers' associations were for the purpose of dealing with others for combating unionism. A well-known example of the latter type was the National Metal Trades Association covering nearly a thousand plants and dedicated to preventing the existence or recognition of unions. Prior to the 1930's and the National Labor Relations Act, which prohibited employer interference with unions as well as requiring employers to bargain with the representatives of their workers, in only a few industries did employers organize to negotiate with unions. These exceptional industries included printing, railroads, coal and glass.

The majority of American employers still bargain on an individual-firm basis but increasing proportions of union members are working under agreements negotiated with a group of employers. Such agreements are more appropriately called multi-employer than industry-wide agreements although in a few industries, including steel, coal, glass, and railroads, the bargaining is close to being industry-wide.

Many small employers have discovered that it is to their advantage to join with other employers in dealing with a strong union even though they may feel that they lose some of their freedom of action by so doing. In the building and service industries where there are often many employers dealing with a single union, employers usually find themselves asked to give the best terms that the union can wrest from any one of them. Yet together they can meet the union with something like equal strength and skill. As a result in the country there are well over 5000 such bargaining associations.

A rather large number of workers in such manufacturing industries as textiles and shipbuilding are covered by regional agreements which bring together for collective bargaining firms which compete in the same labor markets.

Most multi-employer, associations represent firms in the same business, although in a few western cities inter-industry groups represent all types of business in a given town or city.

The primary concern of American trade unions is with the jobs of their members and the improvement of their employment conditions through collective bargaining. From time to time the concept of employment conditions is broadened to include new areas such as employer-financed pension or unemployment funds, but these are changes of degree rather than kind. If the unions demand more control over hiring, firing and promotion, it is not for the purpose of displacing management but rather to increase the job security of their members who fear that management may unilaterally change the conditions to the detriment of a particular worker or group of workers. This fear of arbitrary management is very real even if it is difficult for management to understand, since the agreement often puts into writing practices long established by many employers. If unions increasingly engage in political activity, it is not from a desire of union officers to hold national political office but rather because they believe that legislation plays such a large part in determining the kind of collective bargains they will be able to negotiate with employers. The violent opposition of many trade unionists to the Taft-Hartley amendments * of the National Labor Relations Act stemmed from their belief that their freedom of economic action was sharply curtailed by that law. Increasingly trade union leaders are convinced that the economic policies of the national government vitally affect the employment and incomes of

* In 1947 the National Labor Relations Act was drastically amended to regulate union activity as well as that of management and regulated to some degree the contents of bargaining agreements. A special section provided for a method of delaying and publicizing strikes which in the mind of the President created national emergency situations. Under the present law unions as well as management may not refuse to bargain with each other. Secondary boycotts (sympathetic strikes) and strikes to force the employer to assign work to a particular group of workers are outlawed as well as coercion of employees in their right to join or refuse to join a union.

Under the law employers and unions may no longer agree that a worker must be a member of a union in order to be employed. Where state law allows contracts which require workers to join unions after being employed, the federal law prohibits the discharge of an employee who is expelled from the union for any reason other than failure to pay dues. Among other provisions added to the law by the 1947 amendments were those facilitating damage suits against unions, requiring sixty days' notice before the termination or expiration of a contract, prohibiting political contributions by unions, and requiring union officials to sign affidavits that they are not Communists.

Another federal government agency concerned with collective bargaining is the Federal Conciliation and Mediation Service, which offers the service of its conciliators in disputes which may have a significant effect on interstate commerce. The Conciliation Service has no authority to impose its advice upon the parties but rather tries to use the abilities of a trained and experienced staff to help the parties reach an agreement.

Because of their critical importance to the whole economy, railway and air transportation come under special laws providing for mediation and fact-finding before strikes are allowed.

their members, so as a result they become concerned with government policies and office holders.

Although some union activity must be judged merely as institutional behavior designed to strengthen and further the labor movement as such, and some union political activity is in the nature of citizenship activity such as the promotion of better schools or better race relations, the primary concern of the unions is still centered around the collective bargaining agreement and its administration.

The goals of management are varied and include profit making, market development, efficiency of operations, the continuity of the firm, and good public relations as well as good relations with its employees. Concentrating on efficiency and profit making, the management of most American companies for a long time neglected personnel problems, leaving such problems to foremen and shop superintendents who in turn were also concerned with making a good showing in the areas of first concern to their employers. Faced with the unions' challenge to their authority and what they deemed interference with their inherent rights to make decisions in all areas, American employers have in the past generally been opposed to unions and have dealt with them only if forced to do so by their economic strength or by the National Labor Relations Act under which collective bargaining for the settlement of differences between workers and employers has been the national labor policy since 1935.

Most American employers at the present time have come to accept unionism and the different management-employee relationships that accompany collective bargaining, but some still are bitterly opposed to the principle of unionism. The typical attitudes of American employers toward unions have been often classified as varying from *exclusion* to *cooperation* with intermediate steps of *containment and acceptance and accommodation.*

When the employers' policy is that of union *exclusion*, management tries to discourage workers from joining unions by coercion or by trying to provide the wage and fringe benefits that competitors grant through collective bargaining. Prior to the National Labor Relations Act many employers encouraged pseudo-unions under company domination. At the present time it is chiefly in the southern part of the United States that employers try to discourage union organization.

Faced with a law compelling them to deal with unions many employers grudgingly acted according to the letter of the law but did everything possible to wean the loyalty of the workers away from the union. Under this policy of *containment*, all relations with the union representatives were kept on a strictly "legal" basis, and the scope of collective bargaining was kept as narrow as possible. The company by so doing hoped eventually to rid itself of collective bargaining.

Another attitude toward unionism is that of *acceptance and accommodation*, in which the employer recognizes the union as part of the industrial scene and tries to use collective bargaining to improve its relations with its employees.

Finally there is the relationship of *cooperation* in which the management actually seeks the assistance of the union in production problems which are not usually the subject matter of collective bargaining. The *acceptance and accommodation* situation is more prevalent than either that of *exclusion* or *cooperation*.

The day-to-day relations of management and unions at the shop or plant level center around the administration of the written collective bargaining agreement; therefore it would be well to examine some important parts of the typical collective bargain, or "contract" as it is often called.

Although the chief purpose of a collective bargaining agreement is to establish wages and working conditions mutually agreeable to the parties, the agreements contain a number of other provisions necessary to the smooth working of the agreement. The opening section contains the names of the parties and designates the work unit covered by the agreement, as well as some general phrases about the good intentions of the parties to carry out the provisions of the agreement for their mutual benefit.

The vast majority of American collective bargaining agreements are for a fixed period of time, which is stated along with the procedures necessary to initiate a new agreement when the existing one expires.

Another and often controversial section contains the provisions designed to protect the union as an institution. The "union security" clause may provide for a union shop under which all employees covered by the agreement must join the union after a brief probationary period or lose their jobs. Federal law forbids the "closed shop" agreement under which only union members are hired and the same federal law delegates to the states the authority, which some of them have exercised, to bar the union shop. Such state laws have become widely known as "right-to-work" laws and are strongly opposed by organized labor.

Less valuable, but still desirable from the unions' point of view, are clauses in agreements which provide that union members must maintain their membership for the duration of the agreement. Many managements also agree to deduct union dues from the workers' wages and pay them directly to the union treasurer. By this "check-off" system management avoids having dues collection taking place during work time and the union avoids the nuisance of seeking out individual members in order to get its income.

Some managements insist that agreements clearly state that management has the responsibility and right to the direction of the working force including the right to hire and fire, assign jobs, determine products and production schedules and methods. Such clauses are designed to limit the scope of collective bargaining at a time when union power and influence is on the rise, but managements are not entirely agreed on their usefulness since their existence may suggest that anything not specifically reserved to management is automatically a subject for bargaining.

No matter how carefully a collective bargaining agreement is drafted by experienced representatives of the company and the union aided by their lawyers, differences of opinion arise during the life of the agreement about its meaning and its application to situations that the drafters did not foresee. Therefore, almost all contracts contain grievance procedures which describe the steps by which such differences are to be settled. Such procedures usually start with a complaint from a worker or his union representative that some right of the worker has been abridged by management. The union representative and the lower levels of management try to work out the problem. Failure of a satisfactory solution at the shop level leads to discussions at higher levels of the union and of management, and at this stage a representative of the national union may be called in to provide expert assistance on the union side. Most, but certainly not all, contracts provide that differences on contract interpretation which cannot be settled by discussions between management and union representatives shall go to arbitration and the contract will specify how the form of arbitration shall be selected.

American management and labor alike are quite determined that their basic agreements be arrived at by mutual agreement rather than by arbitration, yet both groups feel that arbitration is the best method of settling disputes over interpretation of such agreements.

Needless to say, the great number of collective bargaining agreements with arbitration provisions has created ever growing opportunities for lawyers and economists to act as arbitrators. The largest corporations and their unions may retain the services of a permanent arbitrator or umpire who agrees to hear all disputes between the parties arising from their contractual relationship; however, the majority of firms and unions select arbitrators on an *ad hoc* basis.

Collective bargaining agreements sometimes provide for boards of arbitration to which each party nominates one or two members, these as a group selecting an impartial chairman. Such a board guarantees that the impartial chairman will know the positions of the parties and also allows for some negotiation under the guise of arbitration. Such an arrangement provides flexibility which may be valuable to both parties particularly since more and more contracts run for a period of three to five years.

If a firm views the collective bargaining contract as a device to contain the ever pressing demands of unionism, it may very well insist on the strictest interpretation of the contract and insist that the arbitrator play a judicial rather than a mediatory role. Less frequently but not uncommonly a union with a strong contract will also insist that an arbitrator interpret but not mediate. But then, in such cases many of the final settlements of grievances are compromises agreed upon by the parties or arranged by the arbitrator who will have acted more like a mediator than an arbitrator.

The number of formal grievances and arbitrations between a union and a management does not necessarily reflect the carefulness with which the contract was drawn nor the changing industrial circumstances, for numerous grievances may be symptoms of poor relationships at the shop level between stewards and foremen, rivalries within the union group or the unwillingness of union officials or foremen to take responsibility for decisions which might arouse antipathy toward themselves.

The part of the collective bargaining agreement which is of most immediate concern to the workers and which generates the greatest public interest is that dealing with wages or more correctly the amount of wage or wage equivalent increases agreed upon by the particular parties.

It is far easier to describe the arguments used by the parties in wage negotiations than it is to state accurately what are the factors which determine the wage rates eventually agreed upon. Since 1941 with a few exceptions the direction of wages has been upward and in such cases the burden of the argument for the changes has been carried by the unions, with the employers arguing not against wage increases but against the amount of union demands.

In the years immediately following World War II general price rises made the cost-of-living argument the basis for most wage demands. During periods of relative price stability a variety of arguments including the need for greater purchasing power and the claims of workers to a share in increasing productivity are put forward by the unions. Productivity increases were incorporated into the General Motors contract with the United Automobile Workers in 1950 and gave great impetus to the use of this argument even though the amount of increase in the general level of productivity is not susceptible of any close measurement.

For most United States industries the post World War decade has been a period of high activity and good profits, so it was natural that the unions should use the ability-to-pay argument singly or along with others. The inability to make substantial wage increases is the other side of the same argument and is used by firms when the situation warrants. This argument coupled with the threat of non-union competition has been used to hold the rate of wage increases in the textile industry well below the national average.

An argument used by both labor and management in nearly all wage negotiations is that of comparison with other groups in the economy, the industry, the region or locality. Union representatives are quick to point to comparable firms that pay higher wages than the employer with whom they are dealing both because they believe such comparisons to be valid and also because their members are quickly aware of such divergencies. Employers are likely to respond with averages for the industry as a whole, local wage levels, or other comparisons which make their wages seem relatively higher.

The postwar years have seen a great increase in pattern bargaining under which the general amount of wage increase for an industry is determined by the settlements arrived at by leading unions and large employers. Whatever settlement is made between the United

Automobile Workers and whichever employer of the big three automobile manufacturers they first negotiate with becomes the "pattern" for the industry, albeit with modifications to fit the special circumstances of other employers and the locals of the autoworkers union with whom they negotiate. Sometimes one firm in a locality is recognized as the pace-setter and other settlements follow its wage agreements.

Whatever arguments a union may put forth for a wage increase or an employer may use to resist one, the final settlement will depend in large part upon each party's estimates of the determination of the other to hold to its position. If the employer feels certain that the union will strike rather than take anything less than a certain amount, he must decide whether to have a strike which will be costly to him whether he wins it or loses it. On the other hand if the union knows that management is determined not to go beyond a certain amount of increase even at the expense of a strike, it must decide how important is the difference between the best management offer and its own demand.

Each of the parties to the negotiation in estimating its own position and that of the other carefully studies the economic position of the firm including its competitors and its markets, the level of employment in the industry and the area, as well as the unions' strength and militancy.

The final agreement reached on wage matters may also depend in part upon what else is written into the contract. Out of the bargaining process which may last days or months it may become clear to the parties that there are a number of possible settlements ranging from a sizable wage increase to a token wage increase accompanied by a number of so-called "fringe benefits". "Fringe benefits" is a misnomer for the very real and also monetarily expensive pension, hospitalization, supplementary unemployment, holiday, vacation, seniority and union security provisions which are bargained on at the same time as wages. In order to make comparisons with what other employers and unions are doing, an estimate of the cost of such benefits is usually calculated on the basis of cents per hour so that the amount of increase published in the newspapers will include these items, which have a calculable monetary value.

In addition to the amount of wages to be paid for each classification of workers, each contract must also include many other provisions dealing with wage questions. If the contract is to last more than one year, it is very likely to contain a provision that either party may on notice ask for a reopening of wage questions after one year. This reopening clause is very important to union officials who must guard their membership against rising living costs and who find frequent pay raises a method of generating interest in unionism. Furthermore, union members bound by a long-term contract become very restless when they see other workers getting increases. Management often prefers long-range contracts that will allow it to estimate more accurately its costs of production. The management and union positions are sometimes compromised in three or five year contracts with certain provisions for annual wage increases in addition to any changes brought about by changes in the cost of living.

Many agreements go well beyond the requirement of the federal law that workers be paid at 150 per cent of their normal pay for any hours in excess of forty worked in a given week. Most common is double pay for work performed on Sundays and holidays. In many cases night workers are paid a "shift" premium.

Job evaluation and piece rate systems provide special problems for the contract negotiator. Since job standards and methods are constantly changing, the contract must provide some method of setting the rates of pay for the new jobs as the changes come about.

Agreement is also necessary for the method of paying the waiting time of piece rate workers and determining the pay of men who are moved from one job to another.

Paid vacations are relatively new for most workers in the United States and the gains in this area are for the most part the product of the collective bargaining of the last two decades. In general, the length of the paid vacation depends upon the workers' seniority with the plant or firm. For most workers the vacation is one or two weeks.

During World War II while the national government's economic policies prevented unions and managements from negotiating wage increases, many "fringe benefits" providing for life, health and accident insurance financed in whole or part by the employer were negotiated. In the postwar years such plans have spread throughout United States industry, and periodically, as part of the negotiations of a new contract, the benefits of such insurance schemes are increased.

The basic retirement benefits for workers in the United States are embodied in the Old Age and Survivors' Insurance part of the Social Security Act of 1935 with its ensuing amendments. This plan, administered by the federal government, collects an equal percentage of the workers' pay from worker and employer and the retired or disabled worker is paid benefits based upon his earnings in all of his employment.

Beginning in the late nineteen-forties many collective bargaining agreements included plans under which the employer would finance sizable supplements to the basic old age and survivors' benefits. The complicated issues of administering jointly such retirement benefits add to the tasks of negotiation and to the bulk of the contracts; these complications have been further complicated by recent agreements trying to provide that the worker shall keep such benefits even if he changes employers.

In the mid nineteen-fifties the most widely discussed feature of major agreements was "the guaranteed annual wage" as many unionists called it or — more exactly — supplemental unemployment compensation. Led by the United Automobile Workers, unions were demanding and getting employer-financed supplements to the unemployment compensation benefits which the various states administered under the general enabling provisions of the federal Social Security law.

Concern of all workers over employment opportunities is reflected in the seniority clauses under which management agrees to lay-off, terminate, transfer and in some cases promote employees on the basis of their length of service with the company, the plant or the shop. Such provisions, particularly where seniority is plant or company wide, become very complex indeed and past arguments over special seniority situations often swell the pages of the more recent contracts. Included in most seniority clauses are provisions to the effect that workers on leave to hold union offices shall accumulate seniority as though on the job. Some contracts provide special privileges for union officers in case of lay-offs. On its side managements try to protect in the contract the shop seniority rights of men who are promoted to supervisory positions at least for their probationary periods.

Our brief outline of the contents and issues of collective bargaining agreements should serve to provide the reader with some understanding of the nature of such agreements even if it passes over many special provisions necessary in any particular labor-management relationship.

As was indicated above, a majority of unorganized workers are still working under contracts negotiated between individual companies and the unions representing their employees. In such situations the final agreements, although much affected by national, regional and industrial trends, are negotiated by the managements and workers aided or directed by representatives of their national union. In those cases where a master agreement is negotiated on some multi-employer basis, many aspects are left to be negotiated at the level of the individual company or plant. As a result, one may conclude that the parties who are to be governed by most agreements have had some part in negotiating all or at least part of the agreements.

The spirit in which this negotiating is done is affected by prior relations between the parties and will in turn affect the relationships after the contract is signed.

Serious students of the collective bargaining process put especial emphasis upon a first contract.[1] They see many present labor-management relationships still reflecting the fact that unions were granted recognition by management within the last two decades as a result of pressure from strikes or the provisions of the National Labor Relations Act which require the management to recognize a union if a majority of its employees vote for it. Whether the situation is a strike or a union election campaign, it evokes strong feelings and strong words on both sides. Management representatives often come to the bargaining table with a feeling that ungrateful workers have been disloyal to the company or have been misled by outside agitators. The union representatives, especially those from the shop, are very conscious of their new positions of authority and are also still in the belligerent frame of mind which led them to join the union when they believed the company to be opposed to unionism.

It requires the utmost skill on the part of experienced national union representatives and real determination on the part of the top management if the bitterness of the recent past is to be prevented from poisoning the negotiations and the future relationship. Much serious study has been given in recent years to the collective bargaining process and the human relations problems involved.[2] Some authorities argue that most important for a constructive future relationship is a realistic recognition by each party of the position and needs of the other. Management, it is argued, must recognize that the union is an entity and needs protection and respect, and a positive step in this direction is to make it the real channel of communication between the management and workers on matters of wage and working conditions. In addition, it must be recognized that the union needs to achieve for its members some immediate gains in order to satisfy in part the promises to its new members. On its side the union must be aware of the company's task of efficient profitable production. The long-run interests of workers and company alike can best be served if the union relationship strengthens the efficiency of the company. Davy[3] in his study of procedure in the negotiating process has made suggestions which experience has shown to be useful when modified to meet the special circumstances of a particular situation. He observes that both the management and union committees should be kept small in order to avoid waste of time and the introduction of irrelevant materials; also if either group is very large some persons are always tempted to play to the audience rather than the issues at hand. Further he suggests that each side have one person clearly in charge and that each side should have the authority to make decisive commitments, even though the union must eventually go to the membership for final ratification. Among other suggestions for smoothing the negotiating process are a number of advance preparations ranging from agreeing upon the exact time and duration of sessions and the procedure to be followed to the exchange of demands and proposals so that each party may study the other's position before the actual bargaining starts. Much time and frustration at the bargaining table may be saved if the parties have agreed in advance on as many facts as possible. In some of the most important industries the experts of both sides work in consultation for months in advance on such problems as the actuarial basis for a pension plan or the cost to the company of each one cent change in the basic wage, etc.

Out of some negotiations come contracts which reflect the grudging respect of each of the parties for the immediate strength of the other, but show no change in spirit; such a contract is viewed as a necessary arrangement until more strength can be marshalled to alter the agreement at the next negotiation. On the other hand out of many negotiations the parties emerge with a real respect for each other, determined to make the contract the working basis for a new and mutually profitable relationship. The very manner in which the news of the agreement is announced to the workers and the public will reveal much about the true relationship which has been achieved and indicate the atmosphere under which the agreement will be administered. A joint statement in which both parties affirm their belief that a workable and reasonable agreement has been reached which they jointly agree to observe both in the letter and in the spirit is considered a desirable way to launch a successful period of labor-management relations. It also announces to the rank and file of the union and the various levels of management that hostilities have ceased and they must now work together. Unilateral announcements from the union and the management about victories achieved are not wise industrial relations policies and portend continued difficulties.

The first contract is usually the most difficult because of the great alteration it implies in the method of deciding labor-management relationships; succeeding contracts will mean less change but any negotiation in which important changes are demanded by either party engenders strong feelings and occasionally long and sometimes bitter strikes. After each agreement the greatest human relations task remains for both parties.

No generalities will cover the many different systems of bargaining and contract administration prevalent in the United States. Two situations, however, describe the methods followed in a great number of cases.

Earlier in this chapter the building industry was cited as one in which collective bargaining has long been established. In this industry the members of the particular craft union work for many different employers and are constantly finding themselves changing jobs and fellow workers. Such workers are represented by a full-time business agent who has a major part in negotiations and almost sole authority from the union side in the administration of the agreement. It is the duty of the business agent to check on all the jobs where his members are employed to make sure that the agreement is being observed. He hears the grievances of the men and takes them up with the contractor with whom he may be dealing on many different projects over the years. Often the business agent is also the employment agency to which a contractor turns for skilled craftsmen and from whom the union members receive information about job opportunities. Since the period of employment on any one job is relatively short, the business agent is given authority to act quickly and decisively in cases of dispute. He usually has the authority to call the men off the job when some matter remains unsettled. The contractor, anxious to complete his construction on schedule, tries to get the matter quickly settled. In this kind of labor-management relationship the employer-business agent relationship is the crux of the matter and experience of many years on both sides has evolved relatively satisfactory working patterns.

In many industrial plants, on the other hand, unionism is relatively new and the organization for handling industrial relations is quite different from that of the building industry. In the typical plant direct contact between management and workers is through the foreman who has direct charge of a group of workers in a department of the plant. This foreman's concern is with production but he also represents management in all phases to the workers. Above the foreman in authority is a superintendent and general manager, the number of layers of management depending upon the size of the plant. For many years management in the United States has recognized the importance of its relations with its employees and most firms have specialists to aid management in its personnel and industrial relations policies. These are generally regarded as staff functions whether in charge of one man or involving a number of departments specializing in recruitment, training and employee relations. In their staff role their effectiveness depends on the willingness of the line management to use their advice and assistance.

On the union side the direct contact with the worker is through the shop steward elected by the men in a department or subdepartment or appointed by the union to serve the group. The steward is a worker and continues as such, often with some provision for time off to transact union affairs. In the union hierachy the next higher level is the local union president who may be a full time worker or in large plants a paid union official. Advising and helping the local union officers and shop stewards is the regional representative of the national union. Like the industrial relations expert on the management side he devotes most of his time to the problems of labor-management relations but generally has more authority on the union side than does his counterpart on the management side. This authority stems more from his work of providing leadership and from his experience than from formal provisions in union constitutions. In addition to his role in labor-management relations, the national representative is the liaison between the local union and the national organization.

Recognition of the crucial role played by foremen in labor-management relations has led American management to put ever-increasing emphasis upon the selection and training of foremen. At one time foremen were selected almost solely on the basis of their skill and ability as production workers; the existence of unionism which has so greatly reduced the foremen's freedom of arbitrary action has in turn forced leadership and ability in personal relationships to become a primary qualification in the selection of new foremen. Many firms have also instituted special training programs for foremen in which they are taught basic principles of psychology and group leadership. For foremen long accustomed to great authority over the workers under them, the readjustment demanded by the advent of collective bargaining is very great and sometimes the most carefully formulated management training program fails to overcome the long practiced system of authority. The dual task of getting along with workers, who if they feel aggrieved can call in their shop steward and set in motion the grievance procedure, and at the same time satisfying managements' need for satisfactory levels of production, puts great strain on this first line of management.

Perhaps one of the most difficult tasks for a foreman is to determine exactly how far top management wants him to go in getting along with the union. Often management is not sure of itself and may be trying to play roles which are somewhat contradictory in themselves. For instance, in all its pronouncements management may be talking about carrying out the spirit of the agreement but at the same time consciously or unconsciously it may be trying to undermine the union by dealing directly with individual employees on matters which have been the subject of collective bargaining and which should be handled through the union.

Again the training program may place great stress upon the recognition of individual differences in human beings, the need for great consideration in individual discipline cases and yet in a particular case the foreman may find himself censured by higher authority for failure to maintain discipline. Management's potential problems in its union relationships are so great in cases involving discipline, work assignment, seniority, etc. that it often removes many such decisions from the foreman, so many that he sometimes feels that he no longer has the authority to carry on his proper functions in relation to the men under him.

As management experience in labor relations grows, such problems are found to be not insurmountable and foremen are taught or discover that the shop steward who was at first regarded as an antagonist may be very useful in helping to maintain discipline, screening baseless complaints, counseling workers on personal problems and serving as an avenue of communication between workers and management.

It is in this latter area of communication that much constructive work can be done through a satisfactory foreman-steward relationship. The steward is also a leader and often has an important influence in shaping the opinions of the men about management activities and intentions. It is the settled policy of many firms to inform the union officers of any important new developments in policies that affect the interests of the work force. The foreman, as part of management, should also know of any changes as soon or sooner than the union so that his position will not be undermined by the union's having information he does not have and also so that he will be in a position to work constructively with the shop steward on issues arising out of the change.

Not only is the foreman's relationship with the men and the shop steward important as a line of communication downward from management but it may be most important as a method of discovering what the workers think of specific management practices and proposed changes. Such information is often of great value to management and when obtained through foremen and the steward may strengthen that relationship rather than create suspicion on the part of the union by having management go directly to the workers.

Selecting and training foremen to work with the union and the shop steward is only part of the human relations content of foreman training programs where managements are anxious to improve their employee and union relationships. Many of the problems that create friction between the workers and supervisors can be avoided if the foreman is skilled in explaining what is expected of workers, in leading a discussion and in explaining management objectives. His tasks of selection, work assignment, and merit rating have to be carried out in a manner that will command respect and acceptance from the workers he supervises as well as from higher management.

The day-to-day relationships at the shop level are greatly affected by the role played by the union stewards as well as that played by the foremen. Management appoints its foremen and, as we have seen in many cases, the foreman has been selected prior to the company's recognition of a union. The union officials do not in most cases select the steward; he is elected by the union members he is to serve.

Whether he feels cooperative or unfriendly towards management is in a sense a reflection of the attitude of the workers who elect him. When the union is new and the members are militant and suspicious of management, they may very likely put forward as their steward a worker whose chief attributes are his ability to rally support against management. Wise managements may recognize this antagonism for what it is and deliberately set about creating an atmosphere of cooperation which will either change the attitude of such a steward or cause the union at its next election to select as its representative a person who is more fair-minded in his appraisal of management.

National union representatives have become increasingly aware of the blockages to a satisfactory labor-management relationship created by a resentful steward and often try insofar as they can to influence the union towards selecting more cooperative members for stewards. Many national unions have shop steward training programs under which shop stewards are taught the basic elements of economics, labor law, and human relations as well as the technical tasks in representing their membership. In such classes skilled union leaders explain their union's view of the functions of management and of unions in general and the economics of the particular industry and firm. The stewards are taught to guard the interests of the membership and of the union, but at the same time they are counseled in the labor-management relationship as it depends upon fair dealings with the foreman and with management. One of the most difficult tasks a steward must learn is how to explain to a worker that a complaint may not be the basis for filing a formal grievance against the company. Union leaders, as well as management, know that some workers feel discriminated against when no basis for such feeling exists. Stewards and higher union officers are sometimes asked to charge the company with violation of contract when they believe the worker is mistaken and there has been no violation. A strong well-entrenched union leadership can refuse to further such a complaint, but a weak union may need all the support it can get and, against its own better judgment, for political reasons back the worker in an unfounded grievance. A sophisticated management, that tries to understand the problems of a union, is able over a period of time to improve its labor-management relationship by helping to build respect for union leadership, so that the union will not have to seek support from individuals or factions when its better judgment dictates otherwise.

While the day-to-day relationship between unions and management rests very heavily on the shop stewards and the foremen, the general direction and overall attitude is determined by the general management on one side and the local officers and the representatives of the national union on the other. We have already pointed out that attitudes of American management towards unions vary from hostility to a desire to work with the union towards satisfactory relationships under which each may achieve its basic goals.

The art of human relations is practiced by managements holding every attitude in the range from hostility to cooperation. Some managements regard human relations programs as a substitute for collective bargaining. They believe, or are led to believe, that if management finds ways of helping individual workers to solve their real or fancied problems they will not join unions or, if they belong to a union, will not support it in basic differences with management. Sometimes such policies, associated with other factors such as high wages, good working conditions, may help keep a union out of a plant, at least for a considerable period of time.

When, however, there is a recognized union with which the management has agreed to bargain collectively, such programs, designed to undermine the union's position or to indicate clearly to the employees that management does not regard the union as being very important or necessary, will immediately foment ill will. The union naturally enough will try to embarrass the company, win the exclusive loyalty of the workers and show its strength whenever and wherever possible. Such relationships are better described as armed truces rather than peaceful labor-management relationships. Many grievance and negotiation sessions are needlessly embittered by the belief of either or both parties that prior to the meeting the other was presenting unfair information to the workers. Much is written about the art of communication in industrial relations and it is undoubtedly one of the most important devices for management to improve its relationships with its employees and for unions to keep their membership informed about current union and collective bargaining problems. But when either party uses the loud-speaker system, periodicals, bulletin boards, etc., to present unilaterally information concerning the contractual arrangements between the parties, it is inviting difficulties in its relationship.

If management is constantly aware of the fact that union officers are elected and are often under criticism from members who aspire to their offices, it can more wisely distinguish matters which should be taken directly to employees from those which should be announced through or jointly with the union. Sensitivity to the total situation rather than standing on management rights is likely to be the best guide for management in borderline situations.

Management cannot be certain that its industrial relations policies, no matter how carefully planned and executed, will guarantee a satisfactory relationship with a union or unions; however, management holds the initiative in so many situations that it can usually influence the collective bargaining relationship more than the union, even if the union leadership is more determined to prove its militancy than to cooperate with the company. Another advantage for the firm is the fact that employees are generally anxious to be on good terms with their employers and will eventually react against union leaders who refuse to meet management halfway in the solution of joint problems.

Once management at its highest policy-making level has determined what kind of union-management relationship it is striving for, it informs all levels of management of that policy and gives instruction on how it is to be carried out. If a company is determined to try to cooperate with the union or unions in its plants and this represents a changed policy, a great deal of conference and training for all levels of supervision is necessary. As we pointed out above, the foremen are particularly important to union-management relations.

Wise management must make up its mind how it will react to the unions' complaints and grievances. Some employers regard grievances as individual nuisances meant to annoy; others see them as symptoms of problem areas where it may be necessary to discuss with the union a way around the difficulty. Some managements will determine to be very legalistic and stick to the letter of the contract forcing each grievance to arbitration unless the union accepts the management interpretation, yet others take pride in almost never allowing a difference over contract interpretation to go to arbitration. From time to time a union finds itself in a difficult competitive relationship with other unions which in a period of rising prices were able to win sizable wage increases or make other gains. Some employers will enjoy the disadvantage of the men with whom they bargain; others may seize the opportunity to strengthen the union, which they hope will behave responsibly, by offering to re-open the wage agreement or by giving some other concession.

Most American managements and unions steer away from such a close relationship that they no longer clearly see the purpose and function of their individual roles, but increasingly they are discovering that in some problems outside the conventional area of collective bargaining they can work together to mutual advantage. Such cooperation is more likely to arise from working together on a specific "problem" than from trying to agree on "principles" of cooperation. Firms in the American garment industry have often called on their unions for help in solving production problems, and many firms have joint labor-management committees on safety.

Much recent discussion and writing about American collective bargaining is based upon an analysis of a number of case studies, made under the sponsorship of the National Planning Association, of the relationships between a variety of firms and the unions with which—by the standards of the Committee—they have had "good" collective bargaining relationship.

The bargaining situations selected for study involved cases which include substantially sized companies in reasonably competitive situations, picking them from important industries scattered over the United States, where a constructive relationship could not be explained by a unique personality or factor.

The final report of the National Planning Association's study lists basic causes of industrial peace.

1. There is full acceptance by management of the collective bargaining process and of unionism as an institution. The company considers a strong union an asset to management.

2. The union fully accepts private ownership and operation of the industry; it recognizes that the welfare of its members depends upon the successful operation of the business.

3. The union is strong, responsible and democratic.

4. The company stays out of the union's internal affairs; it does not seek to alienate the workers' allegiance to their union.

5. Mutual trust and confidence exist between the parties. There have been no serious ideological incompatibilities.

6. Neither party to bargaining has adopted a legalistic approach to the solution of problems in the relationship.

7. Negotiations are "problem-centered"—more time is spent on day-to-day problems that on defining abstract principles.

8. There is widespread union-management consultation and highly developed information-sharing.

9. Grievances are settled promptly, in the local plant whenever possible. There is flexibility and informality within the procedure.

In recent years the term "human relations" has come rapidly to the forefront in discussions of labor-management relations and at the same time a large amount of writing and research about human relations is going on in American industrial and academic circles. An awareness of the special human problems is not new in American industry but the present emphasis on the study of inter-individual and inter-group relationships is a recognition that along with the solution of technical problems there must be increasing concern for human elements in production. At this stage few would claim the existence of a science of human relations in industry; rather, sensitive observers increasingly call our attention to the fact that humans are not machines, that they have feelings and emotions which must be respected in order to get the highest degree of cooperation in the work-place and in labor-management relations.

Much of American management is eager to make use of knowledge and techniques in human relations even though a great deal of the work in the field is still tentative and experimental. As more experience and more truly scientific studies of human beings at work are made, the findings will be used by both labor and management to forge working relations that will come nearer to satisfying the goals of the two parties.

American collective bargaining is still relatively young. The basic outlines are established, but certainly as yet the variety of relationships is so great that it is clear much change is yet to come before a large number of generalizations will be true of all situations.

References

1. Selekman, Benjamin, *Labor Relations and Human Relations*, New York: Mc Graw-Hill Book Company, 1947.
2. Davey, Harold, *Contemporary Collective Bargaining*, New York: Prentice Hall, Inc., 1951, Ch. 11.
   Whyte, W. F. ed., *Industry & Society*, New York: Mc Graw-Hill Book Company, 1946.
   Whyte, W. F., *Men, Money and Materials*, New York: Harper and Bros., 1956.
   Dunlop & Healy, *Collective Bargaining—Principles and Cases*, Homewood, Illinois: Richard D. Irwin Inc., 1953.
   Selekman, Benjamin, *Labor Relations and Human Relations*, New York: Mc Graw Hill Book Company, 1947.
3. Davey, Harold, *Contemporary Collective Bargaining*, p. 269.
4. National Planning Association. *Causes of Industrial Peace Under Collective Bargaining. A Final Report, Case Studies*, Washington, D. C., 1953, p. 93.

CHAPTER 5

ORGANIZED LABOUR AND MANAGEMENT

Part II. The United Kingdom

N. S. ROSS

Faculty of Commerce and Social Science, University of Birmingham

Much theoretical discussion of human relations and management in industry appears tacitly to assume that the firm operates as an isolated unit with a monolithic structure. From some limited points of view, the firm may indeed be regarded as a self-contained and self-sufficient social system but, in practice, it is continuously subjected to external influences and pressures of many kinds and is inevitably involved in a continuous process of comparison which develops a sensitivity towards the outside world that is both stimulating and restraining. External forces, in the shape of government policy, public opinion, and the actions of consumers and competitors, modify policies and relationships within the firm. Trade union organization is a significant influence of this kind, but it differs radically from the others because it can both penetrate directly the social and economic boundaries of the firm and also establish within these boundaries an independent existence whose group structure and objectives may not coincide with those of the firm.

It is this aspect of trade unionism which engenders a sense of frustration and hostility among some managers and employers because it can so obviously be seen to cut across the concept of the firm as a unitary or monolithic structure. Recent sociological speculation and investigation, it is true, have revealed the weaknesses of this concept, but vast numbers of managers are still unaware of the significance of the group structure of their firms and tend to see the trade union as an intrusion into what otherwise they bel[illegible] to be a single, integrated system of relationships. There is, moreover, much in modern theoretical speculation about management which appears to lend colour to this unitary concept. Emphasis on the creation of a common doctrine concerning the objectives of the firm on the integration of individual and group aspirations, and on the notion of formal authority as flowing from a central source suggest an ideal of corporate unity which in the political field has latterly fallen into disrepute. Occasionally, one can scarcely fail to detect something of the flavour of totalitarianism in some of the theorizing about the nature of the managerial process.

Perhaps for this reason, management theorists have avoided discussion of the impact of trade unions and collective bargaining on managerial processes and functions. These are awkward facts which do not fit well into a theoretical scheme which postulates the managerial function as one of integrating a mass of individuals into a viable organization—the firm—capable of surviving under a given set of technical and commercial conditions. It is significant that, although the institutions and processes of collective bargaining are of immense practical importance and make considerable claims upon managerial time and energy, they have been ignored by virtually all who have attempted theoretical generalizations about management. Yet it is clear that these phenomena impinge upon the process of management at many points; that, for example, motivation as a managerial responsibility involves recognition of and adaptation to group goals of many kinds, among which trade union objectives are especially important because they are developed and sustained by a continuing organization usually extending outside the firm itself. This blind spot in management theory is suggestively parallel to the situation in economic theory where wage-theories ignore, or fail to deal satisfactorily with, the existence of trade unions and collective bargaining. It is perhaps because of this, that wage theory is one of the weakest and least satisfactory aspects of economic theory.

What seems to be required is a theoretical approach to management which treats the firm as a plural society rather than as the organic unity which most theorists appear hitherto to have represented it to be. The problem of government of a plural society is not to unify, integrate or liquidate sectional groups and their special interests in the name of some over-riding corporate existence, but to control and balance the activities of constituent groups so as to provide for the maximum degree of freedom of association and action for sectional and group purposes consistent with the general interest of the society as conceived, with the support of public opinion, by those responsible for its government. A free, democratic society is necessarily a plural society and the government of such societies is notoriously a more complex and difficult task than is the case with those whose structure is monolithic and authoritarian in character.

In practice, industrial organization has been, and still largely remains, authoritarian in character and it is, therefore, not surprising that attempts to analyse its principles of managerial operation have tended to emphasize concepts of integration and organic unity. Even where the analysis has pointed to such apparently democratic procedures as consultation and negotiation, these have been represented as techniques of integration or methods of creating a common doctrine rather than as natural features of the firm as a multi-group society. In recent years, authoritarian concepts have been shaken by growing sociological knowledge of the structure of relationships in industry and by the widespread failure of authoritarian methods in dealing with the new situation produced by prolonged prosperity and full employment.

The trend towards a more democratic approach to management has been greatly hampered, however, not only by the forces of conservatism and fear of the unknown, but also by certain very real practical problems, chief among which has been that of clothing power with responsibility. No solution has been found to the problem of giving organizational or constitutional expression to management's responsibility to employees, shareholders and customers and, hence, opportunities remain for arbitrary and unchecked action, and industrial organizations substantially retain their authoritarian character and methods despite the efforts of enlightened industrialists and managers to introduce some elements of democracy into human relations within the firm. Democratic government does not, of course, imply the rejection of authority, but requires that, in some form or another, those exercising power should ultimately be responsible to the governed or their representatives. Arbitrary exercise of power breeds resentment and resistance which finds expression in the creation of forms of countervailing power, chief among which, in the industrial situation, is trade union organization. Thus a very common interpretation of the industrial situation is that of a constant struggle between two highly organized groups, each possessing enormous power which is wielded arbitrarily and without check save that imposed by the threat of equally arbitrary reprisals.

The theory of the firm as a plural society is basic to this chapter whose object is to show, primarily with reference to organized labour and management in the United Kingdom, the practical and theoretical importance of developing such an approach. It is intended to concentrate the discussion on relations at the local level. Although this is the most significant level from the point of view of human relations within the firm, we shall also have to consider some of the consequences of national organization of employers and employees and the associated phenomenon of national collective bargaining.

Since the phrase collective bargaining was first coined by the Webbs at the end of the 19th century, in connection with their studies of the British trade union movement, the activity thus described has developed into a vitally significant feature of industrial relations throughout the modern world. Although collective bargaining can, and does, take place between groups formed on a most informal and loosely organized basis, the development of this procedure in practically every advanced industrial community has resulted in the emergence of a closely organized and highly institutionalized system, the influence of which permeates the entire social structure and profoundly affects the individual welfare of every member of the community. The classic definition of the term by the Webbs emphasized three distinguishing features. In the first place, collective bargaining eliminates and replaces individual bargaining; secondly, it involves the creation and expression of a collective will; and thirdly, its objective is the establishment of the common rule.

The practice of collective bargaining is older than trade unionism itself. Instances of the practice in factories and workshops in which trade union organization is non-existent can occasionally be found at the present day. The situation is not uncommon, for example, among clerical and supervisory workers in respect of whom, in general, trade unionism has made relatively little progress. At this stage, however, initial success in collective bargaining is often the precursor of full-blooded trade union organization without which it would remain a series of sporadic, disconnected efforts, devoid of long-term policy and little more advanced than the technique of the humble petition timorously presented by employees to the all-powerful employer. In fact, it is clear that it is the combination of the method of collective bargaining with permanent trade union organization and its counterpart, the employers' association, that has resulted in its emergence as a social phenomenon of the first magnitude at the present time.

The term collective bargaining, in British experience, covers three main situations. There is the elementary situation of a group of workers in a common employment bargaining with their employer from time to time as the need arises. The second stage finds a continuous association of workers, not necessarily all in common employment—in other words, a trade union—bargaining with individual employers. In the third stage, a trade union or federation of trade unions bargains with an employers' association on a local, regional or national basis. All these situations are to be found in British industry at the present day, but the trend of development is predominantly towards bargaining between highly organized national bodies of employers and employees. It might truly be said, in fact, that this is the logical and inevitable outcome of the grafting of the functions of collective bargaining on to specialized and permanent organizational forms.

This development of the practice of collective bargaining, and the institutional arrangements associated with it, has resulted in a number of important economic, social and political consequences which will be very briefly examined. Primarily, it has resulted in the establishment of parity of bargaining strength between employers and employed. The inherent weakness of the position of the individual in bargaining with his employer has long been recognized, and the part played by collective bargaining in redressing the balance of bargaining power by eliminating the influence of the particular exigencies of individual employees and employers needs no emphasis. Its results can be seen in the steady amelioration of conditions of life and work which has been experienced by the British worker throughout the past hundred years. Collective bargaining also has the consequence of eliminating competitive bargaining and removing the price of labour from the field of entrepreneurial competition. This result inevitably flows from the practice of collective bargaining once a certain degree of organization has been achieved on both sides. Successful trade union organization leads to combination of employers for the protection of their interests. The establishment and maintenance of the common rule is obviously in the interests of employers as a group although it may appear to individual employers, from time to time, advantageous to depart from it. Public opinion of the employing group, therefore, supported in many cases by other sanctions, is heavily weighted in these circumstances in favour of the common rule. As a result, the terms of collective agreements are frequently observed even by those who are not directly parties to them. Although the incentive to break the common rule varies with changes in economic conditions, collective bargaining in well organized industries does, in general, have the effect of removing the price of labour from the field of competition between business organizers.

It may thus be considered to make for the canalization of competitive forces into the channels of technical and managerial efficiency and commercial astuteness, not only by blocking the channel of competitive wage-bargaining, but also by exercising uniform pressure upon all firms, efficient and inefficient alike. Terms which may permit very comfortable margins to efficient firms may squeeze out of existence the profits of less efficient concerns. Pressure will therefore be set up within such firms to adjust themselves to the new situation by technical and managerial improvements. Viewed from this angle, trade union pressure for higher wages and better conditions, sustained over a long period, may represent an important dynamic factor in the raising of productive efficiency and may have contributed to the technological and managerial progress of the past century.

A further consequence is that determination of the price of labour may in certain circumstances become primarily a political or quasi-political issue. This possibility exists where a government feels impelled to intervene directly or indirectly in the public interest. The existence of great national organizations of labour and capital clearly contributes to the creation of a situation in which political intervention may have to be considered. In some countries, political intervention in the determination of wages and conditions of employment has taken a direct form, but in the United Kingdom it has entered into the situation only rarely and then very indirectly as, for example, in 1926 and 1931, and again, in very recent times, in the form of ministerial pronouncements and exhortations on the subject of prices and incomes. The British tradition of industrial self-government, expressed in the institutions of voluntary collective bargaining, has so far been sufficiently robust to deter any direct general excursion by the state into the field of wage-determination even in time of war. Nevertheless, political intervention remains a possibility which may well have been brought nearer by the great extension of public organization of industry as a result of recent nationalization of important basic industries.

Finally, national collective bargaining has resulted in increased public awareness of the economic and social importance of the results of collective bargaining and has thus stimulated criticism of the technique, as practised in this way, on the grounds of its social irresponsibility. There is a growing feeling that it is inadvisable to leave decisions affecting the welfare of the consumer or of the public exclusively in the hands of the representatives of the vested interests of the producers. Widespread development of such opinions will inevitably strengthen the possibility of direct political intervention in the arrangements made between employers and employed. On the other hand, as the representatives of employers and employed become increasingly conscious of the need to consider public opinion, a sense of public responsibility may develop and show itself, for example, by further extension and strengthening of machinery for conciliation and arbitration and by still greater reluctance to attempt to impose solutions by force.

In Great Britain, with the granting of freedom of association, organizations of employers and employed developed over a long period on a voluntary basis with the minimum of control and direction by the state. This voluntary concept permeates the entire structure and working of the system of industrial relations. It explains, for example, the fact that collective agreements are not legally enforceable between the subscribing parties; that legislation guaranteeing recognition and representation has not been thought desirable or necessary; that the state, whilst providing machinery for voluntary use, has not taken powers to secure compulsory settlement of industrial disputes, except in two periods of national emergency, and has assumed statutory power to regulate wages and conditions of employment only in those cases where it can be shown that the non-existence or weakness of organizations of employers and employed makes it unlikely that voluntary machinery for collective bargaining can be established or can work effectively.

The structures and methods which emerged as a result of this voluntary process display so much variety that it is difficult to detect any common pattern. Although employers' associations are almost invariably organized on an industrial basis, the unions have grown in such diverse ways in the course of adapting themselves to the changing environment that it is impossible to fit them satisfactorily into any logical classification of structural types. There is no simple or clear division into craft and industrial unions. Some important organizations like the Amalgamated Engineering Union contain many of the features of both types. At the same time, methods and procedures of government are infinitely varied in detail and although, in general, the pattern is that of democratic representative government some of the features of primitive direct democracy survive in many constitutions.

A trade union, it should be remembered, is itself a plural society containing many individual and group interests based on differentiation of function, geographical location, status and political beliefs. Its leadership is confronted with a problem of adjusting conflicting interests, which is essentially similar to that facing the management of the firm. It has, however, one advantage over the firm; its leaders or managers are constitutionally responsible to the entire membership and not to one section only. This constitutional responsibility is achieved in British trade unions in many different ways. In some, it is secured by conferring authority on elected lay executive committees or councils; in others, by popular election of full-time officers and committees and by many combinations of these methods, reinforced in some cases by elected courts of appeal with final jurisdiction in all disputes between members and those in executive authority. As a rule, also, policy-making bodies such as annual conferences are numerically dominated by lay representatives from local branch or district organizations. In the Amalgamated Engineering Union and the Transport and General Workers' Union, the number of executive council members and full-time officials attending the policy-making conferences is limited by rule. Thus, in most British trade unions, there are adequate constitutional channels for the expression of public opinion together with means of checking any arbitrary exercise of power by officials and representatives. Tyrannical and oppressive acts by those in authority against individual members may nevertheless occur in isolated instances, but it is unlikely that large-scale and persistent acts of this kind could be indulged in with impunity. Moreover, a deeply ingrained tradition of responsible service among trade union officials also constitutes a safeguard. On the whole, the British union official prefers to regard himself as the servant of the members and not their master, a view with which the members are inclined to agree and are usually not slow to enforce.

In the majority of cases, the leaders of British trade unions are very sensitive to the public opinion of the membership and are influenced accordingly in their attempts to reconcile general and sectional interests both in matters of internal administration and in questions of industrial policy. At national and regional levels, relationships and communications tend, generally, to be formalized along the lines of the constitutional structure of the union, whereas the local situation is characterized by much greater informality. In matters of broad general policy affecting the whole or an entire section of the membership, the formal structure of representative committees and national conferences, together with the hierarchy of full-time officials, is usually capable of producing an acceptable formula. This structure, however, cannot deal so effectively with local problems in industries in which conditions vary considerably from plant to plant. To the extent that unions have attempted to deal with local problems of this type, they have been compelled, almost invariably, either to entrust the responsibility to their existing branch organization or to develop additional local machinery for this purpose.

In most cases, the union branch, organized on a territorial or residential basis, drawing its membership from a number of different factories and meeting at intervals ranging from one week to three months, is not a very suitable unit to represent members in day-to-day relations with their employers. The need for action at this level led, therefore, to the evolution of systems of workshop representation which are additional to, and in some cases entirely separate from, traditional branch organization. This has had the effect, in many cases, of interposing an additional link in the chain of communication between members and the union's hierarchy and of isolating the branch still further from the daily industrial life of its members, a fact which may go some way towards explaining the indifference with which formal branch activities are almost universally regarded. Viewed from the upper levels of the hierarchy, the advantages of workshop representation, both in intensifying a union's control of terms and conditions of employment and in taking much of the burden from over-worked full-time officers, may be offset to some extent by a loosening of the ties with the ordinary members and the creation of local centres of power which, unless very strictly controlled, may diminish the authority of regional and national governing bodies and their officers. Most arrangements for workshop representation are in fact compromises between the need to provide members with continuous on-the-job services and the need to retain a central coordinating authority which alone can preserve the existing elaborate structure of national and regional collective bargaining.

From the point of view of relations between organized labour and management at the factory level, the tendency of most of the unions in the past to centralize control of finance and policy was of the greatest significance. This development, which added considerably to the strength and permanence of union organization, was a powerful influence in the evolution of nation-wide systems of collective bargaining in a great range of industries and trades. Collective bargaining on this scale was also encouraged by the belief, shared by the unions and the organized employers, that competitive labour standards were undesirable in a geographically compact industrial community. The result has been that, over a very large area of industry, decisions about wages and the other principal terms of contracts of employment have been taken out of the hands both of individual employers and of local union groups. Thus, unions and employers' associations have tended to be regarded as external agencies, limiting and regulating only the main terms and conditions of employment in the plant.

The development of collective bargaining on a national scale inevitably limited local freedom of action for all parties. This limitation varied in extent with the nature of the industry and of the particular arrangements adopted. Centralized administrations such as the railways and the civil service, with a high degree of uniformity of local conditions and practices, tended to produce centralized structures of agreements leaving little room for local initiative apart from supervision of their application and interpretation of minor clauses deliberately left open for local action. Industries in which local conditions and practices vary significantly, for example, engineering, tended to adopt more flexible arrangements which, whilst establishing general principles and basic minimum conditions of employment nationally, leave considerable freedom for local initiative within the framework of national agreements.

So far, the impact of workshop organization on the structure of national collective bargaining has not been very considerable. The functions of workshop representatives have been limited in most cases to supervision and interpretation in the light of local conditions. In others, however, these representatives have been granted or have assumed power to negotiate, directly with their employers, agreements which provide for improvements or advances on the terms of the national agreement. This development occurs more frequently with firms which are not members of an employers' association because the latter naturally tends to resist such action by individual members. It is not always successful in this, especially in times of labour shortage. Many individual employers are also uneasy, for reasons mentioned earlier, about the development of machinery of union representation within the firm and take the view that unions should confine their activities to bargaining within the external framework of relationships established with the employers' associations. This view ignores the existence of the local as well as the general sectional interests of employees and the tendency for such local interests to seek continuous and organized forms of expression within the firm. The established trade union provides the most obvious basis for achieving this end and, over the years, unions have modified their structures accordingly, even, in many cases, against the opposition of their officials and other influential elements. In spite of doubts and misgivings still remaining in some trade union quarters and opposition on the part of many employers, the trend is towards an increase in the volume and importance of union activities at plant level and it is unlikely that employers will be able to halt, still less to reverse, this movement.

Restriction of local freedom was part of the price that had to be paid to establish the common rule or standard employment practice in any industry. This was the principal objective of British trade unions after securing recognition by employers; union organization and methods were developed primarily towards this end. Hence the concentration on regional and national machinery and the constant drive to extend the area of collective agreements. This also explains the emergence of workshop organization at a relatively late stage of union development even in industries like engineering where local conditions vary tremendously. Regulation of the details of employment in individual factories or workshops seemed of little significance compared with the establishment of a common rule for the industry as a whole, and only when this was achieved could attention be effectively directed to the problem of regulating, in detail, local conditions. Confronted by the rising power of trade unionism, employers, too, were impelled towards the policy of the common rule and their organizations, in general, were shaped accordingly. The importance attached by both sides, and by the state, to the common rule, as laid down by voluntary collective agreements, was vividly demonstrated in the weaving section of the cotton industry by Parliamentary action resulting in the Cotton Manufacturing (Temporary Provisions) Act of 1934 which, for the first time under conditions of peace, gave statutory effect to the terms of collective agreements in industry. Without this support, the entire structure of collective bargaining in the industry was in danger of complete collapse as a result of a process of competitive wage-adjustment on a plant basis in an attempt to ensure that particular establishments secured a share of the greatly reduced volume of trade.

The importance of the common rule extends beyond the immediate membership of unions and employers' associations and exercises a profound influence on non-members. Inevitably, the employment policy of even the most independently-minded employer is related to the standards established by the collective agreements existing in his industry. It is sometimes argued that a "good employer" can be independent of union and employers' association alike but this is, clearly, true only in a very superficial way. An employer is "good" in relation to some existing standard of employment practice and, in an industry where organized collective bargaining takes place, this standard will be established by the terms of the collective agreements. Thus, an independent "good employer" wishing to maintain his position in this respect will eventually find it necessary to adjust his employment policy in sympathy with any significant variations in the terms of the appropriate collective agreements. Equally, the independent employer who has no "good" ambitions will find his employment policy conditioned to a great extent by the existing collective agreements, especially in times of prosperity and full-employment.

The powerful process of equitable comparison, which is always at work, appears to be the rock on which founders the belief that enlightened or progressive employment policies will eliminate trade union organization among employees. Whilst, under existing conditions, such a policy may seem to operate successfully in isolated instances, it clearly depends upon the existence of standards against which comparisons can be made. If all employers were to become "enlightened" or "progressive", enlightenment would cease to be a virtue outweighing, from the employee's point of view, the advantages of trade union organization. Employees, having adjusted themselves to the new standards, would tend to seek further advances. Two developments would then seem likely. Either individual employers would offer still further improvements, thus stimulating comparisons which would lead less favoured groups of employees to resort to organized action to secure similar advances, or employers would combine to maintain uniform standards, a situation tending to favour the retention of the *status quo*, thus giving rise to organized opposition by employees to a policy which appeared to deny them opportunities for further progress.

There are many reasons for believing that any attempt to eliminate trade unions by "enlightened" treatment of employees —a policy described in some trade union circles as that of choking the workers with chocolate—is both impracticable and undesirable. Over a large sector of British industry it would encounter the powerful forces of tradition and institutional loyalties and would be opposed by the long-accumulated force of emotional attitudes and political or ideological beliefs. Moreover, such a policy would eventually come up against the other sectional interests involved, particularly those of shareholders, and the net result might only be to delay the onset of conflict rather than to eliminate it and, in the process, to give more ground than might otherwise have been necessary. The plain fact is that one does not eliminate sectional interests by satisfying them. Sectional interests are inevitable in any highly specialized society and, no matter how satisfied those concerned may be with their current position, awareness of their special interests remains intense. Where there is awareness of a special interest there is always the possibility—some would say certainty—of some form of protective organization emerging amongst those concerned. Trade unions then, as long-established and experienced protectors of sectional interests, would appear to have considerable chances of survival against any onslaught of "enlightened" management and, indeed, if sufficiently astute, might well be able to turn it to their advantage.

Whilst it is true that the unenlightened, inconsiderate and grasping employer has been one of the most successful recruiting agents for trade unions, they do not owe their existence to him but to the deeper social and economic forces to which reference has been made. It follows, therefore, that his conversion to enlightened practices, desirable though this may be in itself, will not deprive trade unions of the reasons for their existence although it may force them to develop new arguments and to offer new services to their members. Finally, advocacy of enlightened management as a solvent of trade unionism, besides being fallacious and impracticable, may have the unfortunate result of poisoning relationships and deepening suspicions still further. It can, clearly, lead to an anti-union label being attached to innovations in the field of managerial techniques no matter how innocuous or socially and economically desirable these may be, thus impeding progress and understanding. Those who advocate a policy of this kind, possibly because they believe in the concept of the firm as an organic unity, may well be rendering a disservice to the cause of better human relations and greater managerial efficiency.

A theory of the management of human relations in industry must, therefore, recognize quite frankly the existence of sectional interests and the fact that groups will organize themselves around them. It must also allow for the fact that external factors and agencies limit, to a greater or lesser extent, freedom of action within the firm. In fact, although it may be a convenient simplification for some purposes, the firm cannot be regarded as a closed system of relationships. An attempt will be made in the following paragraphs to indicate some of the questions arising from the concept of the firm as a system of dynamic equilibrium of a number of separate but interdependent group or sectional interests and to suggest possible lines of approach to their solution.

Clearly, the central processes of the system are the formulation of group objectives, their communication to the interested parties and their eventual adjustment or balancing. The firm is organized around some central objective which is initially determined by an individual promoter or small group of promoters and later maintained, modified and developed by policy-makers who draw their legal authority from ownership of the assets of the business. This objective is expressed in formal organizational terms reflecting the technical and commercial functions involved in its achievement, and the organizational structure thus created is purely functional and devoid of any consciously planned internal social objectives. Legal and functional authority is vested in the owners of the assets or their representatives. In manning the organization, those responsible for its direction offer to satisfy certain individual objectives of those who accept employment, chief among which is, normally, the acquisition of an income. Viewed simply as a matter of establishing contractual relationships in which a certain income is paid in return for specific services performed under certain conditions, the problem of organizing the human cooperation necessary to achieve the firm's objective seems deceptively simple. It is, however, far from being uncomplicated in practice because the motives and objectives of the participants, including employers and managers, are mixed, and because individuals brought together for the purposes of the firm tend spontaneously to establish group relationships whose boundaries and objectives do not necessarily coincide with those expressed in the firm's formal structure and aims.

The task of management in this system of relationships is to reconcile individual and group objectives as closely as possible to the central objective in order to enable the firm to work efficiently towards that end. This process involves making decisions which limit, restrain or reject individual and group objectives and is thus productive of conflict. Managerial action inevitably increases awareness of sectional interests and tends to this extent to consolidate them. The central managerial objective may be imposed on individuals and small groups by the authority and economic power derived from the ownership of the assets of the firm, but this will tend to produce resistance and forms of non-cooperation for which there are many opportunities in practice. In particular, it stimulates organization by employees in order to confront power derived from property with the power that springs from control of the supply of labour and which finds continuing and effective expression in trade union organization. Trade unions do not introduce conflict into the industrial scene. They simply provide a highly organized and continuous form of expression for existing sectional interests among employees. It may be argued that they intensify and prolong conflicts of interest and make more severe and widespread any resulting dislocation of industrial activity. On the other hand, it can be said that, by organizing and focusing group opinions and aspirations, giving them coherent expression and providing recognizable machinery through which to negotiate the necessary adjustment of conflicting interests, the unions contribute immensely to the solution of problems which, because they are inherent in the working relationship, must be dealt with in some way or other by those responsible for the management of industrial activity.

The situation is exceedingly complex because the agencies or groups through which the central purpose must be given effect themselves possess separate identities and objectives. Hence, for example, directives from the top level, after filtering through the subordinate managerial groupings, frequently acquire an interpretation reflecting these sectional managerial purposes. The central purpose of the firm may be considerably distorted in this way, the extent to which this happens being influenced by many factors such as the degree of centralization of authority, the extent of awareness at the centre of the existence of this distorting tendency and ability to control it, the existence of trade union organization. At first sight, the importance of the latter factor in this connection may not be very obvious. Where subordinates have no independent union organization, their superiors can usually block effectively any direct and, therefore, unbiased communication between them and the higher levels of authority, and some deviations from central policy may, therefore, proceed unchecked. When subordinates are organized in a trade union, they become sufficiently powerful either to insist on direct communication with higher authority or to create a situation which will compel authority to intervene, investigate and thus become aware of any deviation involved.

In connection with this feature of direct communication with higher authority by way of the trade union, it is significant that unorganized, non-manual and supervisory groups frequently complain that their aspirations are ignored by higher management whilst those of organized manual workers are given urgent and careful attention. Frustration produced by this situation may affect the attitudes of supervisors and junior managers to trade unions and their representatives, finding expression frequently in carefully contrived minor restrictions and pinpricking actions directed at the union men. Where, as is so often the case, this situation is also reflected in the existence of standing negotiating machinery consisting exclusively of senior managers and the trade union representatives of the rank-and-file employees, the problem is still further aggravated. Those supervisors and managers who are excluded may become resentful towards both higher management and union representatives and may also view the proceedings with suspicion and alarm. They may well feel that their status and authority are diminished by an arrangement which permits some of their own subordinates regularly to meet and negotiate with important members of the higher management with whom they themselves rarely have any personal contact. That a lowly subordinate should enjoy the prestige associated with access to, and personal relations with, those in high places may be hard to bear.

There is, of course, also a real danger that this meeting of representatives of the extreme levels in the firm may lead to neglect of the lower managerial structure as a channel for communicating to employees the policy and central objectives of the firm and to reliance upon trade union representatives to carry out this vital managerial function. Although, as noted earlier, the danger of distortion exists in both cases, higher management is usually able to exercise much more control over the activities of subordinate managers in this direction than it can hope to do in the case of trade union representatives. Clearly, from the managerial point of view, it is unwise to rely solely on the trade union structure in the factory as an avenue of communication. The fact that communication with employees is for some purposes effected through their union organization, far from justifying neglect of the managerial structure, should rather emphasize the importance of this aspect of its functions both to maintain the status and morale of the managers and to retain some measure of control in this significant sector of employer-employee relations. That abdication from this important managerial function is not improbable is indicated by a recent announcement by a well-known firm in the motor industry that in future it will not rely solely upon the shop stewards to inform the employees of its policy and views, but will employ a specialist industrial relations officer to perform this function!

The adjustment of managerial and trade union objectives is achieved by a system of relationships between the representatives of these group interests in which concern for sectional interests is a dominating consideration. Although in the short run each group may make concessions to some concept of the general interest, in the long run sectional interests must prevail or seem to prevail, otherwise the representatives will be replaced. To represent adjustment as being effected by a process of bargaining within the limits of predetermined points of maximum concession by both sides, is an over-simplification which assumes the use of some form of economic calculus. This is not a satisfactory explanation, even in wages issues, since other factors of a non-economic character, such as prestige, group survival, political and moral considerations and so on, are also usually involved. Moreover, it is rare, in practice, for any positions to be absolutely fixed because the limits of concession will depend on the exigencies of particular situations. Bargaining positions emerge, are elaborated and modified in the course of negotiations. They represent, in fact, moveable points, and a large part of the art of negotiating lies in being able quickly to recognize these points, as they begin to crystallize; to appraise the possibility of shaping and moving them in the desired direction and to achieve this before the other party takes up a position which he may feel compelled to defend vigorously. The aim is to keep the position fluid until the possibility of agreement emerges. Obviously negotiations are only possible in such conditions; if fixed positions are adopted negotiation ceases. Since the consequences of failure to agree may range from outright attempts at coercion to more or less mild expressions of protest accompanied by some reduction in goodwill, it is important that negotiators should be able to assess fairly accurately the strength of feeling about the issue and the probable consequences of failure to reach a satisfactory agreement.

The adjustment finally arrived at, therefore, depends essentially upon the personalities, skill and judgement of the negotiators, supported in the last resort by the power they are able to deploy. Issues are not decided by reference to any set of accepted principles save so far as precedents and national collective agreements may serve as such. Indeed, one of the main difficulties of negotiation, and still more of arbitration, is precisely this lack of principles of decision. The idea of settlement or adjustment of conflicting group interests on an objective basis implies the existence of principles or criteria by reference to which proposals can be formulated, tested and decided. In fact, however, the criteria for deciding employment issues are far from being objective in character even in respect of the determination of wages where, at first sight, one might think that an objective basis could be found. Neither the principle of the living wage, the concept of capacity to pay nor the principle of relativity gives any real guidance to negotiators and arbitrators. Because of their vagueness and looseness of definition, these so-called principles are in practice largely of propaganda value only. Expediency and custom or tradition must be the main refuges of those who are required to make practical decisions on these matters. This has long been recognized as the supreme difficulty of arbitration. The Royal Commission on Trade Unions of 1867—69, for example, rejected compulsory arbitration on the grounds that there are no admitted principles of decision on which an arbitrator may proceed.[1] In a recent comment on this problem, it is suggested that the pronouncements of Parliament or of some planning body might serve as principles to be interpreted in detail by negotiators and arbitrators.[2] This, however, assumes acceptance of ideas of economic planning to a degree unpalatable to many sections of the community including the trade unions themselves. Another practical difficulty arises from the fact that prediction of the consequences of proposed changes in wages and conditions of employment is a matter of the greatest uncertainty and it is impossible to estimate in advance the associated quantitative changes in costs, prices and employment. Propositions about incomes in general are of little service since incomes are negotiated in relation to particular situations and their level is indeterminate, being influenced by a complex of economic, social, psychological and political factors.

In the absence of principles, one would expect the distribution of incomes and other benefits arising from industrial activity to be determined by pure expediency with perhaps an occasional touch of crude empiricism. This, it is suggested, is in fact the formula followed by British trade unions and employers in the post-war period, with the possible exception of the short-lived phase of wage-restraint in 1948 and 1949 when, with some important exceptions, the unions and employers accepted the principles of the White Paper on Personal Incomes, Costs and Prices.[3] In this case, acceptance of an arbitrary set of principles or objectives handed down by the planners provided a temporary precision to the aims of trade union wage-policy but, because it did not deal with the fundamental issues of wage determination, the plan created tensions and stresses within and between the unions which inevitably led to its early breakdown. Apart from this episode, post-war claims by British trade unions have been based mainly on the expediency of cost-of-living increases.

One of the significant curiosities of post-war trade union policy was the failure of the unions to react positively to the Labour Government's policy of economic planning. It is true that the Government did not seek powers of control in the labour market, preferring to announce its formal adherence to the idea of industrial self-government, accompanied by exhortations to the parties concerned about the need to give due consideration to the wider interests involved. Since the idea of planning and control of economic activity in the public interest has been quite widely accepted in the trade union movement, the unions, at first sight, might have been expected to accept voluntarily the Government's direction and advice on the requirements of the economic plan. In the event, however, the unions showed themselves strongly averse to accepting the implications of economic planning in the field of wage-determination, preferring to continue to rely upon the balancing of forces in a free labour market. It was this fact, among others, that led some observers to describe the trade unions as the last stronghold of conservatism in Great Britain. In fact, it simply demonstrated instinctive realization by the unions that, as the representatives of the vested interests of employees, they could not be associated with either government or managerial policies without losing their essential character and, therefore, the reason for their existence.

In the absence of other principles of settlement, it is sometimes suggested that the furtherance of some common purpose may serve as a principle of adjustment of sectional interests. Since organized labour and employers are mutually dependent, they may be thought to have a common objective, if no higher than that of joint survival. This, however, is an extreme, long-term position and rarely enters into practical negotiations which are essentially short-term in character. That the relationship is mutually advantageous, for example in providing the participants with incomes, is not sufficient to establish a common purpose in the sense of working towards agreed ends. Recognition of advantages in terms of the production of income, as implied by acceptance of the relationship, does not carry with it agreement to the terms of the distribution of income. Furthermore, there is a whole range of issues such as the distribution of privilege, status and power arising out of the activities of the firm which provides material for conflict.

It is frequently argued that the common objective, on which to base that identity of interest necessary for fully effective co-operation, is achieved by invoking the idea of satisfying a social purpose—usually the provision of goods and services to meet community requirements. Whether this concept makes a significant contribution to the solution of the practical problem of adjusting the claims of sectional interests, is doubtful. Of necessity, the firm has always had an external social purpose, since satisfaction of consumers' requirements is, in the long run, a condition of survival. Nevertheless, recognition of the fact that revenue is dependent on successfully serving the needs of the customer does not *ipso facto* produce agreement about its distribution among those participating in the work. Emphasis on the social purpose of industry may be of value as a propagandist antidote to long and widely held views concerning the iniquity of the profit-motive, but it is not a concept which will revolutionize relationships in industry. It may be useful to demonstrate that, in general, the incomes derived from industry by both capital and labour are socially justified, but this rather obvious proposition contributes little to the solution of the practical problem of determining, in specific cases, the distribution of financial and other rewards or settling questions of status and participation in control. The concept may also be helpful in creating a sense of satisfaction in socially useful work and in heightening the individual's awareness of the prestige and status associated with his employment, but, again, the fact that individuals value non-material satisfactions of this kind does not mean that they are devoid of self-interest and always ready to accept without question whatever share of the fruits may be offered to them. It simply indicates that self-interest and its satisfaction take many different forms.

The effectiveness of the appeal to social purpose is largely a matter for speculation. Under war-time conditions, many sectional aims were willingly subordinated to the national cause, but there is much to suggest that, since they do not possess the dramatic urgency and simplicity of war-aims, it is difficult to present the prosaic facts of national economic policy in such a way as to stimulate the imagination and the emotions of the public so that they perceive some connection between their own actions and the national or social interest. For the great majority, the sense of belonging to a group, which alone makes possible the voluntary subordination of individual to collective interest, appears not to extend very strongly outside the range of the small face-to-face groups of which they are members. Thus loyalties and responses to the needs and objectives of wider groups—the firm, local community and nation—are weak or even non-existent. Unless the social purpose of the wider group can be successfully interpreted in terms of the objectives of primary groups, the objectives of the latter may over-ride those of the former. The argument, however, has now arrived back at the starting point—that the task of management is the adjustment of group objectives—so that the concept of a common social purpose has not really advanced the search for a solution.

There are also practical difficulties in applying the concept of a common social purpose arising from the unrepresentative character of the managerial group from the point of view of all the interests involved. For all legal and most practical purposes, they represent only the owners of the assets. It is difficult for the representatives of any one sectional interest to represent themselves as the arbiters of the wider social interest, and so the analysis reverts to the constitutional difficulties considered earlier. Therefore, it would appear necessary to abandon the approach to the problem of adjustment of sectional interests along the lines of an agreed unity of central purpose achieved by the integration of individual and group aspirations or objectives. From a purely practical point of view, it is doubtful whether high-sounding talk of social objectives will ever succeed in disguising the existence of sectional interests which, to those who share them, possess a very much more immediate and vital reality. The concept of the firm as a plural society, containing many related but separate interests and objectives which must be maintained in some kind of equilibrium, offers a much more realistic approach than that implied in the idea of the firm as an organic or corporate unity.

Satisfactory adjustment or balancing of sectional interests in a plural society would appear to demand six main conditions which must be satisfied by all the groups concerned but especially by that group which accepts responsibility for the government or management of the society as a whole. The first of these is recognition of the existence of these interests and their legitimacy. This implies not simply awareness of their existence but understanding of their character and objectives and their acceptance as a natural expression of the fact that a specialized society produces special interests which demand consideration and a measure of satisfaction if the society is to function effectively. The social and economic history of the past two centuries has discredited the extreme individualist position which sought the maximum social welfare through the free play of enlightened self-interest, but it is by no means certain that the extreme collectivist approach provides a solution which is compatible with the idea of a free society, defined as one which permits a maximum degree of freedom of action to individuals and constituent groups consistent with social standards and objectives approved or accepted by public opinion. In this sense, the concept of social purpose may have some part to play in the adjustment of sectional interests, but only as a limiting or, regulating condition not as a central driving force. The demand, implicit in much modern theorizing about management, that sectional interests in the firm should be integrated in conformity with some common doctrine in support of centrally inspired or imposed objectives, seems to incline rather dangerously towards the extreme position.

The attitude which regards sectional interests as not quite proper and not to be too openly acknowledged, but to be camouflaged or wrapped up in woolly phrases concerning service to some wider social objective, is probably largely the result of a reaction against the extreme individualist position, a reaction which, over the past one hundred years or so, has found expression in various social, political and religious movements and ideologies. The loosening of the old sanctions and the shifting towards organized labour of the balance of power in industry, produced by recent economic conditions, has stimulated a desperate search for a formula which will convert interdependence of group interests into identity of interests. Conspicuous lack of success in this direction suggests that this may be a wrong approach. The fact that objectives are linked does not necessarily mean that they are identical or even capable of being made so. There is much to suggest that, instead of striving for the unattainable, the inevitability of differences in sectional interests should be recognized and attention concentrated on the task of improving the efficiency with which they are managed or adjusted in order that the firm might remain technically and socially an effective going concern.

Recognition by all the groups involved of the existence of the legitimate interests of others is a prior condition of success in this direction. In practice, the main parties in industry have been compelled to adopt a realistic approach and to recognize the existence of other group interests. Although they may have questioned their legitimacy, British trade unions have never doubted the existence of the vested interests of the employers and, of necessity, have acted as, and represented themselves to be, the guardians of the special interests of their own members. Employers, in turn, have been compelled, mainly as a consequence of trade union organization, to recognize the existence of the special interests of their employees and, as a result, have become more clearly aware of the nature of their own interests. From this point of view, organized labour may be regarded as having made a major contribution to the realization of this primary condition for successful adjustment of sectional interests.

Turning to the second condition, it is clear that, without effective representation of the interests involved, a satisfactory and workable adjustment of individual and group objectives is difficult or impossible of achievement. Acceptance of decisions affecting such interests is seriously prejudiced by the knowledge or belief that these interests have escaped consideration because they have been totally or partially unrepresented during the process of decision-making. In practice, representation is effected by formal and informal arrangements. Informal representation is achieved through spontaneous groupings and relationships which develop within the firm and produce their own systems of communication. Formal representation is embodied in the organizational structure of the firm which normally permits, at least on paper, the expression by subordinates to their superiors of views on questions affecting personal interests and in the case of a serious dispute or grievance, may also provide for reference to higher authority. As a rule, however, formal representation of this type is of very limited value in the adjustment of differing interests because its use, if not frowned upon, is frequently not encouraged, especially at the lower levels where it is likely to be interpreted as criticism of the superior and may produce unfortunate consequences. Its most important defect, however, is that, since it is based on the relationship of superior to subordinate, inequalities of status and power exist which make it difficult for the subordinate effectively to represent his own special interests or to feel confident that, where these conflict with the interests of superiors, they will receive fair consideration.

Some senior executives believe that this difficulty can be overcome by proclaiming the policy of "the open door" and inviting direct personal representation from any level. Apart from the obvious threat which such an arrangement constitutes to the structure of authority and responsibility in the firm, it almost invariably fails because strong social pressures of many kinds exist which deter the individual from using this approach. A more serious attempt to surmount the problem takes the form of incorporating into the formal organizational structure a committee, or system of committees charged with ascertaining and representing various group interests and advising management concerning their treatment. Since they have no independent existence, such committees cannot negotiate in the ordinary sense of the term although they may be used by management in settling the details of terms and conditions of employment. They are, in fact, consultative committees and their scope can be extended beyond the consideration of matters strictly related to the terms of contracts of service to cover questions of operational efficiency and associated managerial topics.

The fact that, in many industries, trade unions have accepted, with reservations, the establishment of consultative committees to discuss matters outside the field of terms and conditions of employment, has led to the suggestion that the functions of consultation and negotiation might be combined under a single joint committee. Few, if any, trade unions would agree to this arrangement except on condition that those who represented the employees were in fact the chosen representatives of the union. Even so, many would resist the idea as an attempt to absorb or enmesh the union in the managerial structure and thus reduce it to impotence as a representative of the sectional interests of its members. The suspicion here is that the device of a combined committee would be used to reduce the status of union representatives from that of independent agents, whose position is guaranteed by organizational strength, to that of subservient counsellors permitted only to advise, even on questions of terms and conditions of employment. Of course, the process might well work in the other direction and management might find that a combined negotiating and consultative committee allowed union representatives to bargain and negotiate on matters hitherto regarded as subjects exclusively reserved for managerial decisions. Hence, some managers view with misgiving proposals for combined committees. It is quite possible, in practice, to combine both functions in one committee provided that a clear and agreed distinction can be drawn between subjects for negotiation and subjects for consultation and that both sides are equally able to detect and prevent encroachment of one function on the other. On balance, however, it might appear safer, from the point of view of both sides, to keep the processes separate.

These considerations point to the importance of the contribution which trade unions make towards effective representation of sectional interests by securing formal recognition and by the establishment of formal machinery of negotiation based on independent representation of the interests of their members. The independent status achieved through trade union organization is significant from two points of view. It is this independent source of power, counteracting the power derived from ownership of property, which alone makes possible the control of arbitrary actions and alone can require those in managerial authority to demonstrate that the interests represented to them have been carefully and exhaustively considered. Secondly, the status derived from successful trade union organization enables the representative to meet and negotiate with employers and managers as an equal and thus to approach his task with advantages that can never be enjoyed by the individual subordinate in his own right nor by the committeeman or representative whose position has been created by managerial act and decision. Effective representation of sectional interests necessitates complete independence of status for those who represent them. For the employee, this independence in relation to his employer can be secured only by the trade union.

Where representation is by full-time officials, as is generally the case in national and regional negotiations and also quite frequently in local or plant bargaining, the independence of the representative is clearly established and beyond the control of employers or managers. The situation is not quite so simple, however, where the representative is himself an employee of the firm with whom he is negotiating. Whilst his status and independence as a representative are still established and guaranteed by his trade union, his personal status as an employee remains that of a subordinate, and thus he is inevitably more susceptible to managerial pressure and influence in the discharge of his representative functions than is the full-time union official. The workshop representative or shop steward finds it difficult completely to dissociate his public position as representative from his private and subordinate status as employee, and his awareness of inferiority in the latter respect may tend to produce aggressiveness in his conduct of negotiations. Moreover, since he knows that his rank-and-file constituents are well aware that he can be subjected to managerial pressure and influence, his anxiety to demonstrate that he has remained unaffected may well lead him to put a premium on militancy and to discount the conciliatory approach. Clearly, then, a management desirous of creating effective relationships and machinery for the adjustment of group interests will scrupulously respect the independence of the representatives and will attempt constantly to demonstrate to all concerned that no personal pressure or influence will be brought to bear.

It is recognized that this is often extremely difficult to observe because of the complexities arising from the dual character of the relationship of shop steward or representative to managerial authority, but there are at least two important steps that can be taken. First of all, restrictions on representatives in the exercise of their representative functions can be limited to the minimum necessary to safeguard against possible abuse by individuals leading to the undermining of discipline and authority. In case of doubt, it is probably better to interpret this condition generously rather than the reverse. The wisdom of this course is borne out in practice by the fact that many employers, in the engineering industry for example, have found it useful to provide facilities for union representatives far in excess of those specified in the appropriate national collective agreements on the subject. Secondly, employers can, as a matter of proclaimed policy, refrain from managerial action such as transfer and dismissal in the case of employees possessing representative status, except where circumstances plainly render such action unavoidable, and then only after a full explanation has been given. Transfer and dismissal of representatives can seriously dislocate the operation of machinery of negotiation besides giving rise to considerable suspicion and hostility. Even where strong technical or organizational grounds exist for the action, it is all too easily construed either as victimization of individuals or as an attack upon union organization, both of which are capable of stimulating violent opposition and reprisals. Management may be regarded as having resorted to the use of force instead of peaceful negotiation in relations with organized labour and, in return, union members may feel justified in replying with force.

Questions of the status and treatment of shop stewards and workshop representatives have already caused disputes, some of them serious, in British industry and the indications are that the number may increase unless agreed principles can be worked out for dealing with the delicate issues involved. Certain trade union circles advocate some form of legal protection for shop stewards, but official opinion in the movement, still wedded to the voluntary tradition of British industrial relations, emphasizes that legal protection would necessarily involve some degree of definition and regulation by the public authorities of the functions of union representatives, and that the difficulties of enforcement would limit the value to the unions of such legislation. It is much better, according to this view, to rely upon the strength derived from a high degree of union organization to prevent any victimization and bullying of workshop representatives by their employers.

Some employers reject the idea of special status for union representatives on the ground that, since all employees are engaged on the same contractual basis, it would be invidious to discriminate in practice between one group or class and the rest. This is a purely legalistic argument which ignores the realities of the situation. Union representatives are more than employees. They have important duties and functions within the firm which are additional to their contractual obligations and they stand in a special relationship both to their employer and to their fellow employees. In fact, they cannot be treated just like any other employee. This is recognized by the granting of facilities, even of a minimal character, for carrying out their representative functions and, having gone so far, it is scarcely logical to refuse to extend recognition to cover the minimum requirements of status which are essential to ensure stability and continuity of performance of a task which is vitally important to employer and employee alike.

It might be objected that conferment of special status would make it impossible for management to rid itself of representatives whom it considered to be irresponsible agitators or otherwise unacceptable as negotiators. This is very dangerous ground. It implies that the employer has the right to choose the trade union representatives, and this is a proposition which unions will, quite properly, resist to the uttermost. An employer is, of course, entitled to indicate to a union that for certain reasons he finds an individual representative unacceptable and is reluctant to negotiate with him, but, if he wishes to avoid a head-on clash, he must refrain from pressing the point further and rely upon the good sense of union officers and members to see that ultimately it is to their advantage to have an acceptable representative. It is a very delicate situation for both sides, but there are many ways in which an employer can, without provoking conflict, convey to the union side that a certain change of representation would be advantageous. The situation calls for tact and diplomacy rather than for "strong-arm" methods. Since attempts to remove unacceptable representatives on pretexts such as redundancy or re-organization will almost invariably meet with fierce opposition and will seriously damage relationships and impair mutual confidence between the parties, it is extremely questionable whether an employer will really find it worth while to refuse to recognize the special status of the union representative, with all that this implies for the development of good relations and mutual confidence, in order to retain a weapon of doubtful value which in some circumstances may recoil upon him disastrously.

If sectional or group interests are to be effectively adjusted, it is clear that there must be an efficient system of communications so that the parties concerned can experience free and continuing interchange of views and aspirations. The structure of such a system is, of course, mainly determined by the nature of the arrangements for representation of the various interests, but the mere devising of a structure is not in itself sufficient to ensure that it functions satisfactorily. This depends primarily upon the nature of the relationships between the groups and the skill with which those who occupy the key positions in these groups use the opportunities for communication with others. Communications which pass along the lines of executive authority are almost certain to be formal in character and, since the structure of executive authority is designed primarily to fit the technical requirements of the firm rather than its social pattern, are unlikely to reflect the aims and aspirations of informal constituent groups except where these latter by chance coincide with functional groupings within the firm. Formal communications are chiefly concerned with coordination and control of technical activities and necessarily assume the existence of rights and duties which have been determined by the contractual relationship between individuals and the firm. To this extent, therefore, the formal structure is not well adapted to communicate sectional or group objectives which are social or extra-contractual in nature. This fact may partly account for the aversion shown historically by management to dealing with collective approaches by subordinates. It is true that the informal system of communication, which develops in some form or other in every firm, can be used to transmit group views and objectives, but its effectiveness depends almost entirely on the extent to which those in authority are aware of the informal structure of the firm and on their ability to interpret and assess the importance of information conveyed by these indirect channels. Nevertheless, the pressure of group interests, especially when they achieve continuity and independence of expression through trade union organization, requires modification of the formal structure to facilitate communication. This is achieved by formal recognition of the trade union as a representative body and by the development of relations between union representatives and management at all levels. Some of the difficulties arising from this development, especially its tendency to establish direct communication between the lowest and the highest levels, have already been examined and it is clear that considerable skill and understanding is required to enable a system to work smoothly and efficiently which in effect breaks the formal line of communication, based on the relationship of subordinate to superior. This disruptive feature of union-management relations suggests yet another reason why some managers regard trade unions with little enthusiasm and most theorists tend to ignore the problems imposed by the impact of labour organization.

The consultative committee is another formal development in this field. Indeed, the improvement of communications may well be regarded as its chief contribution compared with which its direct contribution to technical and organizational improvement is insignificant. Consultative committees may be considered to be a development or extension of the informal relationships arising in the working group. In fact, if these relationships are satisfactory, a formal committee is probably superfluous except perhaps in very large firms and, even here, the committee is no substitute for effective informal relations. The technique of consultation, whether by means of committees or by informal personal contact, may go some way towards the solution of the problem of responsibility, which was discussed earlier, by creating and expressing a form of public opinion within the firm in support of managerial policies. From this point of view, consultation is a political technique rather than an efficiency device and there is much to suggest that its continued development will depend more upon wider realization of its potential contribution to the establishment and acceptance of responsible government or management in industry than upon its contribution in the technical or operational field.

The fourth condition for successful adjustment of sectional interests is that of flexibility of group objectives and of central direction and policy. This requires very little comment because, clearly, the more rigid group aims become, the more difficult it is to reconcile differences. Flexibility in this respect is not to be confused with vagueness or lack of definition which can only impair relationships by causing confusion and irritation. It is quite possible to define policy in general terms in such a way that a clear indication is given of the main direction of the objective without specifying detailed requirements and conditions. As a general rule, the greater the detail in which a policy is elaborated and published, the less is its flexibility. The responsibility for ensuring flexibility rests with the leaders of all the groups or interests involved, but may be considered especially heavy in the case of the managerial group since they have assumed the task of holding the firm together as an effective system of cooperation. Fortunately, management as a rule is better placed to secure flexibility of policy than are the trade unions because of the nature of the policy-making process in each case. In the case of management, the process usually involves a relatively small and more homogeneous group of people and, as a result, policy can normally be adapted more quickly and easily to meet changing situations. Trade unions on the other hand, because of very much greater numbers, greater diversity of interests and outlook and more complicated constitutional arrangements, have special problems of policy-making which tend to reduce flexibility. Although the nature and problems of policy formation in trade unions are of considerable importance in the relations between organized labour and management, the subject is too wide and too specialized to be dealt with in a general review of this character.

Ability and willingness to create conditions allowing the maximum realization of sectional objectives is the fifth condition of adjustment. This requires a positive approach to the problem rather than the negative one of rejecting the objectives of others because they appear to conflict with one's own. For example, management might reject a union demand for higher earnings on the ground that it would adversely affect costs and profit margins. This might be perfectly true, given the assumptions that other factors remain unchanged, but if management has the ability and the will to create new conditions—for instance by the introduction of systems of payment by results, technical and organizational improvement and so on—it may become possible to meet the objective of higher earnings at least in part. Such a policy involves mutual recognition of the fact that militant pursuit of vested interests is not necessarily incompatible with constructive co-operation between them and, indeed, that the latter may be indispensable to success in the former.

Another way of expressing this is that the parties must be able and willing to effect changes that may be necessary in order to secure satisfactory adjustment of their objectives. If, however, complete avoidance of change is a principal objective of any group, then a satisfactory adjustment of sectional interests is impossible since this represents an inflexible objective and violates the fourth condition which has just been discussed. It is suggested that the approach envisaged in the condition now being examined is more realistic than that which relies upon appeals to abandon or modify vested interests in the name of some wider social purpose even in the most unlikely event of agreement being reached on such a purpose. The former approach has the advantage of drawing upon the powerful forces of self-interest and, although it lacks the inspiration of high purpose, may at least make possible the attainment of efficiency. In any case, it may be argued that the ultimate ends to be served by such efficiency cannot be determined either jointly or severally by the vested interests contributing to the production of goods and services, but only by some wider public opinion, whether expressed in the market-place or in the councils of the nation.

The sixth and final condition is that the balance of power between the parties should not be markedly uneven. In this respect, trade union organization has made perhaps its greatest impact on the industrial situation by providing the only possible source of countervailing power apart from direct state intervention. It is no exaggeration to say that, without the contribution of organized labour, a voluntary, self-governing industrial society would be impossible. Where power is concentrated in the hands of a single group, the plural society withers and is supplanted by the monolithic. Without trade union organization, the subordinate groups, formal and informal, within the firm are ineffective in controlling and restraining the exercise of power by the representatives of property and must accept their terms without serious question. Quite apart from the grave implications of such a situation for a politically democratic community, it is doubtful whether, in the long run, it would provide the basis for an efficient industrial society.[4]

References

1. *Royal Commission on Trade Unions, 1867—69.* Final Report, Vol. I, p. XXVII.
2. Barbara Wootton, *Social Foundations of Wage Policy,* London: Allen and Unwin, 1955.
3. *Personal Incomes, Costs and Prices,* Cmd. 7321, February 1948. London: H. M. S. O.
4. For a discussion of political implications, see Clark Kerr, *Industrial Relations and the Liberal Pluralist,* Reprint No. 80, University of California Institute of Industrial Relations, 1955.

CHAPTER 6

HUMAN RELATIONS IN THE BOARD ROOM

E. F. L. BRECH

Senior Partner: Urwick, Orr & Partners, London

The connotation of the term "human relations" that has been gaining currency in most industrial countries in recent years refers particularly to the manager-worker context, and more in a formal sense than in respect of informal personal contacts. The "managers" concerned in this connection are, however, at all levels of the organization, including the top levels, for it is widely recognized that sound human relations within an enterprise cannot be attained and maintained unless they have a foundation in policy formulated and supported by those at the highest positions of authority. The main subject-matter of the present chapter is to be the nature and significance of the policy aspects underlying human relations; that is to say, the incidence of the subject of human relations in the policy deliberations of the Board of Directors or whomsoever else form the governing authority of the particular enterprise concerned.

There is, however, another interpretation of the title which has an indirect bearing on the lead given by the Board of Directors to the human relations tone of their enterprise, namely, consideration of the patterns of behaviour and relationships within the Board Room, among the Directors themselves. This is, perhaps, delicate ground on which to tread, but it is as important a matter to review as any other aspect of human relations. It has long been recognized that the tone and quality of an organization are a direct reflection of the leadership and example from the top, and many managers know how much the soundness or otherwise of the human relations atmosphere among employees is determined by the quality of relationships among the managers themselves. The pattern of human relations within any organization is an integral one, linking top management with the points of operation, and, if there is weakness or strained relationship at the higher or intermediate levels, it is unlikely that sound atmosphere and efficient working can be maintained at operative levels.

For the average run of industrial and commercial enterprises, the term "Board Room" is a conventional synonym for the Board of Directors as the formally constituted governing authority of a company set up under any national legislation. The title ought, however, to be taken here metaphorically, to refer to the governing body of any organization, whatever its form; in the first part of the chapter, the matter has relevance also to the single owner-managers who are the heads of the many smaller businesses that are characteristic of western industrial communities.

There is no call, for the purposes of the present context, to go into the niceties of company form, or differences that emerge from different legal systems. The simple supposition can be made that the company or the partnership or the authority is a corporate body established to conduct certain activities, and financed by a group of owners (shareholders) who are usually individuals but sometimes are banks or other financial institutions, or even the State. To enable the enterprise to be smoothly and efficiently conducted, these owners set up a small group of persons as the Directors —chosen either from among themselves or by selection and appointment from elsewhere on grounds of technical and business competence. In Great Britain, it is most common to find the Directors as full-time servants of the company, often holding executive and technical posts within the organization, as well as their membership of the Board. However constituted, the Board of Directors is the legally recognized authority for conducting the affairs of the enterprise on behalf of the owners, in accordance with their intentions, and within the framework of a given code of law. In the main, this law is concerned with the protection of the investors who have contributed to financing the enterprise, and the law seldom seeks to intervene in the affairs of the company unless there is fraud or other illegal practice. Naturally, Company Law varies widely from country to country, but the essentials of the legal framework are similar so far as they bind the Directors in terms of responsibility under the law.

In Great Britain, Company Law requires the Directors to conduct the affairs of the enterprise in terms of the Memorandum and Articles of Association on the basis of which the company was constituted. The Directors are the immediate representatives of the owners, as well as the highest level of government of the enterprise. In German Law, however, these two roles are separated: a body called the "Aufsichtsrat" is the voice of the owners in policy and control, and a separate body called the "Vorstand" is the highest level of direction, composed of the top executives or specialists with the Managing Director. The latter individual is the link between the two bodies, but otherwise membership is distinctive. There is another special feature in that selected representatives of the employees serve as full members of the "Aufsichtsrat" but not of the "Vorstand".

Leaving aside complexities stemming from such differences of legal framework, it can be said broadly that because a Board of Directors stands as the formally constituted governing authority of the enterprise, the first responsibility is a legal one, to ensure that the company's affairs are conducted in accordance with the requirements of its constitution as well as in accordance with the law.[1] The constitution has been laid down by the founder-owners, and includes a statement of the objectives. These are concerned with the manufacture and sale of certain commodities, or the provision of services of one kind or another, or the conduct of some other activities. Out of such activities the owners are expecting to reap remuneration on their investment, or reward for their venture—in the form of profits. From the standpoint of the owners, in fact, the specific purpose of the company is to make a profit for their personal enrichment. Yet nowhere in the Memorandum or Articles of Association (i.e. the constitution of the Company) is such an objective stated: it is implicit in the formation of the enterprise, and figures prominently in the mandate entrusted by the owners to the Directors. It is not at all uncommon to read of shareholders making sweeping changes in the membership of the Board of Directors because they are dissatisfied with the profit-earning of the company and know that better direction of affairs could bring much better returns. There are, of course, some enterprises where the profit objective is minimized or even absent, but the need to cover all costs of operating and to provide for the preservation of capital remains—otherwise the enterprise can only bleed to death. This is neatly recognized in the formulation of one or two of Britain's nationalized industries where the requirement is laid on the Boards by Parliament that they are "to break-even, taking one year with another", interest on capital and provision for replacement being included in the cost elements to be covered at break-even.

A Board of Directors thus has two responsibilities laid upon it by the fact of its constitution—to comply with legal requirements; to earn a profit for the owners. The Directors can, however, accomplish these two tasks only by dint of undertaking much fuller responsibilities concerned with the direction of the enterprise, and this fuller conception of their role has a very important bearing on their contribution to the pattern of human relations within the enterprise.

The fuller role starts in the consideration of the main objectives, as laid down in the Memorandum of Association. It may be a company which has been formed in order to undertake the manufacture and sale of certain lines of products, merchanting them through wholesale channels for home and export trading. Or the founders may be interested only in trading, and are buying their wares from manufacturers, but themselves concentrating on wholesale or retail selling. Or again, the company may be concerned with the provision of services such as transport for passengers or goods, the generation and supply of electricity, the provision of banking, or advertising, or loans for house purchase, or amusement in the form of television or the theatre. The goods or services a company is providing may be used only by the citizens in the home country or may be exported to all quarters of the globe, but wherever used they will form an item in the general pattern of social living. Seen thus in its setting within the community, any enterprise can be considered as meeting certain basic purposes by means of which it becomes an integral part of the working fabric of a modern industrial society. These purposes may be summarized as follows:

1. The company is providing a given range of goods and/or services which contribute to the normal living of the people in the community where it is set or in other parts of the world—things such as food, clothing, or other necessities and amenities of life. In a more primitive world, individuals would have provided all such things for themselves in so far as they existed at all, but the main feature in the development of civilization has been the progressive specialization of activity, coupled with the expansion of exchange in scope and complexity. In the end, an individual citizen buys all that he needs against a medium of exchange called money, and a vast complex system of manufacturing and trading exists to respond to the behests of the money as the expression of his needs and wants.

2. In the course of conducting these activities, a company also provides employment which gives rise to the payment of wages and salaries in money—the medium through which the citizens can buy their commodities and services. This second aspect of social living is closely interwoven with the foregoing and forms the other half of the transaction. It is again a mark of advanced civilization that the individual, instead of absorbing all his and his family's time in occupations directed immediately to their own living, concentrates on a given task for which he receives a given quantity of means of exchange and so is enabled to complete the purchase transaction. The company has not only to pay the persons whom it employs, but has also to make contributions to civic organizations in the form of central and local government through taxation.

3. The company provides also an opportunity for the investment of savings, thereby obtaining for itself the capital needed for the conduct of its enterprise. The savings come either from collective sources through other companies, or from individuals who do not spend currently all that they earn; but in either case the savings come initially from the double-sided transaction of selling and buying which is the economic activity inherent in the life of the community. The motive for saving in the case of the individual is the provision for a later purpose, possibly for times when earnings will no longer be possible.

4. Because of its utilization of such savings in the promotion of greater efficiency of operation, the company is able to pay interest on the capital or savings that it uses, either in the form of a contracted rate of return or in the form of dividends declared on the basis of profit earned. Because such savings or capital are productive, it is legitimate that interest or profit should be paid. And by the same token, it is legitimate that those who forego consumption in order to make capital available should be able to receive the additional income as a reward for their forebearance.

5. The company's activities can contribute to the advancement of the standard of living by the improvement in the quality of the products or services that it offers, or by the development of new products and services, or by improving its methods of working so as to release resources for further production and for contributions to social development in the form of roads, education, and the like.

6. The activity undertaken by the company in the employment of people provides opportunities for the emotional and social satisfactions which are derived from personal association in a given common task. This goes to the roots of the human being by reason of man's gregarious nature and is a facet of human behaviour which remains over in the modern civilized community from man's more

primitive patterns of life, when in earlier times he worked in compact social groups for the direct satisfaction of his needs as part of a communal life.

Few Directors would recognize their own objectives in the form of these six points. Yet, it remains a fundamental truth that all six must be part and parcel of the purposes of any enterprise set up in a modern community; the Directors in their role as the responsible representatives of the owners of the enterprise, accountable for the direction of its affairs, must thereby assume responsibility for the achievement of such basic social purposes. They declare their first "acceptance" in the statement set out in the Memorandum of Association, declaring their objectives in the enterprise; these relate particularly to the first purpose listed above. They recognize the second purpose as "a demand for labour" and they endeavour to fulfil it as best possible through the medium of a personnel policy. By reason of long-standing industrial history, a Director's normal acceptance of this responsibility is limited to a contractual undertaking with individuals on a daily, weekly or monthly basis, but in more recent years the notion has been gaining ground that the employment of people involves also a responsibility for continuing livelihood—in current terminology "full employment". This notion has been evidenced, for instance, by the agreement signed in the United States between some employers and unions providing for "annual contracts of employment" on basic levels of wage covering periods of activity, or of inactivity should there be a recession in trading. Conceptions of this kind are indeed vital to the modern industrial community, if there is to be further progress along lines of automation, whether in manufacturing or in the office.

The third and fourth of the basic purposes listed above would be readily accepted by all Directors, and are, in fact, enshrined in the whole procedure of company activity, including the purchase and sale of shares on the Stock Exchange; through this institution the third purpose provides for additional opportunities of benefit to owners, by means of the derivative exercise of "making a fortune" from capital transactions. The fifth purpose is very largely an extension of the first but is normally seen by Directors of enterprises in a more limited way on the basis of the philosophy that "if we don't go forward, we die". In other words, in order to keep a business in a going state they have to give attention to improvements of quality, of methods, and of efficiency—but seldom is this seen as an activity or an aim with a *social* connotation. This latter, however, is very important, because unless there is a continuous endeavour to improve the effective utilization of resources, the standard of living of the community as a whole cannot progress. The sixth purpose listed is hardly recognized at all among the general run of Directors and tends to be seen as a peculiar quip of industrial cranks!

All six purposes stem from the notion that an enterprise is *entrusted by the community* with some of its own material and human resources for the conduct of affairs and is allowed to take a main share of responsibility for activities that are vital to the living and wellbeing of the citizens. In some states, in fact, this freedom is not given, all such enterprises being owned and directed by sections of State Authority representing the community.

It is the thesis of the present chapter that acceptance of the inherent social obligation imposed by these six basic purposes is of fundamental relevance to a sound pattern of human relations. This is parallel to the legal obligation imposed by the constitution of the company, and, in the last analysis, just as inescapable. Translated into a realistic scheme for practical application, this combination of economic, social and legal responsibilities which is to be laid upon and accepted by a Board of Directors can be formulated into a schedule, parallel to those prepared in many organizations for their senior executive positions. A suggested schedule is given at Appendix A following this chapter. On the basis of such a pattern of responsibilities, human relations fall naturally into the purview of any Board of Directors from the two facets referred to at the outset of this chapter, namely:

a. the direction given in respect of, and consequently the influence exerted from the top of the organization on, the human tone of the enterprise below the level of the Directors themselves;

b. the human behaviour pattern occurring among the Board members themselves in the fulfilment of their corporate responsibilities, together with the bearing that any (adverse) reflections of this pattern, if unfavourable, are bound to have on the effectiveness with which the Board's purposes are fulfilled and the direction of the enterprise carried on.

Each aspect calls for specific treatment and together they form the remaining substance of this chapter.

A. Human Relations Policy and Tone

The key to the Directors' responsibility in this respect is seen in items 6 and 15 of the Schedule. The Board of Directors in its corporate capacity does *not* have a *direct* impact on the pattern or standard of human relations below it, because the effective action stemming from its own decisions passes through the one member who is the "chief executive" and is therefore the Board's link with executive action. It does, however, have a very important role to play in setting the lines to be followed and determining the tone of human relations. All too frequently in contemporary industrial practice, Boards of Directors are apt to leave consideration of personnel policy and human tone to their Managing Director to deal with as he thinks fit, and in consequence this particular aspect of their own corporate responsibility tends largely to be neglected. It must be admitted, of course, that the neglect often arises from the fact that the Directors have not themselves recognized the existence of such responsibility at their own level. Their chief concern in setting the lines of direction and reviewing progress tends to be concentrated on the financial position of the company, on the general sales position, or on matters of further technical development. Provided they are not aware of any "trouble" in industrial relations, they are often content to take for granted that the human facet of the organization is cared for. At times, when evidence of neglect becomes apparent from below, the Managing Director may plead that he "has had no time to give to personnel matters recently"—too absorbed in technical problems of production or research or actively immersed in major sales activities. Equally, he may feel that, having appointed a Personnel Officer at lower level, he has done all that is necessary. The result of this traditional approach at Board level to human relations problems is seen, for instance, in the pattern of affairs in certain sections of British industry recently at the point where a declining volume of business, coupled with improvements in productive method, have brought into focus for the first time in some branches a surplus of employment in relation to a true competitive situation. The story of the human relations tangle of the car industry, for example, is sufficiently widely known not to need further comment in the present context. On a smaller scale, the traditionally negligent attitude of Boards of Directors towards their human relations responsibilities can be seen in the case—unfortunately only too representative of many others—of a medium-sized manufacturing concern set up within recent years under favourable conditions, with new premises and plant and every opportunity of doing things properly from the outset. The owners of the business (who were also its Directors) had every good intention and were fully seized in principle of the importance of giving consideration to establishing a sound level of employee relations. Unfortunately, they forgot to bring their principle forward into practice within the Board meetings, with the result that for several years the executives had to face a gradually worsening position of labour unrest, unfounded but recurrent grievances about working conditions, inadequate consultation, and eventually a situation brought almost to the verge of a strike. Looking back over the position at this point of time, the Directors were able to recognize that they had by reason of such conditions suffered severe financial losses, the extent of which far outweighed the gains that they had attained by their concentration on improvement of the product and of productive methods.

A great deal of the laziness at Board level in regard to human relations stems from the background of British industry, influences dating as far back as the nineteenth century, but more keenly activated by the attitudes of the 1920's and 1930's—periods of heavy unemployment. when labour was cheap and easy to get and many Directors felt that they had no reason to bother about the people that they employed. The bogey of the "dole queue" was their standard! Many of the men at Board level today were then in their prime and the deep-set influences engendered therefrom die hard. Today there is undoubtedly a change in the climate of public opinion and a much greater readiness to recognize responsibilities in terms of sound human relations. But the persistence of the old-time negligent view is still much stronger than it ought to be; it rears its head today altogether too readily in older managers who regret being in a situation of full employment, which encourages employees to be "difficult". They can frequently be heard voicing their laments for the days of pre-war discipline and yearning for the return of the discipline of the dole—perhaps only in a minor form, but at any rate enough to make human relations something about which they would not have to busy themselves!

To make sure that it obtains a sound fulfilment of its own responsibilities, a Board of Directors must give a clear lead for the human relations tone of the enterprise which it is directing, in the form of a personnel policy handed over to the Managing Director, and of a periodic check on him to ensure that, with the cooperation of the executives under his own guidance, the policy is being fulfilled and the intentions of the Board achieved. While this is indeed enshrined in item 15 of the Schedule, such a formal statement of it is of little avail unless quoted, understood and sincerely accepted by all the Directors, individually and corporately—accepted, not in terms of a sentimental notion concerned with "looking after the workers", but in terms of a fundamental social responsibility directed to the attainment of basic purposes and intimately bound up with maintaining and improving the efficiency of operations. Personnel policy and progress should, at Board level, be as much a matter for annual review and annual congratulation as the trading results of the enterprise. On such a basis, the Managing Director starts from strength, and can enlist the full force of the cooperative support of his executives and supervisors, these in turn harnessing the purposeful participation of the men and women employed. That this is no idle fantasy has been proven by many a company. "Consultation in industry" can so easily become—has so often become—but an empty formula, instead of the framework for the steadfast pursuit of worth-while objectives. Advances in technology are, indeed, the keynote to industrial progress in the twentieth century, but even the most daring of them can be nullified by the ill-will of the human members of the productive organism. We are as yet generations away from the day when brains and brawn can be laid to rest, leaving the robots to do everything for us. Progress in electronics and automation—the "blessed words" of the new industrial revolution—does not yet mean the substitution of men by machines; it means rather a change in the form in which the human contribution is made.

So the human being continues to matter! And unless he matters at Board level, he is not likely to matter effectively elsewhere in the organization. The lines along which the Board ensures that its intentions are translated into effective action makes up the substance and detail of personnel policy and practices as discussed by specialists in this subject. There the questions of specifications and standards for employment are considered, to get the square pegs in the square holes; schemes and methods of training for speedy learning of high performance production; accident precautions and positive measures for facilitating health and good working; provision for consultation, for information, for the examination of difficulties and grievances; fair bases for discipline; procedures for promotion, for review of rates and salaries, and a host of detail matters that bear directly on the contentment and efficiency of operatives and clerks at work. The Board does not have to go into all these avenues; it has to indicate the standards at which personnel policy should be applied, and then provide the specialist assistance of the Personnel Officer to advise and assist the chief executive and others in establishing the details to the extent deemed desirable. Some indication of the general framework of a Board's approach is given in a statement of personnel policy laid down by a study group of practising managers and personnel officers some years ago: this is reproduced at Appendix B.

Few firms have gone to the lengths then envisaged, though a great deal of encouraging progress has been made. Indicative of this are, for example, a number of announcements that have appeared in recent years in the national press, over the names of well-known companies as part of their campaign for encouraging good recruitment. The flavour of the announcements is important, because of the emphasis which is given to the importance of personnel policy. Some of the statements have had the substance—and in a few cases also the form—of a declaration of faith in the dignity of man and in the vital part that human values can play in the well-being and progress of the industrial system. Two of these statements, different in purpose and character, can serve to illustrate the many that have appeared:[2]

(a) The first comes from the Esso Petroleum Company; a half-page announcement, headed "Where We Stand . . .", included the following striking paragraphs—

"1. *To the employees*

Since the Employees give their skill, experience, energy and time to the Company, it is right that the Company should secure for them also the material reward appropriate to their efforts and abilities. This reward should at all times be adequate to ensure a decent progressive standard of living, and should be increased as and when individual ability, loyal service and acceptance of greater responsibility make this in equity desirable. A fair system of material rewards will also include facilities for social security, such as pensions and other benefits, supplementary to those already provided by the State.

The Company also recognises its obligation to provide safe and sanitary working conditions and to see that hours of work and opportunities for rest, holidays and recreation are at least as favourable as those observed by other leading companies in comparable operations. Its aim is, by objective selection, to place employees in the work most suited to their abilities and to provide the means for them to improve their performance by training and so advance in their profession.

For the efficient and harmonious conduct of its business, the Company believes in the necessity and value of joint consultation at all levels.

Finally, the Company recognises an employee's religious and political freedom; that is, his freedom to associate or not with any religious body, political party or any lawful society or organization.

"2. *To the community*

Since a company is an integral part of the social and economic life of the community—be it locally or nationally— it is under an obligation to conduct its business in such a way as to further the social and economic progress of that community, or at very least not to impede it.

It has a duty beyond its immediate business of supplying goods and services at the right quality and price; it has a duty of citizenship, of co-operating with the proper authorities at every level of government. In framing its policies, it must consider the aspects of the public interest. In its everyday actions it must practise consideration for its neighbours. It must be an active asset to the community within which it operates, not a passive occupier of space."

(b) The second was an announcement by The Birfield Group (covering several specialist engineering companies), inviting applications for appointments in Personnel Management, with a display advertisement headed "A Lifetime Career in Industrial Human Relations". This included two main paragraphs:

"1. We believe:

... that Britain's prosperity in the next few years; promising a higher standard of life for our children and grandchildren, depends inevitably on our ability to offer goods and services of better quality at no higher price than those of our overseas competitors.

... that Britain can sustain—and improve—its position as the world's breeding ground for ideas, ideals and leaders, if we have the right leadership.

... that Industry must attract the right people and give them the opportunity to develop their abilities to the full.

''2. If you believe:

... that improved relations between all those engaged in Industry depend on dispelling unfounded fears and misunderstanding...

... that most men and women have an inherent inclination to live and work in accordance with those principles which are the basis of our faith ...

... that you have the requisite qualities enabling you to be concerned with industrial personnel relations as a life's work ...".

A Board's concern for the soundness of the human relations within its organization may well measure the difference between success and failure, and certainly between profit and loss. It is again an inescapable responsibility laid on a Board that it must provide for efficient— and continuously efficient— operations in all aspects of its work (items 4 and 18 in the Schedule at Appendix A). Progressive efficiency is vitally inter-related with sound human relations. To recognize this is not to put an "ideal" in a "sordid setting", but to give reality and purpose to a major factor of practical significance that could otherwise so easily degenerate into an empty sentiment.

In a long-standing industrial country like Britain, the contemporary scene is bedevilled by the ghosts of the past, and many of the ghosts wear the shrouds of bad human policies. The driving sentiment of the Trade Union movement is the memory of the unemployment of the 20's and 30's and of the negative attitude of the then employers, unmoved by any sense of social concern and avowedly guided first and foremost by consideration of profit and capital. Behind this lies another memory of longer duration, the handing-down from generations long-since dead of the bitterness and squalor of nineteenth century working conditions, a poverty born of self-centred self-interest. No issue of wages or working conditions in the Britain of our own times is considered or settled solely in the light of the facts and figures of the contemporary scene. Industrial relations have a foundation of deeply-laid fears and phobias—prejudices that have no right still to be alive, but are so intricately interwoven with the pattern of our social fabric that they dominate every situation. Against this background, we stand on the threshold of a new industrial revolution. We can but hope that the Directors whose decisions will launch and lead the new history will this time be wide-minded and long-sighted. Their human relations policy will be the main evidence for their judgment by posterity.

There is today a major difference in the general pattern of industry, namely, that so many of the Directors are also full-time employees of their companies, with executive or technical jobs as well. They will have, in consequence, a far closer appreciation of the repercussions of Board decisions and a quicker realization of the cost of policy deficiencies. They are, moreover, in a position where a professional concern for the efficient conduct of the enterprise is of greater moment than the personal financial benefit of a quickly-taken profit. To that extent, they can be so much in touch in their Board Rooms with the flesh and blood of human relations that the ghosts are returned to their past.

B. The Behaviour Pattern in the Board Room

In turning to the second aspect of the subject, we enter a far more intangible and less factual realm. Here we are dealing with the attitudes and the behaviour of a group of men who, by whatever chance of circumstances, are now associated in a commonly accepted responsibility as members of a Board of Directors. They may in many cases be also holding executive positions within the same enterprise, as a matter of fulltime employment, or they may have no other than a slender and intermittent contact derived from their membership of the Board. How each came to be chosen as a member of the Board may indeed have a great bearing on the competence with which he discharges his share of the responsibility, but it is not an aspect that need be deeply gone into here. He may be a Director because he is one of the men who have got together to form a new enterprise, without any consideration of competence or systematic basis of selection coming into account. Or his Board membership may be the final phase of a long-service career with the company—equally without any regard for his competence to serve at this higher level. The man whose Directorship appointment is based on objective assessment of suitability and fitness for this job may—at least in the normal run of British industry and of commerce—regard himself as an unusual phenomenon! This is an issue which touches very deeply on the subject of the human relations within the Board Room and their influence on the effectiveness of the government of the enterprise.

The first plunge into this maelstrom can be made an easy one by taking up the standpoint of an imaginary listener at one of those "private sessions" that so frequently occur in the pubs or the clubs after office hours, or in the informal gatherings between sessions at a Management Conference. The actors in the scene are a small group of managers—perhaps all from the one firm, or, more usually, from a number of different firms; the only difference that this membership of one or of many enterprises makes lies in the smaller or greater degree of "guardedness" with which the conversation is conducted, of open reference to names, or frequency of unflattering descriptions. The subject-matter of the conversation, the observer would discover, is something to do with "What's wrong with our company?", and he would speedily glean the impression that the companies concerned are governed by Directors who appear to be little more than a bunch of nitwits. Heaven alone knows how they ever got to the level of Directorship! This could only have been by some malicious machination, for their own personal ends! The companies, it seems, suffer from complete absence of policy or from grave weaknesses in policy where some is formulated. There is lack of decision; there is no control, and there appear to be more or less frequent appointments which are completely incomprehensible to this intelligent group of men chewing the situation over round the bar. No technical developments take place at the behest of the Directors, and, for some peculiar reason, those Directors stymie their own best interests by failing to come to grips with long-standing issues, etc, etc.

That little scene is not exaggerated and can be confirmed from the experience of any one who has mixed with the rank and file of managers; there is among the men at lower levels a great deal of serious reflection on the competence and attitude of Boards of Directors. It may be argued in reply that such managers and lower managers do not really know what they are talking about, and that most of their observations could be little more than biased and uninformed conclusions. Yet, the frequency with which this little scene is reenacted and the similarity of the content on each occasion must lead an observer to feel that they cannot all be so very wrong.

Apart from gleanings from imaginary incidental conversations, realistic pictures can be presented from personal observations of what takes place at Board meetings. Findings from this source tend to suggest that a great deal of the hearsay evidence is, unfortunately, well-founded and cannot be dismissed as exaggerated. For a professional Management Consultant to present illustrations of his own experiences at Board proceedings is a delicate and difficult task, but the importance of the matter justifies the attempt.

The following "snapshots" ought perhaps to be prefaced by the novelist's cautionary convention that "nothing in this story has any reference to any real situation or person"—except, of course, that on this occasion all the stories happen to be real. They will be recognized by many readers, but, fortunately, they will always be related to the reader's own experience and thus wrongly identified. Fortunately, too, the ***dramatis personae*** are unlikely to be any more successful at identification—however many heads caps may fit!

Case A

This is a manufacturing and trading business, with family ownership now in its third generation. Its particular field of product has undergone only minor technical change in recent decades, and the business is today of medium size, having had little expansion in the present generation. The main growth took place in the second generation, when the family head carried the business from a small unit to one of the leaders in its own field. In recent years, there have been quite important opportunities for diversification of product and for a gradual change-over to parallel fields, using the same basic technology of production with appropriate modifications but based on new materials. To take advantage of these opportunities requires imaginative thinking in technical and marketing fields, yet offers a magnificent chance to start up a new phase of vigorous life which can run ahead for another three generations of family prosperity. If the company fails to take advantage of these opportunities, it will continue for some time on its present scale of operations along its traditional lines, will continue to earn mediocre profits, but is likely before long to enter onto a phase of gradual decline in profitability and size. This is indeed a remarkable challenge and a weighty responsibility to put on a Board of Directors, with a ready outcome in renewed life or lingering decay.

The Board of Directors has six members, of whom three are from the family and three not. Among the family members, the first to consider is the Director holding the joint offices of Chairman and Managing Director. He is the son of the second generation father who turned the business from its small one-man size into a considerable and respected concern. This son was brought up in the business but, because of his father's prosperity, he lived "like a gentleman". There was no need for him to show the same zest as his father, and it is more than likely that as a younger man he was stifled by his father's prosperity and self-confidence. Today he would be assessed as an average-to-poor chief executive and chairman. He succeeded his father at his death about 15 years ago. The second family Director is a younger man, a cousin of the foregoing and responsible for technical developments. He is not, in fact, the holder of any technical qualifications and was given this post, with a seat on the Board, some years ago after he had been working unsatisfactorily and unhappily in another concern—his return to the family Board being regarded as "maintaining the interests of the family". By virtue of his field of responsibility he is supposed to keep abreast of technical developments, and he does a reasonable job in acquiring information and building up files on relevant matters. He also does quite a good job in the way of technical appraisal of current developments elsewhere, but is not able fully to appreciate the significance of what he is appraising or to translate it into terms that would have a bearing on the technical and marketing policy of the company. No action results from his reports, even when they are valuable or useful—this for the very simple and human reason that the Director in charge of production matters has no time for this Technical Director and despises all his work.

The third family Director is an older man again, an uncle of the Managing Director and the father of the man just described. Over the years, he used to be concerned with the quality of basic materials and with their purchase, as well as with one or two related technical matters. He is now retired from all full-time responsibilities, but retains his seat on the Board and attends most of the Board meetings. He never really got on well with his brother whilst he was in full-time employment, probably largely because there was a mutual dislike between their respective wives; so, for the present moment he does not really count for much, but, once again in the interests of preserving family unity, he is allowed to sit around and give all the appearances of being a responsible member of the Board, even if virtually an outside Director. He has no big shareholding in the company and his main concern is probably to protect the position of his son, against pressures from the non-family members of the Board.

Of the three non-family Directors, the first is the man responsible for production and manufacturing. He has risen from the ranks, has been with the company for a great many years, and was the mainstay of the second generation father in the process of building up the business. He has no formal qualifications, but has a very good experience and knowledge of the trade and is a man of very sound competence in what today would be called a practical old-fashioned sense. He is reliable, does a very good job in his responsibility for production; he is undoubtedly the chief reason for the continuing success of the business, such as it is. He was made a Director by the second generation father a couple of years before the latter died. He cannot see that there is any need for technical changes, and attributes the difficulties of trading to changes in economic conditions which are no doubt temporary, feeling that one day things will go back to what they were in the good old days. The suggested move into new products leaves him completely uninterested and he has no regard at all for any active research work in any such directions. It is possible that in part these views are determined by an unconscious realization that he has now only very few years to go; he is thus not particularly keen on being personally embroiled in far-reaching technological and manufacturing changes. As a result of this attitude, he is in frequent conflict with the Technical Director, but no outcome of such conflicts is ever reached. The Chairman's tendency at Board meetings is to gloss things over and leave matters to be reconsidered on another occasion—the situation clearly puts before him a human relations problem that is far too thorny to be taken up openly!

The next Director is the man responsible for sales, who is also the Sales Manager directly governing all sales activities. He has been with the company only five or six years and was brought in by the Managing Director through personal acquaintance. He had a career in the trade elsewhere and acquired the reputation of being a sales executive of good quality. He was made a Director from the outset, this being one of his conditions for joining the company. He has proved to be a reasonably successful sales executive along traditional lines, but shows little imagination and has no experience of developing into new fields of product. He gives the impression of being quite unable to understand the economic trends of the industry and knows nothing at all about the contemporary conception of "marketing". He has to struggle hard as Sales Manager to maintain the volume of sales, and does so with the support of some quite good salesmen along traditional lines, but not by any carefully thought-out policies or programme of sales development. He is a man of pleasant personal make-up and gets on well with all the other Directors, largely perhaps because his contacts with them other than at Board meetings tend to be superficial, except in the case of the Managing Director.

The sixth member of the Board is an outsider and is serving on a part-time basis, with a general responsibility for financial advice. He is not, however, responsible for financial control or the accounting activities of the company, though the Chief Accountant is expected to look to him for particular guidance on financial matters when so instructed by the Managing Director. This outside Director was also brought on to the Board through personal acquaintanceship with the Managing Director and has been with the company a little less than two years. He is a man of standing in local circles and his appointment was agreed to by the Board, less because of any contribution that he could make from a financial standpoint than for reasons of prestige that his name would bring to the company. He is an individual whom one would describe as a good type and sensible, but he makes but a small contribution at Board meetings, appearing to be somewhat lost in the intricacies of the human relations pattern among his fellow-Directors.

The Secretary of the company is the full-time member of staff who is also the Chief Accountant; he attends at Board meetings in his capacity as Secretary, but is expected in his other role to present the financial figures and statistical data on the Managing Director's behalf. He does not play any responsible part in Board proceedings —which is perhaps a pity, because he is a man of good competence with far-seeing insight into business affairs. He has been with the company several years; he gets on very well with all the Directors, though less well with the Managing Director than with the others. One would say that there is a mutual lack of warmth between these two, largely because the Secretary-Accountant can see through the façade put up by the Managing Director, and the latter is well aware of the scrutiny that is going on inside his subordinate's mind!

An unseen observer watching the proceedings at meetings would very speedily appreciate that this Board of Directors is not functioning in its proper role at all. It is not dealing effectively with the policy matters that are coming up before it and it is not giving any sort of lead, still less a reliable lead, to the Managing Director, and through him to the executives—this weakness being the greater when it is appreciated that two of the principal executives, responsible for production and sales, are sitting at the Board table in their directorial capacity. That there is a good deal of important matter for consideration and decision is obvious from the company's position and from the new trading opportunities before it. The observer watching Board meetings would also become aware of the fact that there appears to be a good deal of important discussion going on among these Directors on a one-to-one basis, outside the Board meetings altogether and that apparently quite a lot of major issues of a policy nature are being considered and decided without coming to the Board formally at all. On the other hand, it would become apparent, too, that the Managing Director is deeply immersed in details of production and technical development to an extent that goes far beyond what the chief executive's role should be, and that at Board meetings a great deal of time and attention is devoted to such detail as ought strictly speaking never to appear on the Board table at all.

Board meetings are held monthly, with agenda and supporting papers properly prepared; this the Secretary sees to in his usual competent way of going about things, but, in spite of this formal guidance, the content of discussions goes far and wide and is mostly vague and woolly under all items. It is quite frequently clear that the two part-time Directors are out of their depth so far as interpreting matters coming forward is concerned, and are unable to relate particular considerations to their context. Neither wants to ask what may appear to be foolish questions to get the background of a particular matter, and each appears to be making his own interpretation as best he can. For the uncle, this interpretation is based on his own past experience and occasional conversations with his son between Board meetings. For the outside man, the basis has to be his own assessment of what he hears, plus what he is told by the Managing Director when they meet outside Board meetings; in consequence, except on matters which are strictly financial in their connotation, he can hardly avoid neglecting the opportunities for exercising correcting influences on the company's affairs at Board level. So far as the manner of Board proceedings is concerned, the most outstanding characteristic is the vagueness and confusion of discussion; in addition, there are frequently occasions when an acrimonious exchange of views ensues and, sometimes, outright conflict, some of it largely personal in content and origin, going back at times to early phases of family history. It is clear that there is at

Board level no unity of interest for the direction of the company and certainly a quite inadequate appreciation of the serious situation which is confronting the business in the present generation.

The outside observer making his appraisal would perhaps say that the main fault lies in the lack of competence of all the Directors! A great deal of it, however, lies in the very poor human relations pattern, for which the Chairman plus Managing Director must take a large measure of responsibility. Unfortunately, he is himself something of a visionary in outlook, very unsystematic in his general approach to things, and somewhat influenced by an ambition to be recognized in the trade and in the locality as being as important and able a man as his father was before him. For this ambition, unfortunately, there is no foundation. In many respects, though, he has sound ideas, particularly in regard to the development of new fields of product and the use of new materials, but all such ideas are frustrated by his inability to get understanding or support at Board level; this in the main is a by-product of the unfortunate human relations situation there. For his own part, he displays a partisan attitude in regard to the family Directors, stemming from dislike of his cousin and complete lack of respect for his uncle. These emotional feelings never fail to come out at Board meetings and undoubtedly colour his behaviour as Chairman of the Board. Many of these weaknesses in personal make-up, of course, affect his position as Managing Director as well, and consequently the company suffers doubly. If there had been a Managing Director of sound competence and ability—obviously of far better calibre than anyone at present on that Board—he could have done a lot to counter the weaknesses at Board level. He could, for example, become a focal point of better Board proceedings, even without being Chairman, and he could certainly ensure that there is a better executive grip on the members of the organization below the Board level, and particularly in the integration of the senior Production and Sales Executives, in spite of their membership of the Board. This is, however, something of a hypothetical consideration, for it is highly unlikely that a Managing Director from outside could be appointed, or any such appointment even considered. In the first place, neither the Production Director nor the Sales Director would be likely to support the appointment of someone over themselves in their executive capacity. Not that either of them would not immediately agree to the unsatisfactory standard of managing directorship exercised by the present incumbent; but each would feel that he himself ought to hold *that* position. Further, all things considered, it is highly unlikely that the present Managing Director would be willing to give up his position.

For the purposes of the present context, it is not necessary to find the solution to this problem—only the moral matters: the extent to which the conduct of the affairs and the future progress of an important business can be placed in serious jeopardy by reason of an unsatisfactory human relations situation within the Board of Directors.

Case B

This is a company in a very different situation from the previous one. It is a large business, not yet 25 years old, and built up on the energy of one man during this period, today recognized among the leaders of its own field. It is a public company with a large outside shareholding and there is no family interest, nor is it likely that a family patrimony will be built up. The one-man "boss" who is now Chairman of the company, but not Managing Director, has been assisted over the years by several men personally selected to work closely alongside him, and the greater part of the growth took place for war-time and immediate post-war purposes. The Chairman, a man now past middle age, is still full-time in attendance and takes a vigorous and active interest in all the affairs of the company. He is a man of high level of personality and of very keen intelligence. He is liked and respected throughout the company, but tends to be aloof, except with his immediate associates; in consequence, he is little understood and is as much feared as he is liked and respected.

The Board is composed of eleven Directors, nine of whom are full-time members of the organization with executive or technical responsibilities, as well as membership of the Board. The two outside members have been personally selected by the Chairman, one in recent years and one a longer time ago, to assist him, not so much by their membership of the Board, as by their personal support and contribution in discussions outside Board meetings; one of them has played a quite important part in assisting the financial transactions involved in the expansion of the business. All the full-time members of the Board are men who have grown up with the Chairman in the course of building the business. Some of them have clearly defined spheres of responsibility, largely by accident of the role that they are playing; for example, one who is responsible for research and technical development. But most have self-carved roles in the manufacturing and trading of the business either at home or abroad, often involving an ill-defined mixture of production and sales responsibilities. There are three main products, with a rough divisional structure so far as manufacturing is concerned, but with sales conducted largely on a regional basis at home and a "free for all" basis abroad. Two of these Directors carry the title "Joint Managing Director", but nobody really knows what responsibilities they are supposed to carry out, nor does this ignorance really seem to matter. Not even the two concerned have a clear idea of what they are supposed to be doing, other than to ensure that the individual activities of the other Directors do not redound to the detriment of the company. In other words, the only clearly identified aspect of top management is that of coordination.

The whole conduct of top management appears to be based on a philosophy of "give and take", plus "old boys who have grown up together", plus a very large sprinkling of "looking after each other". Perhaps the latter facet of relationships—particularly when taken in the context of the widespread knowledge that "the old man can be ruthless when circumstances seem to him to necessitate it"—is the strongest force that keeps the harmony of the full-time members of the Board, both at Board level and in their executive roles. The company's anecdotal history is replete with stories that stand as tombstones in the memories of the present Directors, relating to former colleagues who fell foul of the "old man", to become the unfortunate victims of his ruthless action. The Chairman's basic characteristic is a respect for "success" in the material sense of the term; he believes in the philosophy that "a man does his best work when he is left to fend for himself and to protect his own interests against the outside world". It is a variant on the widely accepted philosophy of "divide and rule", with perhaps a touch of Machiavelli, and it has even been voiced by the Chairman in the somewhat crude form that "if you look after yourself, your service to the business can be taken for granted". Needless to say, the monetary rewards offered to the members of this top management group are high. In other words, the rewards for looking after oneself— and incidentally after the business—are commensurate with the Chairman's belief in this philosophy.

Board meetings are monthly, but in between the formal sessions there are frequent meetings, large and small, either among some of the Directors themselves or of Directors plus their immediate subordinate managers. Every Director has responsible to him various executives, but not all at the same level of responsibility. Each tends also to have one senior member of staff in a confidential "personal assistant" capacity, kept closely alongside himself with the particular purpose of keeping ears and eyes open and acting as what would be called in modern language "the protective radar screen". Naturally enough, this individual shares in the high level remuneration by which self-protection is rewarded.

An observer at Board meetings would find a picture of harmonious discussion, with perhaps just the occasional flare of conflict; seemingly, an atmosphere of good relations and a quiet pursuit of sound progress in the company's affairs. Now and again, matters are considered, discussed and decided in a way which might cause a man of honest proportions to raise his eyebrows, but nonetheless there is a seemingly strong unanimity in the interests of the company. It is unquestionably a very successful company and has been very much helped by the economic conditions in which it has grown up. The realistic observer who cares to take his eyes off facts in order to gaze at the crystal ball might be tempted to say that if at any time the company hit adverse economic conditions, it would probably suffer very badly.

The observer, however, who looked just at what he saw in the Board Room would come away with a quite false impression of what is really going on. If he could listen in an analytical sense—as it were, between the lines, or listening to what is *not* being said—he might glean a great deal more; and if he could be in personal contact with the members of the Board when they are not sitting in their corporate capacity round the Board table, he would realize how much the harmonious unanimity of the Board Room gives a false picture! With adequate opportunity to lift up the stones here and there and so really find what is going on, he would see the whole of this top management group involved in a complex interwoven pattern of human relationships of a quite ugly kind. The philosophy is indeed working as it is intended to! There is no mutual trust among the Directors, save in incidental pairs here and there. There is a strong and continuous jockeying for position, with the eleventh commandment very clearly in evidence—"on no account be found out by the old man". There is strong and widely accepted encouragement to selected subordinates to work "for the support of our side" and against the other sides, and there is a great deal of time and energy lost to the service of the company by the Directors and their senior staffs in defending their positions and protecting their own interests. Contentious issues, or deficiencies which might reflect on individuals at top level, are by mutual agreement blatantly glossed over and suitably "explained" so as to be kept out of the Board Room, in the interests of mutual protection, so that the old man does not get to know about them. His aloofness and his own unquestioned singleness of purpose in pursuit of the business preserve him from misgivings or from anxiety to see what is really going on outside the Board Room and outside the immediate circle of persons with whom he is prepared to come into contact.

None of the Directors is of outstanding competence, though all are men of ability, who have contributed seriously to the building up of the firm and have carried out a sound job of work in spite of difficulties. The ugliness of the human relations position can be seen only in the repercussions that it produces among the managers at lower levels and in the inability to get many issues decided. There is a great deal of inefficiency and a considerable amount of cynicism among the members of staff at lower levels; the company pays high salaries to its senior staffs even outside the Board Room and offers admirable conditions of service, so that the cynic is reinforced in the feeling that "you are bribed to live their way of life——even if you feel that a different way of life could redound more to the efficiency of the company and to the assuredness of its future progress".

The human relations pattern in the Board Room prevents the laying of a sound foundation for coordinated thinking for the future of the business, and one could hazard a guess that if by a stroke of ill fate the Chairman were to be removed by an accident or illness, an extremely serious and somewhat chaotic situation would ensue; there *could* be no one to take over at Board level such cementing as is already done, little though it is. One could safely bet on a period of internecine conflict, which could spell for the company a serious setback, if not disaster. The gazer into the crystal ball foreseeing adverse economic conditions might enter on the same bet, for the stress imposed by adversity, even with the Chairman still in office, could fragment the superficial unanimity produced at Board level by the philosophy of self-interest and mutual protection. Only solid and stable human relations in a team can withstand the stresses and strain of adversity.

Case C

This is a medium-large concern, relatively new in its present form, progressive and profitable, and in all respects a sound and well conducted business. At all levels it has well qualified members of staff, thoroughly competent in the conduct of their responsibilities. The Board consists of a Chairman, who serves the company on a part-time basis, a full-time Managing Director, and four executives who are also in charge of production and sales, with three specialist or technical members, one of whom is Secretary. By anyone meeting these eight full-time members of the Board they would be sized up as sound men of good competence, well chosen for their jobs, individually imbued with a high sense of responsibility and carrying out their tasks in a satisfactory way. But attending at Board meetings after individual contact with the members, one is quickly aware of something seriously amiss. Board proceedings appear to be well conducted; agenda, documentation and treatment are all good, yet there is an air of unhappiness about, and the discussions and deliberations lack the vigour and the fullness of participation that would be expected from the personal assessment of the individual members. Closer observing and listening for a while would enable the critic to diagnose two particular difficulties, which undoubtedly play a big part in producing this air of unhappiness, and in consequence limiting the usefulness of the Board's proceedings.

The first is the attitude of the Chairman, seen in the form of a great readiness to "smack people down", obviously done with great relish. More than that, one can see that he encourages his colleagues to put themselves up, so that he can smack them down, and that he seeks opportunities to get one member of the Board taking a crack at another. The Chairman is a public figure, and, while undoubtedly a man of competence, holds himself higher in his own esteem than other people might feel is justified. To the outside observer he gives the impression of "play-acting" when he is presiding at the Board meeting, and he is obviously too self-centred to appreciate the reactions of his behaviour on the other members, even though they are persons with whom he has been associated for some years and who have a good measure of respect for his known abilities. Because the individual members are competent in themselves and able to get on satisfactorily in their jobs, the adverse repercussions in this Board atmosphere are not serious, and the main safeguard lies—fortunately—in the high competence of the Managing Director.

With his subordinate executive colleagues outside the Board meetings he can make good the deficiencies of policy thinking and the lack of serious review of progress, and thus overcome the shortcomings due to the Chairman's unfortunate influence on Board proceedings. The Managing Director is a highly competent man, quiet and reserved in character, well-liked and respected by all his colleagues, particularly because of the steps that he takes to promote and keep harmony among them outside the Board Room. He enjoys their respect the more because he suffers with them from being "smacked down" on occasions and because he is frequently prepared to offer himself as the target to safeguard one of them.

The second difficulty arises from an opinion shared jointly by the Chairman and the Managing Director, that they do not believe in the proper definition of responsibilities of executives. Accordingly, although by title each of the eight full-time members of the Board has a mandate that appears to be broadly clear, there is a great deal of confusion over respective responsibilities in action, and many of these difficulties are seen reflected in Board discussions. Among the latter there comes the frequent occurrence of the difficulty as to whether or not a particular Director "represents" his field at Board level. Because of the good personal feeling among members, serious difficulties in action do not result in strained relationships, but the lack of clarity about respective responsibilities reinforces the personal position at Board meetings: no one individual need participate in discussions except when his "own field" is specifically and clearly being referred to, and thus he reduces the risk and the opportunity of being smacked down. There is a great loss to the company, because there is a mutilation of the corporate sense in the proceedings of the Board, and a reduction of the sense of sharing a common corporate responsibility for policy and progress. The full benefit of the specialists is also not attained; for example, the Accountant member of the Board, a highly competent individual, has developed excellent control techniques, but these are not adequately used, partly because of the feeling that they are imposed by the Chairman and the Accountant, and partly because of the lack of open mutual discussion as to the significance of situations revealed by control data. Equally, the specialist member of the Board who is responsible for personnel relations loses a great deal of his effectiveness within the Board, and in the orgzaniation below, because there is no mandate which clearly expresses his role; he again is a sound individual, but of quiet personality, and accordingly there is no driving force behind his advice. The factories have local Personnel Officers attached, but the personnel services afforded reflect the strength or weakness of the individuals concerned and do not reflect anything like a common policy or approach, simply because the Director responsible at Board level would hesitate before he gave any cause for anyone to allege that he was "interfering".

These weaknesses are, by comparison with the two cases previously illustrated, small and almost unimportant; but to see this company in action at Board level does bring home the fact that a great deal of potential advancement is lost because of a situation of mutilated personal relations.

Case D

This again is a publicly known company, providing a service instead of being in the manufacturing field. Over the years, it has taken its share of ups and downs, but on the whole has been sound. Yet, it could be very much better than it is. It has a Board of Directors of eight members, none of them with more than a few years' service, and again a part-time Chairman. There is no family ownership or interest. The Managing Director is a full-time member, as also are four other Directors, two in executive positions and two in specialist technical positions. The remaining three are outsiders, serving on a part-time basis and brought in by mutual agreement of the full-time members. The positions of Chairman and Managing Director are regarded as "plums", because of the public standing of the company and because of the opportunities that their holders would have for getting recognition in other fields, including openings for advancement to bigger companies. The Chairman is currently known to be looking around for his next appointment on a bigger scale, and it is widely known inside the concern that the Managing Director would be quite willing to better himself elsewhere, if the opportunity came along. In these circumstances there is ample scope for jockeying, and all the Directors, whether full-time or part-time, have ambitions to move up and can see opportunities for their own progress—not *all* the Directors, because one of them is too old to be much bothered with further advancement, and one other is sufficiently realist to recognize that he has not the ability or experience to be chosen for higher things.

Board meetings are held fortnightly, and proceedings deal with a lot of executive detail which, strictly speaking, ought not to come around the Board table. The reason is obvious—all Directors, full or part-time, must keep themselves in the picture from every point of view, if they are going to be able to seize the opportunities for fulfilling ambitions as and when they arise. In consequence, many issues are discussed at great length far beyond their need. On the other hand, many issues are deferred again and again because they are rather too ticklish to decide—in the sense that anyone taking a strong position on any such issue might prejudice his own standing! The momentum of a well-balanced business keeps the concern going successfully, responding broadly to outside conditions which in recent years have generally been favourable. Attention devoted to technical development is good and accounts to a very large extent for the continuing progress of the concern, in spite of the deficiencies at Board level. The efficiency of operations and of administration is patchy, and insofar as an overall assessment could be made, "mediocre" would be the most apt description. Under sound direction this position could be very *easily* improved, because there is a great deal of goodwill among the executives at lower levels. Unfortunately, there is also a great deal of unhappiness among these executives, largely a reflection of the inadequate leadership from the Board or through the Managing Director. There are individual executives who work well at their own jobs uninfluenced by the unhappy atmosphere in which they are set, but there are others to whom this unhappy atmosphere is a matter of emotional importance, and they find themselves hanging back, doing just the minimum of work to keep the job going; they have no leadership from the top, no sense of appreciation, no real forward programme to work to in the interests of continuing progress; they are aware of deficiencies in top management decision and of consequent inefficiencies, but, except in a few cases, they have no personal urge to struggle against these difficulties in the absence of coordinated interest and support from above.

The Managing Director's main interest is to "manage" his Board, that is to say, to prevent the Directors from "interfering" with his running of the concern or from formulating policies and taking decisions that he personally would not like. Among his friends and associates outside he is known to speak in this way about his Board, and to give the impression of *his* role being that of forming policy and running the show, with the Board as a kind of advisory body, which he can listen to or not at will, and the members of which depend on him for all the sound decisions that will keep the company profitably in business. He is a strong personality and of good competence, and he could do his top executive job extremely well, if his sights were set right instead of being clouded by the over-concern with personal ambitions. It is difficult to say precisely, but it is probable that he is keenly interested in becoming Chairman of the company, not so much because of the office itself but as a potential avenue to financial opportunities and public honours. By the same token, other Directors are too much concerned with maintaining their own respective positions, in the interests of fulfilling their own ambitions, to be able to get a grip on the Managing Director and so maintain their own corporate control of affairs, ensuring that he serves as their executive instrument, while retaining policy formulation clearly and corporately in their own hands.

This case presents an illustration of a fallacy common among Managing Directors, especially among those who have grown up within a business and have built up the Boards of Directors alongside themselves, parallel with their own growth; also among those Managing Directors of strong personality brought in to an old-established concern over the heads of the existing executives. The fallacy is that of conceiving their role, as this one does, as that of "running or managing the Board", instead of seeing themselves in the correct dual role of sharing the corporate responsibility of the Board plus serving as the chief point of executive interpretation and action. This is a fallacy undoubtedly produced by over-concern with prestige, and it has the unfortunate consequence of leading Managing Directors to overlook the great value that is contributed by objective review from several minds together, with the critical appraisal of interested colleagues sharing a mutual responsibility and anxious to help. Corporate guidance of a Managing Director, whether of strong or weak personality, is impossible if Directors are distracted by personal ambitions, and the repercussions of this situation on the morale of the executives at lower level is a usual phenomenon.

In this case the human relations pattern at Board level is not exactly poor, but it is equally clear that there is a sufficient weakness in the human pattern to have important and unfortunate consequences on the efficiency of the enterprise.

Most readers who have experience of top management or membership of Boards of directors will shake their heads over these cases and agree that they reveal a sad state of affairs—one hopes they will be able to add that no such situations occur in their own enterprises! It is, of course, likely that even those Directors who are set in the midst of such situations would not readily recognize it, and, still less, admit it. For, such a situation, once admitted, gives a compelling obligation to do something about correcting it or to get out entirely. The cases cited are bad ones, because their intention is to reveal how an unsatisfactory human relations pattern at Board level can have distressing consequences elsewhere, but they are not unrepresentative of many businesses in industry—the professional Management Consultants see this to such an extent that, in private conversations, they frequently voice their amazement at industry continuing to run as successfully as it does! However lamentable the admission, objective appraisal leads to the view that there is a great deal of mediocrity widespread among the Boards of Directors. To this situation there is no short-term remedy, and the main hope for improvement rests on the fact that within very recent years there has been a marked and rapid advancement in the standards of selection and training for management positions at the intermediate levels of organizations. Logically, this development *ought* to carry many better men to the top ere long.

One of the major puzzles of industrial progress is reflected in this hope; it can be summed up in two questions:

(a) Why is it that so many of the wrong men get to the top?
(b) What happens to the good younger men on the way up?

It is a frequently seen experience that good men making progress in larger organizations are, at middle age, appointed to membership of the Board of Directors. The outside observer may have the hope that a measure of leavening is about to take place, yet, strangely, no such consequence ensues; the good younger man himself seems to become infected with the general mediocrity that he has joined. Is it because he has become disillusioned? Is it that he has become for the first time aware of opportunities for personal ambition, and has become overlaid with such attractions rather than with the ideal of service within a profession? Or is it just that the struggle to maintain a strong independent standard at a better level than the average is too great for any one man to carry on single-handed?

The other aspect is easier to understand, i.e. the wrong men getting to the top; the very characteristics that make these men "wrong" are the ones that supply motive power to efforts for advancement. Ambition and power-seeking provide motive force of greater strength to men who do not have the inherent basic competence than to those who start with a strong foundation of real intellectual and personal ability—a driving force that enables the ambitious and the power-seeking to give thought to their own advancement while better men would be absorbed in doing the job and serving the cause.

These are issues leading deeply into the jungles of personality comparison and into the intricate problem of selection for advancement. They are too tangled and far-reaching for further pursuit here, and the only relevant conclusion from observations is that neither good human relations within the Board Room nor sound human relations policy from the Board Room are ever attainable on the basis of absorption in personal ambitions and power politics.

To attain a sound pattern of human relations in and from the Board Room, what is required at the level of the Board, in terms of its attitude and proceedings? Without going here to the lengths of a detailed answer, the following main factors can perhaps provide a summary.

(a) The Role and Objectives of the Board

There must be a right outlook and attitude on the part of the members of the Board, recognizing that they are fulfilling an important objective role in the service of their enterprise, as well as in the service of the community. To such aims considerations of their own personal benefit and advancement must be subordinated. Obviously, a Director of a company, particularly if he is also deeply concerned financially, is entitled to pay some regard to his own progress, his own remuneration and the preservation of his own capital values. The question is one of perspective. The best advancement of personal interests comes from the attainment of a good job competently done, and if the Director's first concern is to the service of the enterprise to which he is accredited, the rest is likely to follow.

A Board's role must of necessity start with acceptance of legal responsibilities, but these must immediately be supplemented by reflection of the wider responsibilities that the Board automatically and implicitly assumes from the very act of constituting the company as an operating economic unit—as summarized in the six basic items listed on pages 136–8 above, and portrayed in the Schedule at Appendix A. These are responsibilities corporately accepted and corporately shared in fulfilment. The individual members of the Board may have particular backgrounds or fields of personal interest, but insofar as their membership of the Board is concerned, they will subordinate these to the interests of the company as a whole; or, rather, will use their specialized channels of interest as the avenues of contribution to the common corporate objectives.

(b) The Attributes of Directors

The personal factors required for membership of a Board are those of a good top manager, with special emphasis laid on objectivity of view, maturity of judgment, cooperativeness in attitude, coupled with the ability to be self-critical and to receive criticism from others, to remain detached from a situation even though being part of it, and to have a high degree of self-responsibility to the point of being able to act against one's own interests, when interests of the concern or of the community require it; with all this must go an ability and a readiness to see other people's points of view. There is as yet no clear knowledge of the factors that determine success in top management—whether lying in the make-up of personality, or in the balance of personality and competence, or in energy and vigour, or in innate flair. There is, however, experience enough to show that a high level of personal make-up and sound attitude at Board level is the only guarantee of good human relations at the top of and throughout an organization.

So far as competence is concerned, Directors need to have a thoroughgoing knowledge of the management process and what it entails in practice, including the measure of social obligation that is inherent in management responsibility. In addition to specific technical or financial competence in given directions, they can be expected to show acquaintance with economic trends and influences on marketing or new developments, an understanding of factors in design and the significance of design in relation to marketing and costs; in special fields, they need the ability to consider and review policy on long term as well as for immediate purposes, and to have a full appreciation of the significance of a "management development programme" as a basic foundation for the future continuance of the organization. That no mention is being made of need for knowledge of developments in the field of human relations is deliberate—at the point when a man is chosen to be a Director he ought already to have a sufficiently full understanding of this field and an adequate appreciation of its contribution to management and direction; if he has not, there is very little chance that he will be able to acquire it adequately in relation to his Board membership.

Does all this suggest that there could be a cadre of Directors, persons found to have all-round competence and thus able to hire out their services specifically for membership of the Boards? The only answer to this could be "God forbid"! It is already a common pattern in the British commercial world to find men with a dozen or more Directorships, not just as names accredited to non-operating companies, but in the sense of being members of active Boards. How can a man undertake correctly his responsible participation in Board membership on this basis? Yet there is value to Board responsibility and proceedings from having one or two members who do not serve the organization on a full-time basis. The "outside Director" can bring to bear an objectivity that cannot be so well attained in Board members whose full-time livelihood is gained within the corporation by dint of carrying as well an executive or specialist responsibility. Frequently, the outsider is a representative of special financial interests or of other parties with which the company has associations, and it may be necessary to provide for such representation on the basis of a suitable formula; but, if he has only this "watching of interests" role, his value is likely to be mutilated and his contribution to a sound human relations pattern impaired, if not nullified.

There should indeed be only the one basis of selection or appointment to Board membership, namely, that the individual concerned is of competent calibre, whether he comes from within the company or from outside. The logic of systematic attention to "management development" implies that there is growing up a body of men and women with much greater knowledge and experience of good management practice, coupled with personal characteristics that have been nurtured in directions of maturity and cooperative responsibility. Thus, in time, there could be available large numbers of potentially well-fitted Board members—reaching a Board by promotion from within, or in some way having the opportunity of serving as the "outside mind" on the Board of another concern.

At that stage of progress in British industry many of the contemporary weaknesses in human relations should be relics of the past.

(c) The Board's Officers and Proceedings

The foregoing comments apply to all members of a Board, irrespective of their particular participation in its affairs. There are, however, two members who acquire special responsibility at Board level by virtue of office, namely, the Chairman and the Managing Director. This is not the place in which to undertake a detailed analysis of their respective roles, but only to glance at these roles from the standpoint of contribution to the smooth working of human relations within the Board proceedings, and to the effective application of personnel policy.[3]

In this particular context the Managing Director is the less important of the two officers, though from the executive standpoint his importance is very much the greater. The Managing Director is, in effect, the executive servant of the Board of Directors and is required to carry into practice for them the policy that they have laid down. In many companies, the Managing Director is the key personality, and the main "representative" of the owners of the business, particularly if it is a family concern. To that extent he sees himself as virtually *the* Board, or certainly its most important member, and thus comes to regard his role as that of managing the Board; perhaps it is he who has seen fit to appoint the other Directors or to allow them to be appointed, and he may like to refer issues to them to get opinions. He certainly does not see himself in correct perspective as *their* executive instrument! With a Board properly constituted, the Managing Director will gain significantly if he is able to see himself in his true dual role: at one and the same time being a Director, on all fours with the others and sharing their corporate responsibility, and yet being also their chief executive, the link between policy and its application, and the main channel through which all effective action is attained in accordance with the Board's intentions. A difficult role this undoubtedly is, and its correct discharge has an important repercussion upon the effectiveness of the Board itself and an attainment of a sound human relations pattern within the organization.

The Chairman is in a very different position. He also is a Board member and therefore a full participant in its corporate responsibility, but his special task is *only* at Board level. He is elected by the

Board members to preside over their meetings, to ensure that their deliberations are soundly and correctly conducted, and to see that the affairs of the company are properly watched over by them in all respects. He is not an executive at all, but is a subordinate of the Board in the sense of having to be bound by their decision in majority vote. His presiding at Board proceedings can be the decisive factor in the effectiveness or otherwise of those proceedings, and in the attainment of reliable and clear policy, with adequate relation to performance and progress. It is for him to ensure that there is orderly and efficient conduct of proceedings, with objective thinking and appraisal of the issues under deliberation, and full discussion, yielding contributions from all Directors. It is he who must ensure that the primary concern is focused on the interests of the company and that there is a cooperative attitude directed to fulfil the corporate responsibility; in consequence, it is he who must see that a sound pattern of human relations is always in evidence within the Board Room and maintained sufficiently sincerely to ensure that it is reflected in policy through the Managing Director as part of the normal attitude of management practice below. Analytical review of the position of the Chairman and the nature of his role goes a long way to indicate that there is value in having the Chairmanship held by a member separate from the office of Managing Director. The man holding both offices cannot serve the Board adequately as Chairman, and certainly cannot discharge the "elder statesman" aspect which has so big a part to play in the maintenance of the human relations pattern at Board level.

In his ordinary role, the Chairman can gain a major contribution to good Board relations from *systematic* proceedings—adequate preparation of matter and good documentation of items for discussion; strict chairmanship to obviate irrelevant and discursive discussion, and to call for clarification when needed; the attainment and recording of clear decisions; the bringing forward of matter that has had perforce to be deferred; the use of standard data for presenting essential control information. With all this, a stern regard to keeping Board deliberations at the right level and avoiding the all-too-easy slipping into details of executive matter—yet ensuring that the Board is adequately informed of the progress of the company's affairs. Through the Managing Director contributions to progress can be received from subordinate members of the organization, and through his reports on performance and position the Board can see that its intentions are being fulfilled. This in the realm of human relations as well as of profits.

It has been the thesis of this chapter that good human relations in the Board Room, and imparted from the Board Room to the organization as a whole, are a reflection of the adoption at Board level of a correct role, supported by adequate competence and sound attitudes—among the latter a genuine acceptance of a sense of social obligation. Whether individuals may like it or not, membership of a Board of Directors imposes such an obligation by the very fact of the constitution of the enterprise, setting out to participate in the socio-economic activity of the industrial system by which the citizens of the community (and of the world at large) provide for their living, their livelihood, the future well-being of their children and their posterity. Once the Board of an enterprise decides to use the human and material resources of the community, through the mechanism of exchange, for the furtherance of objectives that will earn profit for the venture, again through the mechanism of exchange, it incurs responsibility for ensuring the efficiency of their enterprise, so that the resources taken up are effectively used to the benefit of the community as well as to the profit of the venturers. This is no idealistic philosophy, but a simple fact of industrial life. It is overtly confirmed in the position of the Directors responsible for the governance of the public corporations, including the British nationalized industries: there are no owners to take a personal profit, and the Boards of Directors owe their accountability to the representatives of the citizens. They have—or should have!—as much concern with efficient and profitable operating as the most individualistic of private "capitalist" owners. The difference lies in this, that to the one the social obligation is direct and declared by statute, whereas to the other it is unidentified and unrecognized.

If the corporate responsibility for the dual obligation of serving the interests of the company and contributing to social well-being were accepted by Directors everywhere, there would be no problems of human relations in the Board Room. Concern with worth-while objectives would absorb the attention and focus the mental energy which go at present to conflicts on grounds of personal competition, and so often poison the human atmosphere.

This approach to human relations at Board level has a very important relevance to the further development of our industrial society. Under present-day conditions, we have in front of us the herald of a new industrial revolution likely to have far-reaching repercussions on efficiency, on employment, on earnings, on the progress of the standard of life and of social stability. Potentially, this new revolution is a source of very high contribution to social advancement. Actually, it is already a source of loss of employment and earnings, and of serious troubles in labour relations. Only a wise and socially responsible approach to policy for automation within each industrial or commercial organization can avoid such serious troubles being the commonplace accompaniment of technical development in the future, thwarting the reaping of the potential social harvest. Recent events in Great Britain have shown only too clearly how the fullness of such benefits turn on the concept of human relations in the Board Room, whether literally or metaphorically interpreted.

APPENDIX A

SCHEDULE OF RESPONSIBILITIES[4]

The Board of Directors

is appointed by and responsible to the shareholders owning the enterprise for the direction and overall control of its activities. The responsibilities falling to its jurisdiction may be summarized as follows:

1. To direct and control the affairs and activities of the enterprise in fulfilment of the objectives laid down in the Memorandum of Association.

2. To ensure that the Company's legal obligations are appropriately discharged and that in all activities there is due conformity with the Articles of Association, and/or with the intentions of shareholders as resolved in General Meeting.

3. To formulate general policy for the conduct of the activities of the enterprise, in fulfilment of the objectives defined, in conformity with the intentions of shareholders, and in accordance with the Company's natural social responsibilities to the community.

4. To direct and control the affairs and activities of the enterprise in such an efficient way as to ensure the attainment of adequate profits to provide for continuity and to provide to the shareholders a fair and reasonable return on the capital invested.

5. To determine the range and volume of trading to be undertaken in fulfilment of the objectives. (This responsibility may often be discharged by approving proposals or budgets submitted to the Board by the Managing Director).

6. To lay down broad lines for the guidance of activities to be undertaken, within the framework of general policy, in the major subdivisions of management action, e.g. production, distribution, finance, personnel, research and development, public relations.

7. To ensure that the Company's executives and officers pay regard to the maintenance of good reputation for the quality of products or services provided, for fair standards of trading, and for honest dealing.

8. To ensure that capital and operating finance are adequately available to support the range and volume of trading approved, together with authorized future extensions thereof.

9. To maintain continuous control over the Company's affairs and activities through the consideration of reports, accounts, and statistics submitted by the Managing Director, and to compare the current and anticipated position with the requirements of policy and of approved range and volume of trading.

10. To maintain continuous control over the Company's financial position in the interest of ensuring the continuing availability of resources, the protection of the shareholders' ownership, the safeguarding of the capital assets, and the due provision of profits.

11. To ensure that adequate regard is paid to the custody and maintenance of the Company's physical assets, and adequate provision made for replacement due to wear, obsolescence, etc.

12. To authorize capital expenditure and the disposition of profits or losses accruing in the conduct of the Company's affairs; to sanction the purchase and sale of lands, buildings and other (major) assets, including the acquisition and disposal of patents.

13. To appoint a Managing Director clearly responsible for the interpretation of policy into instructions for executive action, and to be satisfied that his discharge thereof is in conformity with policy and the Board's intentions.

14. To ensure that the Managing Director creates and maintains a sound structure of management responsibilities, duly delegated as appropriate.

15. To ensure that the Managing Director develops and maintains a sound "tone" of human relations within the organization, in order to promote the morale and therefore the efficiency of the management team, and through them of all personnel.

16. To sanction or confirm senior executive appointments, including salaries and conditions of service therein.

17. To provide for the availability of continuous information about current and future economic conditions that bear on the Company's activities.

18. To ensure that adequate provision is made for the stable continuity of the Company in regard to technical development, volume of trading, finance, and management competence.

19. To ensure that relevant new developments in technology are adequately appreciated and brought to bear in the formulation and modification of policy.

Special responsibilities

To safeguard the maintenance of coordination in the higher levels of management by ensuring that no Director (other than the duly appointed Managing Director) undertakes independent interpretation of policy or exercises executive authority "on behalf of the Board".

Subordinates

— in relation to any executive or administrative action following from Board proceedings:

The Managing Director.
The Secretary.

— in relation to any public statement or action as well as in relation to conformity with the Board's decisions:

The Chairman of the Board.

APPENDIX B

Aims and Principles of Personnel Policy for Industrial Organizations[5]

A. *Aims:*

1. To enable the organization to fulfil or carry out the main items which have been laid down as the desirable minima of general industrial employment policy.

2. To ensure that the employees of an organization are fully informed on these main items of policy and to secure cooperation in their attainment.

3. To provide within the organization such conditions of employment and procedures as will enable all employees to develop a sincere sense of unity with the enterprise and to carry out their duties in the most willing and effective manner.

4. To provide the organization continuously with adequate competent and suitable personnel for all levels and types of occupations required.

B. *Principles:*

1. To establish and maintain a Personnel Management Function, responsible to the Chief Executive and adequately financed for the fulfilment of its responsibilities.

As a corollary, the broad lines of the Personnel Policy of the organization should be defined by the Board of Directors on a parity of importance with other major aspects of policy.

2. To guarantee to all Employees a right of personal and confidential access to the Personnel Executive(s) or the Executive acting in that capacity.

3. To afford the greatest possible degree of stability in employment.

This implies:

(a) Opportunity of permanent and continuous employment for competent employees.

(b) Adequate and objective methods of selection prior to engagement and of review during employment.

(c) The provision of appropriate training facilities (within or without the enterprise) to enable employees to secure the competence required:

(i) for effective performance of duties; and
(ii) for promotion when so selected.

(d) The filling of senior vacancies by up-grading and promotion, so long as actually or potentially competent candidates are available.

(e) A guarantee against unfair dismissal.

(f) Adequate consideration of the influence on employment of the organization's policies and plans regarding production and distribution, so as to avoid employee displacement so far as that is at all possible.

4. To observe the recognized standards of Fair Wages. (This would not preclude the determination of standard Job Classifications and Base Rates or the operation of Output and other Bonus Schemes, provided they fall within the definition of Fair Wages).

5. To guarantee fairness in the maintenance of discipline and to encourage employees to accept responsibility for discipline.

6. To maintain a high level of working conditions, but regarding as a minimum the fulfilment—in letter and spirit—of the Factories Acts and other industrial Legislation and Regulations, with particular reference to adequate provision for the prevention of accidents, the rendering of first-aid, and the safeguarding and maintenance of health.

7. To establish effective procedures for regular consultation between Management and Employees, in a genuine desire to keep Employees fully informed of all matters bearing on their employment and to enable them to contribute to the effective management of the enterprise.

8. To welcome and accord full freedom of association in membership of Trade Unions, but to accord equality of treatment to members and non-members alike.

9. To assist Employees in the development of social, educational and recreational amenities and to encourage their collaboration with nationally or regionally established facilities; also to avoid the provision of facilities as an inducement to employment.

10. To maintain these aims and principles of Personnel Policy without discrimination—though with the necessary differences of application—in respect of all types and grades of Employees, using that term in its widest sense.

References

1. So far as Great Britain is concerned the legal position of the Board is very well presented in *The Company Director* by Alfred Read, Jordan & Sons, London, 1953.

2. These two excerpts are quoted with the permission of the Companies concerned, and the author records his appreciation of their cooperation.

3. For a fuller study of the roles of Chairman and Managing Director see E. F. L. Brech, *Organisation: the Framework of Management*, London: Longmans Green & Company, 1957, Chapter VIII "The Responsibilities of Top Management".

4. Extracted from Brech, *loc. cit.*

5. Extracted from the Report on *Administrative and Executive Problems in the Industrial Transition from War to Peace*. Part I—"Personnel". Published by the London Centre of the Institute of Industrial Administration, 1945.

Chapter 7

HUMAN RELATIONS, MANAGEMENT AND SIZE

R. W. REVANS

Professor of Industrial Administration, University of Manchester

I Introduction

Consider Fig. I, which shows how often the individual workman gets hurt in mines and quarries employing different numbers of men. Each line is drawn for a whole industry; the three lines together represent over a quarter of a million accidents occurring to a million men. These results show that, in Britain, individual miners and quarry workers tend to have more accidents as the mines get bigger; the law of increasing risk to any particular man is that it goes up as the logarithm of the size. In America the result is quite different; the rate rises to a maximum in mines employing from 100 to 300 and then falls quite sharply.

Table 1 was prepared in 1869 by Sir J. Y. Simpson, the pioneer of anesthesia. It describes (for those days, before the development of antiseptic surgery) the risk of dying, after the amputation of one of the four limbs, in hospitals with different numbers of beds.

These figures show that the chance of dying after an amputation in the largest hospitals was, in 1869, about three times as great as in the smallest; and four times as great as in one's own bedroom.

Table 2 is taken from a publication[1] of Princeton University on industrial relations in 82 factories near Trenton, New Jersey. It shows the distribution by size according to whether the factories have had strikes in their histories or not. This shows that the probability of an industrial dispute rises significantly as the plants increase in size.

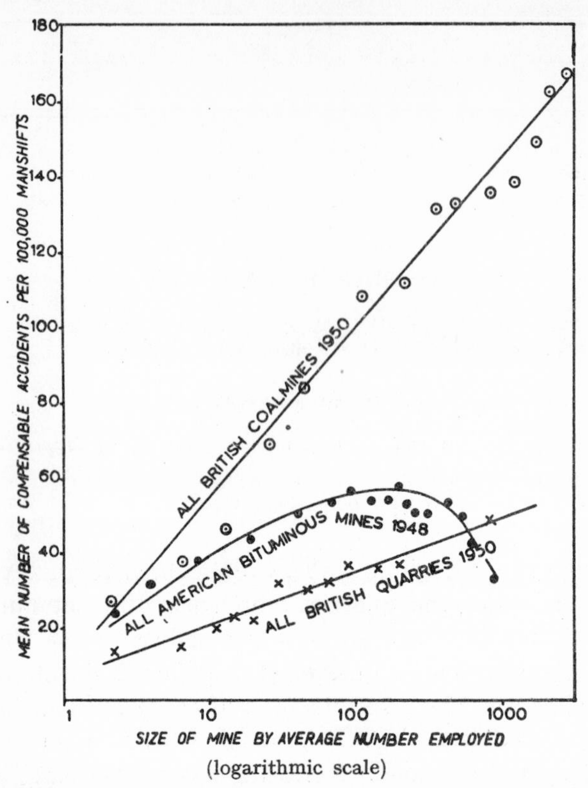

(logarithmic scale)

Fig. I. Relation between mean accident rate and mean group-size of all British coalmines and quarries 1950 and of all American bituminous coalmines 1948.
(Sources: Ministry of Power and American Bureau of Mines)

A study[2] of the total absence rate for the year 1950 among the men at 91 factories belonging to the same British company shows a correlation with size of + 0.447; this is very highly significant, and shows that the likelihood of any individual man being away ill on any particular day tends to be larger in the big plants than in the small; the rate in the units employing less than twenty was, on average, only about one quarter of that in those employing over three thousand.

Fig. II shows, for the year 1950, the percentage of miners, employed in mines of different sizes, who bought the National Coal Board's magazine *COAL*. It refers altogether to the 450 mines that sold the magazine, approximately half of those managed by the Board.

Table 1

Size of Hospital	Death Rate
1st Series – In large and metropolitan British hospitals, chiefly containing from 300 to 500 beds or upwards, out of 2089 limb-amputations 855 died, or	1 in 2.4
2nd Series – In provincial hospitals containing from 201 to 300 beds, out of 803 limb-amputations 228 died, or	1 in 3.5
3rd Series – In provincial hospitals containing from 101 to 200 beds, out of 1370 limb-amputations 310 died, or	1 in 4.4
4th Series – In provincial hospitals containing from 26 to 100 beds, out of 761 limb-amputations 134 died, or	1 in 5.6
5th Series – In provincial hospitals containing 25 beds or under, out of 143 limb-amputations 20 died, or	1 in 7.1
6th Series – In British private country practice, with the patients operated on in single or isolated rooms, out of 2098 limb-amputations 226 died, or	1 in 9.2

Table 2

STRIKE EXPERIENCE BY SIZE OF PLANT

Plant Size by Numbers Employed	No. of Plants having Strikes	No. of Plants having no Strikes
Up to 100	1	11
101 — 200	3	7
201 — 500	16	14
501 — 1000	11	7
1001 — 2500	7	2
2501 — 5000	2	0
Above 5000	1	0
All	41	41

(The equality of the totals is, of course, coincidental)

It suggests that the willingness of the man to buy the magazine falls off as the mines get bigger. Fig. II also shows for England and Wales only, the percentage of men (in all the collieries of each size group with National Savings Schemes) who subscribe for Certificates; it can be seen that on average this is independent of the size

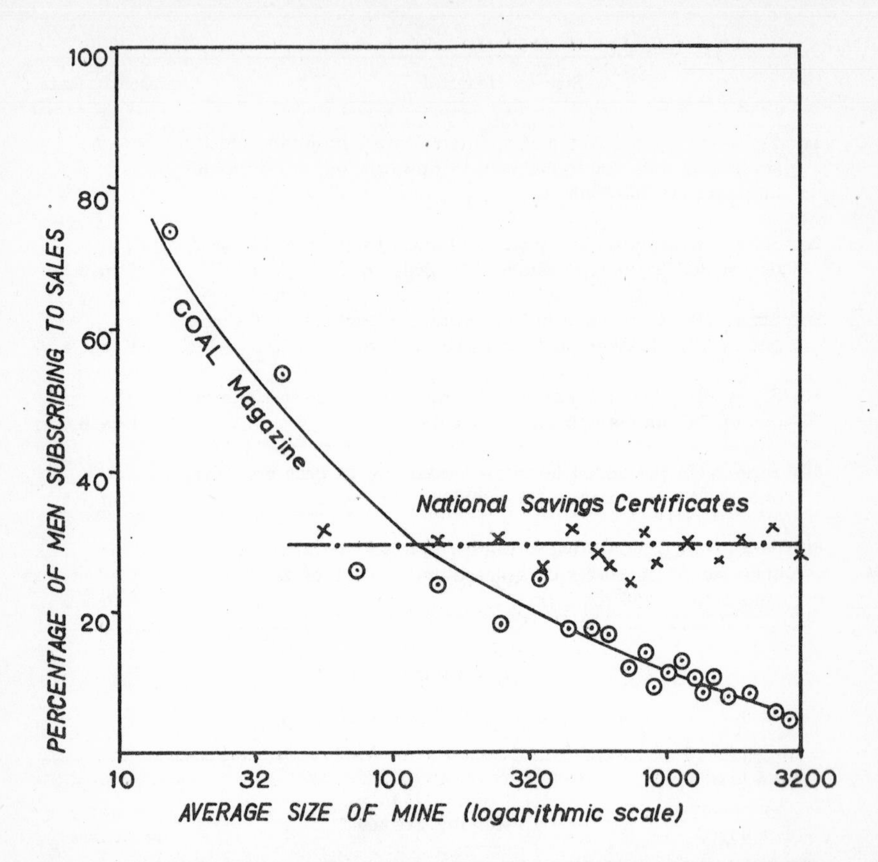

Fig. II. Percentages of all miners employed (at participating mines only) who subscribe to (i) NCB Magazine *COAL* and (ii) National Savings Certificates.

of the mine. These results refer to 531 mines (all those with schemes) out of a total for England and Wales of 721. Neither conclusion to be drawn from Fig. II is thus likely to be biased by sampling errors.

Table 3 shows the average output of coal per man per year from 1948 to 1953 inclusive, for all National Coal Board mines employing over 250 men, according to the number of men on books.

This suggests that there may be assignable reasons for men to work less effectively in large mines than in small. But the decline in annual average output cannot be explained by the larger mines employing relatively more non-productive workers. (It will be shown later that the men in the larger mines work fewer manshifts

Table 3

AVERAGE OUTPUT OF COAL PER MAN-YEAR FOR ALL N. C. B. MINES
1948—1953

Size by No. of Men on Books	Output per man-year in tons	Size by No. of Men on Books	Output per man-year in tons
250 — 499	264	1500 — 1999	314
500 — 749	279	2000 — 2499	298
750 — 999	287	2500 — 2999	298
1000 — 1499	308	3000 & over	272

(Source: Annual Statistical Digests, Ministry of Power.)

a year, but there is evidence, in the Digests, that the shift output —as well as annual attendances—also falls off with size.)

The Annual Report of the Chief Inspector of Factories, 1956, shows that, in British Industry, the compensable accident rate rises steadily with the average size of the factory. He suggests that this is purely a statistical effect, caused by the mere grouping of factories by size into one table; the smaller ones seem inherently less dangerous by the nature of the hazards of their trades. Thus a corresponding table from American mixed industry, supplied by the National Safety Council, Inc. is of interest. It is drawn from 3500 manufacturing plants and shows the opposite trend, a strongly declining size effect.

Table 3 (a)

ACCIDENT FREQUENCIES, IN LOST TIME ACCIDENTS PER MILLION MAN HOURS, AT 3500 AMERICAN PLANTS BY NUMBERS OF PERSONS EMPLOYED

Numbers Employed	Lost Time Accidents per million man hours
Below 25	25.9
25 — 49	21.4
50 — 99	17.4
100 — 199	18.2
200 — 499	12.3
500 — 999	11.8
1000 & over	9.2

It is interesting to compare this trend with the American curve of Fig. I, showing how the accident rate falls only in the larger mines.

We may conclude from these numerical results that some ostensible aims of human beings are difficult to achieve in large organizations;* these statistics suggest that size may have a disabling effect on human cooperation. The following pages discuss this in more detail.

II Historical

It has been known from the earliest times that getting large numbers of people to share in a common task is often difficult and sometimes impossible; to manage successfully the business of a thousand people is more than twice as difficult as looking after five hundred, and looking after five hundred is, in turn, more than twice as hard as managing two hundred and fifty. Whatever form of expression one chooses—to manage, to control, to exercise authority over, to direct, to organize, to be responsible for, or simply to look after—the practical difficulties of what one does increase more rapidly than the number of persons being managed.

One of the earliest references to this effect is to be found in the Old Testament[3]; this describes how Moses attempted to settle the troubles of the Israelites in the desert by dealing with their complaints personally. Since he was unable to give enough time to them and to his other duties, his arrears of work mounted up and those who wanted to see him on important business were kept waiting "from morning until night". His father-in-law, Jethro, advised him not only to draw up a proper scheme of delegation, appointing subordinates in charge of groups of tens, fifties and hundreds, but to make clear what matters could be delegated to them, at different levels, to deal with. What is of interest to us now, however, is that Jethro perceived that a poor organization (in this case one that was slow in taking decisions) would also affect the morale of the multitude and ultimately diminish the prestige of the leader.

A second writer of antiquity to mention size-handicaps is Aristotle. In his Ethics[4] he says, "A state cannot be made out of ten citizens, and one which is made out of ten times ten thousand is no longer a state"; in his Politics[5] he says of the too large state, "Who can be

* As this chapter is being prepared for publication The Howard League for Penal Reform has begun a campaign for smaller prisons, on the grounds that, in the larger ones—with 1000 or more prisoners—the governor is too busy with "administration" to find time to do his proper task. *Manchester Guardian* Oct. 8, 1956.

the general of a mass so excessively large? And who can give it orders, unless he has Stentor's voice?". He suggests that a stable constitution demands that the citizens of a state must "know one another's characters".[6] Aristotle's ethical and political ideas were reflected in industry, for the manufacturing unit proper in Greece was very small compared with those of modern times; one Cephalus, who at the end of the fifth century employed 120 men making shields, was regarded as the largest employer of the age. A few mines were said to employ about 100.[7] It is, again, of interest to remember that modern sociologists have put five hundred as the order of size of a successful factory, since beyond this limit the employees cannot discriminate between their less familiar workmates and complete strangers. They could not, as Aristotle would require "know one another's characters", and it is suggested that, when this limit is passed, the morale is no longer stable and is readily disturbed by rumour.*

These references are to social organization; the control of large bodies of men collected together for technical achievement does not seem to have attracted the writers of antiquity in the same way, perhaps because questions of industrial democracy or labour management did not arise in slave societies. Real strikes, however, did occur in Asia Minor in Roman times among those workers who were no longer serfs.[8] But the multitudes of peasants who hauled the stones for the Pyramids must have needed elaborate organization; it is astonishing for how many centuries a relatively small aristocracy could keep in subjection, by the influences of religion, kingship and the lash, hundreds of thousands of serfs, employed in the erection of enormous monuments, in the digging and maintenance of canals and other large-scale enterprises. Rostovtzev observes, however, that passive resistance, or "folded hands", was traditional and became very common in the Hellenistic period and during the Roman protectorate.[9] In Roman times the management of the slave labour forces that manned the manufactories and constructed the palaces, amphitheatres, baths, granaries, aqueducts and so forth was in the hands of managers who were themselves generally slaves; their own corporations (collegia tenuiorum)

* In the winter *Proceedings of the British Institute of Management 1948/9*, No. 3, Sir Charles Renold (then Chairman of the Council) gave it as his opinion that under modern conditions the optimum size of unit would be between one and two thousand people. See Table 3; the facts of this table were not known to Sir Charles when he expressed this view.

combined a professional with a religious character but pursued no economic ends. In the Augustine period we read of factories with hundreds employed, making flour and bread, and pottery and earthenware lamps; mass production of this kind was usually done by slaves, and the free generally carried out their trades in small private workshops. The description of a vast iron works by Diodorus is not now regarded as representative—or even true.[10] Towards the end of the fourth century the large manufactories had disappeared and there was no room for large-scale industry or trade; the economic historians fail to agree upon the reasons for the comparative failure of the organizational genius of the Romans to develop large-scale industrial production.

In Western Europe the growth of large-scale industrial enterprise begins with the invention of the weight-driven clock; social regimentation demands the regularity of fixed hours of work more than it demands either capitalism or machinery. But in the early days of the woollen industry there was active opposition to the growth of the factory system, that is, to the employment of workers on looms owned by the capitalist and set up in his premises. In 1339 Thomas Blanket was indicted at Bristol, together with the mayor and bailliffs, for concentrating hired workmen under one roof; in 1555 the Weavers Act of Philip and Mary, which forbade the setting up of more than two looms in any woollen weaver's house, was partly occasioned by the fear that larger factories might offer scope for agitators to stir up rioting and disorder. It was also to prevent the decay of skilled craftsmanship, on the assumption that the large factory could be filled with untrained workers. But it had already been shown that neither of these typically modern fears—that factories lead to riots and destroy skill—was necessarily valid; the famous Jack of Newbury (John Winchcombe), who died in 1520, is remembered as having successfully organized a mill employing seven hundred workers, maintained at a high level of morale and efficiency. The happiness of his factory, as well as its size, is suggested in these enthusiastic terms by Thomas Deloney, writing in the same century.

> Within one roome being large and long,
> There stood two hundred Loomes full strong:
> Two hundred men the truth is so
> Wrougt in these Loomes al in a row.
> By euery one a pretty boy,
> Sate making quils with muckle joy;

And in another place hard by,
An hundred women merily
Were carding hard with joyfull cheere,
Who singing sate with voices cleere.
And in a chamber close beside,
Two hundred maidens did abide,
In petticoates of Stammell red,
And milke-white kerchers on their head.

The quality of his products is suggested by the advice of the English envoy at Antwerp to the Protector Somerset to send over "a thousand of Winchcombe's kersies" in discharge of a debt. In 1546 William Stumpe, a clothier of Malmesbury, rented Osney Abbey to employ two thousand workers to make cloth; he had already taken Malmesbury Abbey for the same purpose and there is no evidence that he managed either enterprise without success.[11]

It was, however, the British coal industry that established the large unit as the normal form of industrial enterprise; those who know the industry well today, and who have a sense of history, would probably explain (and perhaps forgive) the low standard of its present management for this reason alone. It seems to be a general law of social history that those who pioneer successfully invariably fall behind the newcomers, by resting on the assurance that what appears to bring success at one time must necessarily continue to guarantee it. However this may be, there is evidence[12] that in the reign of James I, a mine at Bedworth in Warwickshire provided maintenance for 500 persons; Nef estimates that half the miners in the whole country at the end of the seventeenth century were employed in pits with over 100 workers, and that there were about 50 such pits.[13] He adds "It is unlikely that, at this time, the average number of workers to an enterprise in any other of the chief British industries, or in any of the privately-owned continental industries, was nearly as large as in British coal mining".

The essential features of a modern factory are an integrated process, a common power supply and a single management. The first example of this, using not steam but water power, was in the Derby silk-throwing mill of the Lombe brothers, described by Daniel Defoe in 1742.[14] This building, 500 feet long, with about one hundred thousand independent movements of its mechanisms, employed three hundred persons, and earned for one of its owners a knighthood, an immense fortune and the grateful acknowledgments of his fellow-countrymen. His technical ideas had been stolen from

Italy with the connivance of a priest[15], and some indication of the human relations within the factory has been given to us by one who experienced them. "To this curious but wretched place I was bound apprentice for seven years, which I always considered the most unhappy of my life . . . I was too short to reach (the engines) . . . a pair of high pattens were lashed to my feet, which I dragged after me till time lengthened my stature . . . the severity was intolerable, the marks of which I yet carry and shall carry to the grave".[16] There is little reason to suppose that this writer was less humanely treated than his fellow-workers, and none whatever to suggest that this large mill differed in its conditions of labour from the others that were rapidly modelled upon it.

It was the eighteenth century that produced the modern fuel-powered factory, when the steam engine was harnessed to the loom for the first time. As in the slave societies of antiquity, so in Lancashire two thousand years later it would be exaggeration to say that considerations for the well-being of the workpeople entered much into the character or policies of the management. Yet, for all the abundance and cheapness of labour, for all the avalanche of exploitation brought down by the collision of capitalism with technology, for all the rapacious talents of organizers like Arkwright, no factory of the mid-eighteenth century was supposed to have employed more than about six hundred persons[17]—only as many as the cleaning staff in some engineering works today. There must have been some cause, internal to the organization of the factories, at work generally to prevent their unlimited expansion, since even by the year of Waterloo the average size of the labour force, men, women and children, in 41 Scottish mills was only 244; of 48 in Manchester only 270. By the end of the century the Soho works of Boulton and Watt—regarded by Urwick[18] as the first "scientifically" managed enterprise of modern times—was said to employ a thousand.[19] These averages are no larger than of Lombe's silk mill at Derby described seventy years before by Defoe; the invention of steam power had still not enabled the mill owners to bring a new order of scale into the field of textile production.

The average size of the cotton factory is not much greater today than it was in 1815. According to the latest Statistical Digest (1956) less than half the six thousand odd textile factories employ over 100 workers; only four percent over 500. The factory virtually failed to grow under the impact of mechanization, and its size hardly changed even throughout a period when, as at no time since, it was coming face to face with large-scale new ideas. Dr. Kay, one of the Poor Law Commissioners, estimated in 1835 that the average size of the 169 newly mechanized mills in Lancashire was still only 255.[20] But if the impact of technology had (and continued to have) little effect upon the scale of management, it was not without a contribution to its philosophy. The weak spot in the industrial system was the nature of the human beings it employed; they rebelled at its pace and they tried to escape its monotony. Andrew Ure, who also published his *Philosophy of Manufactures* in 1835, observed "By the infirmity of human nature, it happens that the more skilful the workman, the more self-willed and intractable he is apt to become, and of course the less fit a component of the mechanical system in which he may do great damage to the whole."[21] It was, to Ure, the factory that offered an escape from this eternal dilemma; the introduction of machinery would make strikes impossible, for the machine would "strangle the hydra of misrule." The regimentation thought possible in the large factory could be expected to regulate the movement of every man and every machine. "When capital enlists science in her service, the refractory hand of labour will be taught docility."[22] For all this the "science" remained a pure technology; it made no contribution whatever to understanding the problems of handling human beings either better or in greater numbers. Even a penetrating observer like Comte, who clearly distinguished between the scientist and the industrialist, and who saw the need in actual production for a third type of professional man, the engineer, different in kind from both, did not have anything to say about problems of management as such; finance, science, and technology were enough.

There were, of course, a few factory owners at this time who had concepts of human relations different from those of Andrew Ure; there had always been such men as Jack of Newbury. Already in the eighteenth century, the Ashtons of Hyde in Cheshire had provided welfare arrangements for their employees that would be regarded even today as useless luxuries by some employers. Indeed, Robert Owen, who employed 1700 hands in his New Lanark mills, was thought, at the time and by his own workpeople, to carry his welfare arrangements too far. One woman who had left his employment, when seeking work in another factory, said, in 1816, "There had been a number of new regulations introduced. They had got dancing masters, a fiddler, a band of music; there were drills and exercises and they were dancing together until they were more fatigued than if they were working."[23] A century and a half later, a sensitive observer might have detected a yearning after the same despotic philanthropy in the professional activities of the Miners Welfare Commission; it is clear that the human problems of the large organization are not solved—perhaps not ameliorated, perhaps even worsened—by adventitious goodwill engineered away from the working place. Nevertheless, Owen may be rightly regarded as the pioneer of personnel management, if only for the persistence with which he advertised the true nature of the problems created by bringing together so many employees in one enterprise, and for his very practical contributions towards solving them.[24] The factories of Boulton and Watt at Soho, Birmingham, and of Wedgwood at Etruria had sick clubs for their workpeople, as well as dispensaries and schools, before the end of the eighteenth century; Boulton and Watt men were engaged by written contracts for periods of up to five years, anticipating American factory policy by nearly two centuries; above all the partnership seems to have studied the problems of management as such—problems of the measurement, flow and timing of work; of the collection and use of statistics and costs; of the analysis of methods and processes[25] so that those whom they employed were able to believe that they served an undertaking which neither wasted their time nor insulted their self-respect. The devotion to the firm of men like William Murdock is an eloquent testimonial to this singular example of eighteenth century enlightenment; the builder of the first locomotive, who could have made a fortune by his inventions, preferred to work at a guinea a week for two employers whose optimistic mottoes and constant practice were "Honesty is the best policy", and "A hard bargain is a bad bargain." But having mentioned this handful of philanthropic exceptions we cannot see the total picture in any different light; and modern industry has probably inherited, from the terrible circumstances of its birth, a hatred of machinery, regimentation, large factories, large coalmines and, by derivation, large corporations. In these later days, of large motor works, large shipyards and large trade unions, it is our business to collect and to interpret the facts about sheer size.

The nineteenth century, at least in Britain, opened the struggle between employers and employed that was the inevitable product of the factory system; it produced the present day division between the managers and the managed, a division more important than that between the rich and the poor, making of Britain two nations more divergent than any envisioned by Disraeli in *Coningsby* and *Sybil.* Industrial society became increasingly preoccupied with questions of conflict, at first with the fight to establish trade unions, and then to preserve them against political attack and judicial undermining; it became involved in conflicts about legislation for health and safety, about hours, wages and the employment of women and children. But while all this was going on, and while the sweeping progress of invention and discovery was making possible such miracles as the Exhibition of 1851, the size of industrial undertakings was hardly changing. The average labour force employed in the engineering industry in 1870 was only 85; for cotton it was 177 and at ironworks 219. In the miscellaneous light metal trades of Birmingham and Sheffield it was 11 and 22 respectively.[26] None of these figures would have seemed remarkable to Cephalus; to Jack of Newbury and William Stumpe they would have seemed remarkably small.

A generation later the conditions of employment in London came under the indefatigable scrutiny of Charles Booth; much of his work describes the revolting conditions in the small workshops of East London, and, if the expression of so feeble a preference is permissible, the balance of his opinion favours the large employer. He points out, for example, the advantages of the larger match-making factories in diminishing necrosis among the girls;[27] that larger drapers shops pay better than smaller, although the small shop tends to train more thoroughly;[28] and in a general discussion of large and small organizations favours the larger because they have wider opportunities, for example, to use machinery, and to employ better methods, better management and better sanitation, whence they should be able to offer more regular employment. He does not, however, fail to see the evils generally attendant on the large organization, particularly the business corporation without a conscience.[29] Yet it is significant that, although Booth's work was throughout a vivid tract against the physical evils of the times, against slums, against poverty, against disease and against all the social ills that these brought with them; and although he advocated the need to reform conditions in the small workshops as well as in the large[30], to prosecute the small exploiting landlord as well as the large, and to do all else possible to combat the hidden degradation of the sweating system; in spite of his eloquent sympathy for those whose physical sufferings he mourned, he saw that ultimately the total problem was one of "social size". London was too big; public opinion was too lax; the opportunities for evil too easy and the instruments of chastisement too frail. But the promise held out by the reforms of social administration that had by that time seized men like Booth were already beginning to have their effect in other towns. "It is not one experiment, but hundreds or thousands that are being made, all over the country, with varying aims and under varying auspices. The Local Government Board may cluck from its coop, but the young birds will run far, and, if they are ducklings, will take to the water. London differs only because of its size. It is the ugly duckling of this story."[31] We see other aspects of this same problem still; if the motive to exploit and to snatch at the expense of others is economic, it is nonetheless society that approves and that grants it expression; the sociologist is overhauling and may supplant the economist as the prophet of political action and understanding.[32]

III The Size Effect

In the structure of British industry today the large organization, except in fields where size is an inevitable ingredient, is still comparatively uncommon. One does not now build a railway except to connect towns widely apart, and this cannot be done without employing scores or even hundreds of thousands of men to run it; one does not sink the shaft of a coalmine to fall short of reaching the seam, and this, with coal at a thousand yards down, cannot be done for less than ten million pounds; to make such expenditure worthwhile it is necessary to employ thousands of men underground. But in other fields, such as manufacture, building, distribution and shopkeeping, there is frequently no overriding need for the enterprise to be large, and large organizations are often correspondingly rare. Table 4 gives the size distribution of firms in all manufacturing industry and in the chemical, engineering and textile industries separately in 1956.

There are naturally slight differences between these size distributions when they are studied in detail. For example, textiles, an old industry, has a low proportion of firms employing above 1000

Table 4

PERCENTAGE DISTRIBUTION OF ALL BRITISH MANUFACTURING ESTABLISHMENTS BY SIZE, JAN. 1956

Size of Firm by Numbers Employed	All Industry	Chemical	Shipbuilding Engineering Electrical	Textile
11 — 24	27.6	23.6	24.9	16.1
25 — 99	45.9	41.2	42.4	44.6
100 — 499	21.6	27.0	23.5	35.4
500 — 999	3.0	5.0	4.9	2.9
1000 — 1999	1.2	1.9	2.8	0.7
above 2000	0.7	1.2	1.5	0.2
Total Numbers.	56,313	2,239	8,886	6,210

(Source: Annual Abstract of Statistics, 1956. Table 147.)

persons; both chemistry and engineering have high ones. But even so, all fall off pretty steeply after passing out of the 100/499 class. It is not unreasonable to suppose that this common pattern is the expression of some set of factors common to all industry, and that the variations it displays are merely casual modifications producted by the particular conditions of industries using different technical processes.

Many reasons are given to explain the survival of the small unit; some of these are as simple as those mentioned by Jethro or Aristotle; others are set out in sophisticated arguments about managerial ability, productive efficiency, geographical location of plant, elasticity of markets, availability of manpower and so forth. In his treatment of the subject Professor Beacham puts the factors that determine the size of firms into four classes—technical, marketing, financial and entrepreneurial. His reference to good human relations as such is short and secondary; they "may be a source of important economies to the small firm. The importance of this factor is recognized by many of their larger rivals who spend large sums on labour management and welfare schemes to secure the willing cooperation of contented employees."[33] It must, of course, be the professional view of economists that good industrial relations have direct pecuniary explanations in all circumstances. Other writers who have set out to explain why firms take up the sizes that they do are Prof. E. A. G. Robinson in *The Structure of Competitive Industry*, 1931; Prof. Sargent Florence in *Investment*,

Location and Size of Plant, 1948, and *The Logic of British and American Industry*, 1953; and R. Robson, *The Size of Firms in the Cotton Industry*, Manchester Statistical Society, November, 1949.

Management Factors and Efficiency

Most writers recognize the entrepreneurial factor to be important, and by this factor is mainly implied that judgement of affairs which enables the manager rapidly and effectively to trim his decisions to the emergencies of the outer world—to know when to buy cheaply, to foresee the need for a change of design, to sense the market in such and such a quarter, to engage in a timely trial of strength with the union, to make an offer for the growing business of a rival and so forth. But of recent years the ability of the manager to get his own subordinates to carry out what it is he thinks should be done has come to be recognized as the greatest and most essential quality of all. This is something quite different from what is canonically regarded as "sound business sense". It is an ability to recognize that the problems of a factory are problems of government, and that the authority of the manager is granted to him by the consent of those he manages and not merely purchased from them by the contract of wages that he has entered into. This consent is, in turn, dependent upon his ability to get the men to understand what he is trying to do and to convince them that it is being done in the most sensible manner; what the workman needs is the belief that his manager can manage. There are many factories in which this belief either struggles for its existence or is already dead. Sir Reginal Verdon Smith, Chairman of the Bristol Aeroplane Co. Ltd., has brought the views of an anonymous sociologist to reinforce his own view of this problem of industrial authority:

> "... there is one area of industrial activity in which, though much has been done at the periphery, very little has been accomplished at the heart—the area of human relations in industry. We all deplore the strikes and conflicts, the arbitrary and undisciplined behaviour of many trade unions, and we sometimes criticise managements for mistakes which cause situations to get out of hand; but do you realise just *how* fundamental, *how* intractable, this question really is at heart? Look at it in terms not of those directly involved in the immediate battles but from the point of view of the sociologist. The other day I came across the following paragraph: 'Of supreme importance in industrial societies is factory organisation, regarded as a political problem. The industrial

revolution brought with it a political problem largely new to human civilisation, that of organising hundreds of thousands of human beings in a single enterprise, without the use of slavery, and by means other than those of military command. In practice, the first methods used, including the terms of payment, the conditions of employment, and the type of command-and-obedience required, provoked bitter resentment and led to the outstanding social breach of industrial societies—the breach between employer and workman.'. . . "[34]

The handful of illustrations given in the Introduction show that, if one interprets such failures of morale as accidents, strikes and absenteeism as responses to the system of authority at the factory, it is at once evident why these failures of morale are more probable in the big organizations. Leaving aside the personal abilities of the individual members of the management, it is evident that in the large or complex organization it is going to be difficult for those who take the decisions to be confident that they are both relevant and intelligible. Before attempting to define what this may mean in more rigorous terms, it is interesting to see what Sir Oliver Franks has to say:

"Really large-scale organization compels men take to many decisions at a point remote from the places where their decisions will take effect. They work on paper. The in-tray and the out-tray symbolize the situation. It is easy not to see beyond the paper and hard to preserve a lively awareness of the real issues, human and material, on which the decisions are made. . . . (There is) a permanent tendency in large-scale organization to play safe. A good deal of coordination is inevitable; it does matter if one department of an organization gets seriously out of step with another. Really difficult cases do require a second opinion, and sometimes a more experienced and authoritative decision. At the same time, a continuous effort of will is required to take all the decisions that are possible as soon as they can be taken and to use the facilities for coordination only where necessary and not as a refuge. Organization on the great scale brings many awkward decisions with it. The capacity to decide wisely and take responsibility is not common: the easier path of delay is a standing temptation."[35]

We may prune Sir Oliver's passage of its emotional abstractions and say that he sees the disadvantages of size as two dimensional; there is a tendency to vertical separation because reports or decisions may have to travel up and down; there is a tendency to horizontal separation because of the need to consult at the same level. These tendencies may be represented in the form of a cross, picturesquely described to the writer by one managing director, after a long squabble with his sales, design and production staffs on the one hand, and with his employees on the other, as the cross which every managing director has to carry. It may well be that on which British management as a whole will be crucified.

The effect of vertical separation may, other things being equal, be measured by the size of the organization. In a number of homologous units, such as coalmines or single-purpose factories that differ only by size and not by process, the administrative distance from the point of operation at the coal face or the bench to the manager in charge will be directly proportional to the logarithm of the size, if the span of control is taken as constant throughout the unit. For if the span of control (the number of men reporting to any other man) is equal to r, and if A is the number of workmen and n the number of levels of supervision, then n is equal to log A taken to the base r. In practice r is not constant, neither in any one mine nor between mines. The existence of these variations means that a precise mathematical statement of the relation between the size of the unit and the number of stages of authority is impossible. But for working purposes (and for averages over large groups), it is not improper and is certainly convenient to say that, broadly speaking, the number of stages of authority from the manager to the workplace is proportional to the logarithm of the numbers employed. Hence, when a manager has to take decisions about affairs at the working place, the opportunities of misinterpretation within the vertical management chain are, on average, proportional to the logarithm of the size of the unit. They arise both in the passage of reports upwards, whereby facts are altered or suppressed and opinions or insinuations are introduced as facts; they arise in the passage of decisions downwards, whereby instructions may be varied, misinterpreted or knowingly misrepresented as the situation appears to the intermediary to warrant. What is more important still is that both upwards or downwards a report or an instruction may simply be overlooked or forgotten. However this may be, we may now interpret Sir Oliver's use of the word "remote" to a first approximation, at least, as measuring the double distance over which the communication is made, and say, as a general rule, that this is proportional to the logarithm of the size of the unit.

Expectation and Experience

At this point it is convenient to introduce the concept of expectation and experience. It is, for the purposes of this chapter, assumed that men are more likely to cooperate with the ostensible aims of the unit at which they work, if the management regards it as a principal aim to provide them with whatever it is they need to achieve those aims.* It is, therefore, assumed that the morale of men will decline when they see, or believe that they see, decisions being carried out that appear to those men to be irrelevant to the situations calling for decision. If men *expect*, on the facts of a situation as they see them, a particular line of action to be taken at the place of work, and *experience* a different one, their morale will change insofar as their experience differs from their expectation. As a rule, decisions fail to meet situations as the men see them, because the men are not aware of all the facts. Hence morale suffers. But at times managements seem to the men to rise above themselves and take decisions better than the men expected and morale improves. On this very elementary line of argument we may say that morale is measured by this difference between expectation and experience, that this difference is measured by Sir Oliver's "remoteness" and that this, in turn, is measured by the logarithm of the size of the unit. If we then assume that the morale of the men is measured by their willingness, or ability, to join in the pursuit of the aims of the organization, we should expect to find the statistics of cooperation in some way dependent upon the size of the unit. The easiest measures of cooperation are, firstly, willingness to turn up to work (attendance); secondly, disposition to withdraw from work involuntarily (accident risks); and, thirdly, determination to withdraw deliberately (strikes). Some of these measures are shown in their relation to size in the next paragraphs.

Absence and Size

Fig. I showed that compensable† accident rates among miners and quarrymen in Britain are statistically proportional to the logarithm

* This is an assumption that would perhaps not be denied explicitly, but one encounters frequent instances of its implicit rejection. The writer has frequently met the argument that it is "a good thing" deliberately to keep foremen just a little short of supplies in order that they may be continuously on their toes, alert to intercept whatever may come their way in the stimulus of competition with their fellows; or else in the belief that a ready supply of materials leads to waste.

† A compensable accident is one involving absence for more than three days.

of the size of the mine. Supporting evidence of the same effect has been found in a study of five randomly chosen gas works in the London area; the range of size was from 67 men employed to 3430; the average duration of absence from accidents per man in each works over the five years from 1948 to 1952 varied from 112 to 199 hours, and the correlation of this absence with log. size was + 0.91, which is significant at 3 %. A similar correlation is visible in the absence rates in the 67 gas works in the area administered by one of the Regional Gas Boards. If a composite morale index is constructed from absence sick, absence injured and absence without leave, its correlation with size of plant over the whole region is + 0.62, which is highly significant.

It is necessary to show that these size-effects are proper to the unit itself and are not social effects due to external causes. Small gas works are usually in small towns; it may be argued that life in the small community is more leisurely and that the size-effect belongs to the locality and not to the unit. Some valuable work on this has been done by S. Wood, Chief Statistician of the General Post Office, who shows (in an unpublished report) that female operators in large telephone exchanges have significantly more absence than those in small. Small exchanges are defined as those employing less than thirty operators, and small exchanges in rural areas show the same absence rates as sub-exchanges employing less than thirty girls in large cities. These effects are consistent and obtain whether the girls are married or single; they suggest, therefore, that the size-effect is internal to the units themselves.

Further evidence that the size-effect in accident rates is both genuine and probably independent of the physical environment is shown by the experience of employees of American hospitals. An analysis of the accidents occurring during the year 1953 in 4,680 hospitals selected at random was conducted jointly by the Bureau of Labor Statistics and the American Hospital Association; the period at risk is the equivalent of a year's work of 837,500 employees, which is greater than the exposure period of all British coalminers for a year. The overall rate, given as the average number of disabling accidents per million employee-hours worked, was 8.6; this is, in the words of the Commissioner of Labor Statistics, "certainly not as good as one might expect in an activity devoted to personal health and well-being." It is also remarkable that an activity so devoted should show so strong a size-effect. This is set out in Table 5.

Table 5

WORK-INJURY FREQUENCY RATES IN AMERICAN HOSPITALS, 1953, BY TYPE AND SIZE OF HOSPITAL

Size of Hospital by Number of Employees	Accident Rate and Type of Hospital				
	General Hospitals	Mental Hospitals	Tuberculosis Hospitals	Special Hospitals	All Hospitals
Less than 10	2.5	6.3 (Less than 10 to 20—49)	7.5 (Less than 10 and 10—19)	2.9 (Less than 10 and 10—19)	2.6
10 — 19	2.5				3.2
20 — 49	4.1		9.1	9.3	5.0
50 — 99	4.5	8.1	7.4	6.7	5.1
100 — 249	5.3	7.6	8.0	8.6	6.0
250 — 499	6.2	8.7	12.6	9.5	7.3
500 — 999	7.4	15.4	16.4	13.4	10.0
1000 — 2499	8.4	21.0 (1000—2499 and 2500 and over)	13.8	25.5	13.5
2500 and over	10.3		—	—	12.4

(The failure of the entries in the final column to rise steadily throughout is manifestly due to the fact that the largest size-class contains no tuberculosis nor special hospitals, and probably only a few mental hospitals, since for these the two final cells are bracketed.)

If we confine our attention to the largest homogeneous class —the general hospitals—we find these figures not incompatible with the main result found from the size-trend in the accident rates among British miners and quarrymen, namely, that the average rate is proportional to the logarithm of the number of persons employed.

On page 179 there is a reference to a study by The Acton Trust of absenteeism among the men at 91 factories. The strong size-effect that this displays is confirmed by Table 6, prepared from absence figures among coalminers for the year 1942, when the coal industry was still privately owned. The table shows the average absence at all mines employing between 10 and 100 persons (smaller) and at all mines employing over 1000 persons (larger) in the seven major coalfields of Britain.

1942 was in the middle of the War when the average national absenteeism rate, taken over *all* persons in employment was about five per cent. Hence the miners in the smaller pits were two points worse than the national average; in the larger they were six points worse. This shows that, whatever may be the causes of absence

Table 6

AVERAGE ABSENTEEISM IN 1942, IN ALL LARGER AND SMALLER COALMINES, BY COALFIELDS

Coalfield	No. of Mines		Average Absenteeism %		Standard Deviation %
	Smaller	Larger	Smaller	Larger	
Scotland	108	12	5.65	7.50	3.25
Northern	92	45	6.72	8.41	3.34
Yorkshire.	42	56	10.02	13.73	3.07
North Midland	27	35	9.05	14.19	3.33
Midland	61	20	7.71	13.45	3.96
Lancs and N. Wales .	41	21	7.43	13.12	3.65
South Wales	79	29	7.51	10.98	4.24
Great Britain.	450	218	7.15	11.66	3.83

(Source: Ministry of Power)

among coalminers, it is not by any means simply because they work underground, or do particular operations. Miners in small pits do jobs similar to those of miners in big pits, but they are not as markedly bad attenders. It is the fact of being a miner in a large mine that is associated with high absenteeism. The national average, taken here as five per cent, is of course drawn from all factories of all sizes and this in itself conceals a size-effect. Using the figures from which the above table was constructed, it is possible to show that, if absenteeism follows a logarithmic law (as it appears to), the inherent absence of the individual miner is about four and a half per cent. By "inherent" is implied that residue independent of the size of the mine in which he works, obtained by putting the number employed in the mine equal to unity.*

Two further studies, each of eight groups of factories belonging to two companies with headquarters near Manchester show a very strong logarithmic size-effect in absenteeism. A firm making electrolytic products, with 8 factories ranging from 70 to 2000 employees; and another making chemicals, with 8 factories ranging from 150 to 3500, both showed logarithmic relationships with

* It is interesting to develop the proposition that absence among coalminers is so strongly a collective phenomenon. If absenteeism, which in 1955 was about 12 %, could be purged of these size factors, the effect on output might be considerable.

linear correlations of absence on log. size more significant than at the 5 % level.

Punctuality as well as absence may also show a size-effect. In such comparisons it is necessary to be reasonably certain that it is the factories rather than the local transport systems that are being compared. The records of the five gasworks mentioned on page 196 are free from this objection; all were served by the London Transport Executive. In order to show that, at least for these workers, there is a length-of-service effect as well as a size-effect, Table 7 shows the distribution of lateness by length of service as well as by size of works. The longer the men remain at any works the less liable they are to be late; this may, perhaps, be regarded as the time equivalent of the size-effect. It is a convergence between management and men over time just as the size-effect may be regarded as a divergence over "space"—although bad attenders will normally be more readily discharged; the closer (in terms of administrative distance) that management and men are together the better their joint efforts, and this contiguity may be built up by the alternative route of long service. In the smallest works the 27 men who had more than 10 years of service were, over a whole year, late only 8 times in all; in the largest works the 305 men who had served less than a year had *before completing their year* already been late 2806 times.

Table 7

TIMES LATE PER MAN BY LENGTH OF SERVICE AT FIVE GAS WORKS, LONDON, 1952

Size of Works by No. of Men	Times late per man by Length of Service in years					
	Below 1 year	1 — 5 years	5 — 10 years	10 — 15 years	15 — 20 years	over 20 years
67	3.4	1.4	1.7	0.8	0.0	0.1
240	5.2	4.3	7.1	1.9	2.8	2.3
460	15.5	10.6	3.8	8.4	3.2	2.7
790	10.2	9.3	5.9	5.0	3.3	3.4
3430	9.2	9.9	7.4	6.6	5.2	2.7

(Source: Acton Society Trust)

Industrial Disputes and Size of Undertaking

On page 179 there was a brief reference to a size-effect in the incidence of industrial disputes in American factories. The illustration may not convince, since the total of occasions on which a man or any given number of men could be drawn into any disagreement with a manager depends upon the number of men. A thousand men, for example, might find ten times as many opportunities for complaining about the state of their machines or the quality of their raw materials as a hundred men working under identical conditions. Hence the trend of Table 2 may not be surprising.

The existence of a true size-effect in disputes is, however, revealed by the figures for the British coal industry. Strikes are notoriously difficult statistical material, for they have not only a frequency distribution, but a severity distribution as well. A hundred strikes that last an average of two shifts among an average of a hundred men are not as disastrous in their effect on output as a single coalfield strike involving a hundred thousand men for a month. The index that will be used here for suggesting the loss of morale at any particular colliery is therefore the tonnage lost in disputes per man per year; the *total* tonnage lost in strikes would naturally tend to be greater at a large pit than a small, even if its relative strike proneness were less. But the *average tonnage lost per man employed* does not suffer from ambiguity. Whether or not tonnage rather than shifts should be the index does not matter since, as Table 3 suggests, the differences between the outputs per manshift averaged over size classes is small.

The results of strike losses for the period of five years from 1949 to 1953 for all mines in Yorkshire and in the bituminous coalfield of South Wales are shown in Tables 8(a) and 8(b). These two coalfields and Scotland account for nearly all the coal lost in disputes in this country; Scotland is, however, not treated here because many of the strikes in the smaller mines of Lanarkshire may be a rear-guard action against the total closure of the coalfield; they are not necessarily evidence of failures of the internal morale of the pits involved, and may even be manifestations of an otherwise healthy solidarity among the men.

These tables, referring to the five years of strike experience of nearly a quarter of a million men in over two hundred mines, show beyond doubt that the willingness of the individual miner to join,

Tables 8 (a) and 8 (b)

INCIDENCE AND SEVERITY OF DISPUTES AT ALL COLLIERIES IN YORKSHIRE, AND IN THE BITUMINOUS COALFIELD OF SOUTH WALES, IN RELATION TO TOTAL SIZE OF COLLIERY, 1949—1953

8 (a) — Yorkshire Coalfield

Manpower Group	No. of Pits	No. of Disputes	Tonnage Lost	No. of Disputes per 1000 Men	Tonnage lost per Man
Below 500	28	79	42,100	11.1	5.94
501 — 1000	25	275	168,953	14.6	8.97
1001 — 1500	20	386	399,240	15.8	16.39
1501 — 2000	21	482	454,285	13.6	12.82
2001 — 2500	8	256	282,282	14.4	15.98
Above 2500	12	824	763,963	24.5	22.70

8 (b) — South Wales Bituminous Coalfield

Manpower Group	No. of Pits	No. of Disputes	Tonnage Lost	No. of Disputes per 1000 Men	Tonnage lost per Man
Below 500	35	204	123,229	16.0	9.69
501 — 1000	40	575	437,997	15.9	12.14
1001 — 1500	23	525	389,833	20.1	15.01
1501 — 2000	6	172	244,321	16.4	23.39

(Source: National Coal Board)

and to remain out with, his mates in a strike goes up steadily with the size of the mine. It would be rash to suggest the form of the strike-size relationship, since the factors at work in the precipitation of strikes are immensely complex and size is only one of them. For all that we may, perhaps, single it out as the most important; there is no consistency in the form of the wage issues for which men appear to strike—except in their consistently irrational complexity. For we note, firstly, that the overwhelming majority of strikes occur among piece-workers, and, compared with the non-piece workers, these are the plutocrats of the industry; and, secondly, that when all piece-workers in pits that do not have strikes are compared with all piece-workers in pits that do, we find the non-striking pits earn on average about a shilling a shift *more* than the striking. But since men who strike sacrifice their five-day-week bonus (which is payment for a sixth shift every time they work a week of five others), this difference of a shilling is probably not significant. Whatever may be the occasions of strikes it is extremely doubtful if the basic causes are pecuniary. It is therefore interesting to study their size-distribution by occasion.

All these disputes in Yorkshire were officially reported as having a particular cause. The mines in which they occurred are here classified into three size-groups; each size-group was chosen so that it employed approximately one-third of the Yorkshire labour force. There were, as a result of this size classification, 67 mines designated as small, 30 medium and 18 large. The disputes were allocated between these size-classes, and entered into one of two classes of reported causes within each size-group. These classes of causes were either monetary or non-monetary. If the dispute arose—or was reported as having arisen—over questions of wages, allowances or price lists, it was classified as having a monetary cause. If it arose over a refusal to accept alternative work, to await repairs after a mechanical breakdown, or because of alleged bad conditions, or for any other non-monetary cause, it was so classified. The total number of disputes so studied was 1,726, or all those reported in 1949—50—51 and —52; they are distributed over the three size-groups and the two classes of reported causes as shown in Table 9(a).

Table 9 (a)

Distribution of 1,726 Disputes in Yorkshire, 1949—52, According to Size-Group of Mine and Reported Cause

Size-Group by No. on Books	No. of Mines	Total No. of Men on Books	Reported Cause	
			Monetary	Non-Monetary
Below 1,250	67	42,600	248	162
1,250 — 2,000	30	47,500	262	280
Above 2,000	18	45,500	320	454

(Source: National Coal Board)

Table 9(a) suggests that the size-effect has little to do with wages, allowances and price lists. The miners in the larger pits are not much more sensitive to money issues than are those in the smaller. But they are more sensitive, man for man, to non-monetary issues; those in the largest pits find nearly three times as many opportunities during the year to dispute factors other than monetary ones as do the men in the smallest pits. It is not unreasonable, as a working hypothesis, to suggest that these other factors have something to do with the difficulties of remoteness confronting the managements of the larger mines. (The Princeton study (Page. 178) showed that the larger factories had higher average hourly earnings but also tended to have more strikes).

It is of interest to partition the reported non-monetary causes yet further. They may be classified under four main headings:

(a) Personal arguments with the management, to include disputes over other men being dismissed, reprimanded or suspended; objections to attitudes of particular officials on particular occasions; questions of personal allowances—house rent or coal and so forth—or on promotion or grading; miscellaneous matters such as perquisites, loss of tools, breaches of Fatal Accident Agreement and so forth.

(b) Criticism of the organization as such, including disagreements over tasks set or methods to be adopted, and refusals to accept reasonable alternative work in emergency.

(c) Objections to environmental conditions, including refusals to complete work left over from the previous shift.

(d) Impatience at mechanical breakdowns, followed by walking out from place of work.

The classification of the 896 non-monetary causes in the 115 mines is shown in Table 9(b), broken down into the same three size-classes by these four sub-classes of reported causes.

Table 9 (b)

CLASSIFICATION OF 896 NON-MONETARY STRIKES IN YORKSHIRE, 1949—52; BY OFFICIALLY REPORTED CAUSE

Size-Group	Reported Cause			
	(a) Personal	(b) Organization	(c) Environment	(d) Impatience
Small	32	73	52	5
Medium	24	144	95	17
Large	33	210	152	59

This table shows that, in spite of their greater total readiness to strike, the men in the larger mines do not fall out with their officials over personal matters more readily nor bear their managers more ill will than those in the smaller. (The differences in col. (a) are not significant). Dissatisfaction over organization shows precisely the same size-trend as that over environment, so that the distinction is probably not a true one; both kinds of dissatisfaction, which between them account for nearly half of all strikes, monetary included, show a strong size-effect. It is these sources of discontent that probably form the background of the poor human relations in the coalfields generally, but in Yorkshire and South Wales they actually precipitate stoppages. Column (d) lends a good deal of colour to this view; the size-effect for strikes precipitated by interruptions to the tasks upon which the men are currently engaged is extremely pronounced. The men in the largest mines are relatively ten times as responsive to interruptions to the rhythm of their work as the men in the smallest; it is not known whether the interruptions are in fact more frequent or whether the men are simply more sensitive to them. Both causes are probable; when men have been interrupted once or twice their irritation on the next occasion may prove decisive in their withdrawal.

It may well be that the apparent failure of the authority of management in the larger organization is the appearance inside industry of a well known sociological effect—that the social conscience is difficult to arouse in the large community. The incidence of crime is, for example, greater per 100,000 inhabitants in the large town than in the small; the percentage of persons on the electoral roll who vote at municipal elections is smaller in the large borough than in the small. There may be a sense in which the sales of the N.C.B. magazine *COAL*, referred to on page 179 and Fig. II, display the same trends of "political attachment" as do the voting returns at the municipal elections. The interest of those who work in the large organization is more difficult to arouse than that of those in the small. It is not that the magazine is necessarily more difficult to market in the larger pit, for there is on average no difference between the large and the small pits in the success of their organizations for the voluntary purchase of National Savings Certificates, as Fig. II shows. The Coal Board is, to the miner, probably personified by the pit and the management of which he has experience; when the one is large and the other remote his response is like that of the municipal voter in the large town: he is, in general, not interested. There is reason to believe that other large concerns selling house magazines have a similar experience to that of the Coal Board.

Size and Human Efficiency

In his final analysis the economist will argue that the survival of a business or industrial institution is determined by its financial efficiency. If, judged against the conditions in which it exists, a factory, a shop or any other enterprise ostensibly aimed at creating value for its owners succeeds in doing so at a level of efficiency not significantly lower than the average level of its competitors engaged on the same mission, then that institution will normally survive. In the long run, sentimental, irrational or uneconomic beliefs exercised to maintain, for example, antiquated family cotton mills or research projects on perpetual motion are, it is said, bound to perish because they must lose money, if not absolutely, then at least relatively to newer mills or more rational research projects. It is interesting to glance at how far these considerations might apply to the efficiency of industrial or business concerns of different sizes.

Table 3 shows that the output of coal per man-year reaches a maximum in the size range of 1500—2000 men employed. Over the years 1948 to 1953 the mean annual output of the man in the largest mines of all is 42 tons less that of the man in the mine of approximately half the size. These figures are, of course, averages taken over the whole industry and conceal wide variations in the figures for individual mines in any particular size-group. For all that, the lesson is quite clear: the capacity of miners to get coal out of a British pit rises to a maximum at about 1700 men employed and thereafter tends to decline. An analysis of wage costs per ton shows the opposite trend: these costs decline up to the figure of 1700 and thereafter rise again. It has already been shown that in the larger mines the men work fewer shifts per year, so that the decline of annual production is partly, but not entirely, explained by this. There is also a fall in average output per man-shift. We do not know enough about the other factors that determine total efficiency to comment upon their relation to size. All we seem to be able to conclude is that we do not know enough about how to manage a very big coalmine to be able to rely with confidence upon

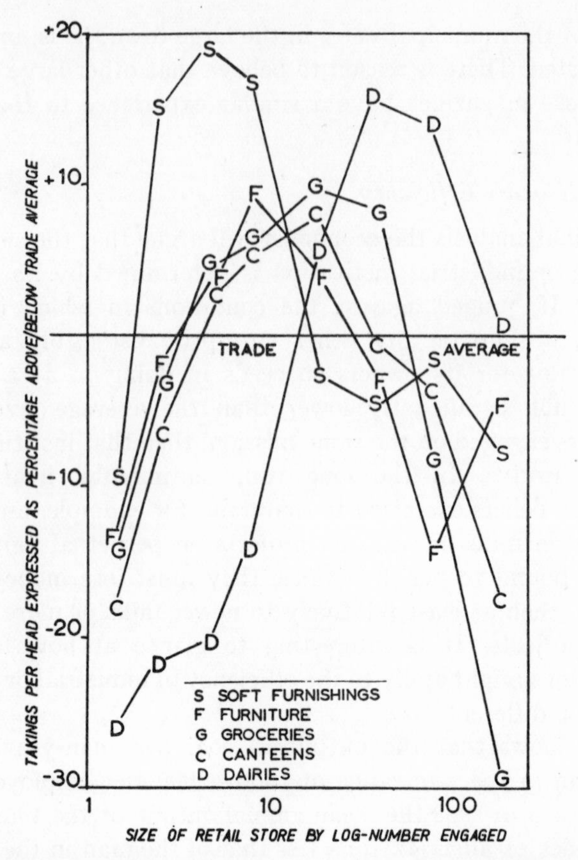

Fig. III. Sales per person engaged in relation to trade average, 1950, by size of store.

the cooperation of the miners employed in it. The current troubles (Feb. 1957) at the works of Briggs' Motor Bodies suggests that this cooperation has also eluded the management of that enormous concern.

The evidence in the field of commerce also suggests that human efficiency depends upon size to such an extent that the reasons for this should be better known. In Fig. III are shown the average sales per person engaged (not per sales assistant) in five kinds of retail units in 1950 by size of unit, as compared with the average sales per person over the trade as a whole. The trades concerned and the number of shops in each trade for which the five trends are drawn are soft furnishings, 4,254; domestic furniture, 6,276; groceries, 94,965; canteens, 21,367; dairies, 8,759. The five selected trades are the only ones in the official report covering the size range to over 100 persons engaged.[36] Fig. III shows how the efficiency with which employees are able to sell rises to a maximum at a medium size of working unit and thereafter declines. It is also of interest to study the effectiveness with which the employee of the company-owned unit sells compared with the employee of the working proprietor in a store of the same size; in all types of store —however large—the sales per person engaged are higher when the proprietor works among his staff. It is difficult to see how these differences—whether by size-trend or ownership— can be explained in other than social terms.

IV Supervision Effects

All that has so far been said has considered the unit—factory, gasworks, retail store or coalmine—merely as having a particular size. The question arises as to the extent to which the management "structure"—by introducing subordinate size-patterns—influences the response of the workpeople. This is simply Jethro's question: is the large organization made more effective by appointing group leaders who know what their duties are, and who have the means of carrying them out? The evidence drawn from the statistics of the coal industry suggests that this effect, namely, the influence of group size as well as of total size, is of fundamental importance.

It is necessary to introduce the concept of supervision ratio; that used here is given by the average number of junior officials per hundred workers underground. In practice this average may vary between pits from three to fifteen. The mode is between seven and eight. In Table 10(a) is shown the distribution of all N.C.B. mines by size and supervision ratio given in ten main classes. Five intervals classify by total tonnage raised, which is a fair indication of overall size; two intervals of supervision ratio are added, so that

Table 10 (a)

Distribution of N.C.B. Mines 1953 by Annual Tonnage Raised (Thousand Tons) and Supervision Ratio

No. of Junior Officials per 100 Employees Underground	Numbers of Mines by Tonnage Size-Classes				
	Below 100	100— 200	200— 350	350— 700	Above 700
8 and above . .	119	64	56	29	6
Below 8	131	139	118	130	38

all the pits are further grouped according to whether they have less than 8 junior officials per 100 men or not. Those with 8 or more will tend to have working groups smaller than those with less than 8.

The format of Table 10(a) is used to set out the effect of closer supervision (smaller working groups) upon the various indices of morale: firstly, improved attendance; secondly, safer working; thirdly, better human relations. This is done in Table 10(b) where the three lines set out

(i) the difference in the annual number of shifts worked per man at the coal face;
(ii) the difference in the mean underground accident rate;
(iii) the difference between the percentages of pits in the sub-classes involved in disputes.

These differences are obtained merely by subtracting the average of the index for the pits (in any size-group) with ratios of below 8 from the average of the index for the pits (in the same size-group) with ratios of above 8.

Table 10 (b)

EFFECT OF SUPERVISION (IN ALL SIZE-GROUPES OF MINE) ON ATTENDANCE, ACCIDENTS AND STRIKES, ALL N.C.B. MINES, 1953

Morale Index	Difference in Morale Index by Tonnage Size-Class (Thousand Tons)				
	Below 100	100 — 200	200 — 350	350 — 700	Above 700
(i) Attendance .	+ 14	+ 2	+ 6	+ 3	+ 6
(ii) Accidents . .	— 10	— 16	— 22	— 7	— 35
(iii) Strikes . . .	— 15	— 10	— 37	— 22	— 36

These results show that in all size-groups of mines (by tonnage raised) the pits with the higher supervision ratio have, on average, a better attendance at the coal face, a lower accident rate and a smaller probability of being involved in a dispute than those with the lower supervision ratio. In other words, the size-effects already traced in the mines as a whole can also be found in the sizes of the working groups within the mines. It is suggested here (but without satisfactory evidence) that the entirely different shape of the accident-size relation for the American mines, shown in Fig. I, is due both to better overall management and to local supervision in the larger units. The general aim is for one supervisor to five men, more than double the intensity of supervision in this country, and, moreover, of a higher individual standard.[37] Research into this effect, which can be detected in other American industries, is urgently needed.

The supervision exercised by an industrial safety officer is not strictly of the kind suggested in these paragraphs. Nevertheless, one might expect to find that an intensive safety campaign, conducted by officials charged with the responsibility for identifying and removing the causes of accidents, would have the same general effect upon the accident rate as an increase in the number of foremen. The following paragraph, taken from Bulletin 1164 of the U.S. Department of Labor, "Work Injuries in the United States during 1952", lends colour to this view.

> "The larger establishments, which can afford trained safety engineers and which conduct intensive safety programs, generally have the lowest rates. Usually the medium-size plants have the highest rates, and the smallest establishments show rates somewhat below the medium-size plants but above the average for the industry. In 44 of the 132 manufacturing classifications for which size tabulations are presented, the highest rates were found among units with 100 to 249 employees; in an additional 38 of the industries, the highest averages were reported by plants with 50 to 99 employees; and in 24 industries, the highest rates were recorded in small plants, with 20 to 49 employees. In 15 industries, the highest rates were reported by units with 250 to 499 employees; and in 6 industries, by those with 500 to 999 employees. However, in 3 industries, the highest rates were reported by the smallest plants, with less than 20 employees and, in two others, by large units with over 1000".

The general size-effect in American manufacturing industries thus resembles that of the American coalmining industry. If the explanation of the last paragraph is correct it is apparent that the responsibility for the size-effects in British industries lies largely with their management organization.

The Morale of Individual Collieries

Table 10(b) and the arguments of the preceding paragraphs may be criticized on the ground that they refer to size and supervision *classes*, and not to *individual* mines. Such criticism could never destroy the argument that both size and structure are significant in determining morale, but it might legitimately claim that, compared with other factors, such as thickness of seam or age of colliery, either size or structure were comparatively unimportant in determining the morale at any individual mine. It is, therefore, profitable to study a number of otherwise comparable individual collieries, and for this purpose two reasonably homogeneous families of mines have been selected. The first is the whole Yorkshire coalfield of 115 mines; the second is the sub-group of the twenty largest mines in Yorkshire.

For the purpose of this study of separate mines a new index of morale, here called L, consisting of the total tonnage lost per man employed, both from compensable accidents and from disputes, was worked out for every colliery in Yorkshire over the five year period 1949 to 1953. This index L is therefore a measure of the extent to which the average miner in any particular colliery was away from work, either because he was engaged in a dispute or because he was injured. It may be an unsatisfactory index, since it does not account for voluntary or sickness absence. That may well be so, but lacking any reliable data on absenteeism it was decided to use the sum of the dispute and accident losses alone. These at least omit from the analysis the deliberate acts of the individual men in staying away; the index L is composed mainly of factors over which the average man exercises no volition; he is carried by his fellow-workmen into the dispute and suffers accident without conscious connivance. The following symbols are also used: M = total number of underground workers; D = number of deputies per 100 underground workers.

(i) For all 115 Yorkshire collieries, the partial correlation coefficients are LM.D = + 0.58 and LD.M = — 0.25. Both of these are significant, so that there is an increasing coal loss per man with total size independently of supervision; and a decreasing coal loss per man with increasing supervision independently of total size. These figures confirm Table 10(b) of averages for the whole industry.

(ii) For the 20 largest mines in Yorkshire the results are generally the same but reveal more strongly the importance of supervision at the place of work. The 20 large units form a group more homogeneous than the above 115, since these 115 vary in size over a range of nearly fifty-fold. This size variation is much greater than the structure variation (as the variation in the number of deputies per 100 men may be regarded) and may, as it actually does, tend to suggest that the correlation of morale with overall size is much greater than with supervision. If morale depends upon the capacity of the central management of a colliery to coordinate the work of all the deputies as well as upon the capacity of the deputies to look after their individual districts, one would expect the effect of the central management to come out strongly over a fifty-fold range of size. The importance of the place held by the deputies might, on that account, tend to be obscured, since the range of the average number of men under the deputies is about three-fold only. Hence it is reasonable to study the effect, not only over the coalfield as a whole, but over the 20 largest pits, in which, since they each employ over 2,000 men, the central management is in all cases remote from the deputies, and absorbed in a considerable task of total coordination. The first order correlation coefficients now become: LM.D = + 0.41; LD.M = — 0.63, showing that in these very large mines the dependence of L, the morale index, upon the number of deputies per 100 men is now greater than its dependence upon the overall size. Whereas, holding the structure variate D constant, the dependence of L on M is barely significant (+ 0.41 for 20 pits is only just significant), the dependence of L on D, holding the size variate M constant, is very highly significant (— 0.63 for 20 pits could not have occurred by chance once in 200 times).

It may be said that although the statistics show some effect of size and supervision on morale, these effects are nevertheless trivial compared with other factors such as geological conditions, the history of labour relations, wages, managerial temperaments and so forth. This is not so. For these 20 large mines the total correlation coefficient of L on M and D together is 0.71. This means that, for the 20 largest mines in Yorkshire, one half (the square of 0.71) of the variations between the morale indices is associated with size and supervision. All the other factors in which the pits differ account only for as much variation in their morale as do the differences of size and structure.

Morale and Thickness of Seam

It is important to show how, if at all, the composite morale index, L, depends upon the thickness of the seam in which the men work. For it is often suggested by mining engineers that accidents are more likely to take place in thick seams than in thin, and that men working in thick seams, by being able to move about along the face, will more readily spread disaffection among their colleagues than men working in thin. The argument runs that the bad morale of the large mines—with heavy loads on both undermanagers and deputies—is mainly due to the thickness of the seam that the large mines tend to work. The methods of partial correlation enable us to answer these arguments. For if the variate, T, for average seam thickness, is introduced, one finds for the 115 collieries in Yorkshire that LT.DM = + 0.06, which is not significant. Thus, if all the pits in Yorkshire were of the same total size and had the same number of deputies per 100 men, there would be no relation between the morale index and the mean thickness of the seam. It is not, in other words, the height of the seam that encourages a high accident rate or many strikes; the responsibility for poor morale is to be found in the large overall size of the mines and the large average number of men under the deputy. The appropriate correlation coefficients LM.DT and LD.MT are + 0.55 and — 0.22, both of which are highly significant for 115 units. These results suggest that it is not geological conditions but the layout and management structure of the large mines in Yorkshire that makes them continually full of labour troubles. The thick seam theory of discontent is not even half true.

Supervision Effects Elsewhere

There is evidence of this supervision effect in other fields. At a large chemical works near Manchester an investigation of the tasks of the maintenance department, then employing 1000 men under 50 charge-hands, showed delays in completing tasks that suggested to the engineer-in-charge the need to think afresh about his supervisory schemes. He discovered that by raising the number of charge-hands to 76 he could reduce the number of tradesmen and other maintenance workers to 800, and thereby obtain a higher standard of maintenance. The supervision ratio was approximately doubled, but the total cost of doing the job better was greatly reduced. The engineer's explanation was quite simple; the supervisors now had time to provide the men with what they needed to do their work, and to spend more time on planning what their work should be. In consequence, the tradesmen and their assistants formed groups that worked more effectively.

Another illustration is given by a study of the accident rates in the

26 separate departments in which the largest steelworks in Asia is organized. This employs nearly 25,000 persons, and the operational departments range in size from the roll-turning shop with 125 on the books up to the sheet mill with over 2,000. There are altogether over 2,600 in the various machine shops, but it is difficult to decide whether or not these should, for this purpose, be counted as one command or not. Again the miscellaneous labour department aggregates over 2,500 and, although those in this department must obviously work in distinct operational commands, they are, like the machine shops, taken as one department for this study. For the years 1952 and 1953 the total number of lost time accidents for the whole enterprise was 2391; the correlation of departmental accident rate with departmental size was + 0.476, which, for 26 departments, is significant at less than one per cent. If the machine shops and the miscellaneous labour department were taken as several smaller departments, the significance would be greater still; the result, however, is already highly significant without this legitimate interpretation of the data.

The Relation between Overall Size and Supervision

Table 10(a) shows an important effect, namely, that management is so built that the supervision ratio tends to fall off in the larger pits. This effect, of tending to have large working groups in large units, seems to be found in industries other than coal. Where the manager has a heavy task, so also do those he is trying to control; not only does he have more subordinates coming to him with their troubles, but each subordinate probably has more troubles to bring. This effect is visible even in the staffing of hospital wards; the number of beds per nurse increases as the hospitals get bigger and, hence, tends to throw more problems on the individual nurse as well as on the matron to whom she answers. For a typical Region the figures for the general hospitals, classified as Acute or Mainly Acute, are set out in Table 11.

In Table 11 the "expected" numbers of nursing staff are those which would result if all nurses in the 60 hospitals were shared in proportion to the numbers of beds. According to this datum, in the larger hospitals seven nurses are doing more than the work of nine in the smaller, supposing that all four size-groups of hospitals are working under equal pressure to the same point of efficiency. This suggests that, as in coalmines, the management of the large unit

Table 11

NURSING STAFF PER 100 BEDS BY SIZE OF HOSPITAL; ALL GENERAL HOSPITALS UNDER A REGIONAL BOARD, 1955

Size by No. of Beds	No. of Hospitals	Total No. of Beds	Total No. of Nursing Staff (Actual)	Total "Expected" No. of Nursing Staff	Difference (Actual less "Expected")
Below 50	18	511	312	288	+ 24
51 — 100	9	643	393	319	+ 74
101 — 300	23	3921	2236	1947	+ 289
Above 300	10	6277	2730	3117	— 387
All	60	11412	5671	5671	—

tends to be under stress at all levels. It would be improper to suggest that the remarkable figures given by Simpson (Table 1) are in any way dependent upon this doubly increasing load; Simpson was well aware that, in 1869, the danger of the large hospital was in its being crowded; he understood that the dangers of cross-infection went up rapidly with the total number of beds. For all that, in an institution like a hospital, with the tradition that the nurse will stay at her task whatever happens, it would be equally improper not to ask whether, in addition to the normal difficulties of managing the larger unit, there is not some additional load resulting from the relatively fewer nurses per hundred patients. Again we know next to nothing of the social forces at work to determine the relations between patient, nurse and matron.

The Endicott Survey

The effects of increasing the supervision ratio in a factory in order to maintain or increase efficiency have been admirably documented by Walker and Richardson.[38] Their work describes how a 5,000 man American plant with production problems of overwhelming complexity was set, at the outbreak of World War II, the following three-fold task: to double its manpower, to decimate its inventory (unfinished work or parts) and to reduce its mean period of delivery from three months to one. The key to the success in having achieved this three-fold objective was the refashioning of the foreman's task: he was put into direct touch with his men by the abolition of the grade of charge-men, and into direct touch with his divisional chiefs by the abolition of the grade of departmental manager; he was encouraged to go directly to other foremen for supplies or services that he knew they could give him; he was charged with training and rate-fixing for the men under him; he was given clerical assistance; and the number of men under his control was, in the key departments, reduced from over 60 to under 30. He was, as Jethro advised Moses, given authority and opportunity to know what his job was and to do it so that the management structure did not become clogged with matters needing decision at inappropriately high levels. The results of the Endicott reorganization are entirely consonant with the scattered evidence of the last few paragraphs; industrial morale begins at the point of work and will tend to be good if the supervision there is good.

V MANAGEMENT INFLUENCES ON MORALE

Even though it has been possible to show that, in the largest coalfield of Britain, the variations in morale from pit to pit are highly dependent upon size and supervision, and are not, as some suppose, dependent mainly upon seam thickness, we are still far from understanding the incidence and effects of other influences. Consider, for example, the story told by Fig. IV which shows in two separate parts the movement of accident rates at the fourteen most homogeneous large pits in Britain between 1944 and 1951. These pits are in the same geological coalfield and all work one and the same seam and no other seam. Between 1944 and 1947 all fourteen pits have accident rates more or less randomly distributed between 110 and 220 compensable accidents per 100,000 manshifts. At nationalization, however, a line was drawn across the coalfield, and six pits were given to one local administration and eight to another; for this reason the accident rates of these two groups are recorded separately over the whole period. It is apparent that there is a strong tendency for the accident rates of the individual pits to settle down at two significantly different group levels. In one group, after nationalization, the good pits catch the bad habits of those formerly bad; the bad ones admitted into the other group even become the best in it. It is impossible to deny the permeation of each group with a spirit of either security or danger; it is no less impossible to escape the conclusion that the medium of permeation is some aspect of the group-management, especially since the high-accident six have both bad strike and bad production records, while

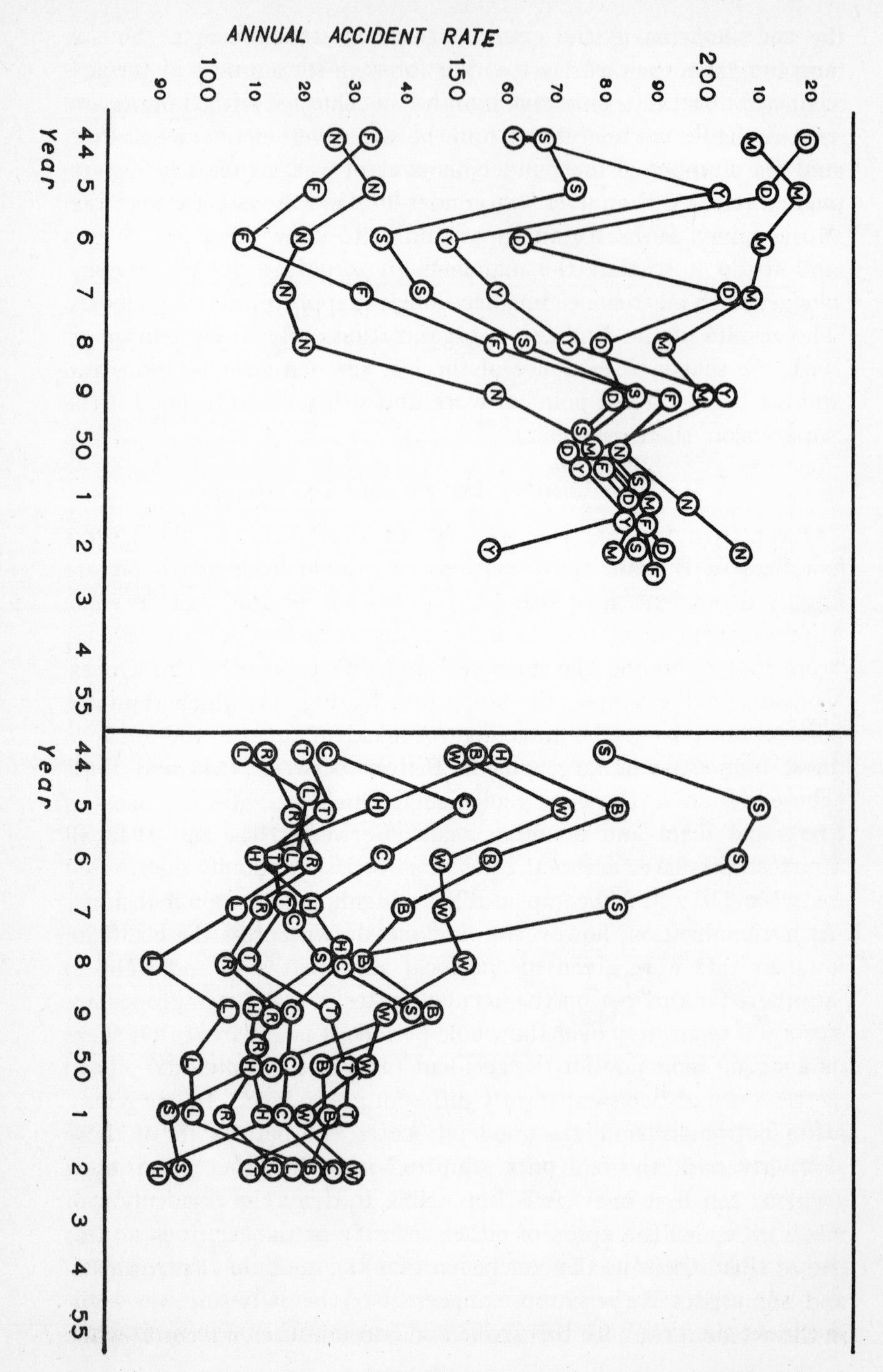

Fig. IV. Showing trends of accident rates at two geologically comparable colliery groups.

the low-accident eight are excellent in both these respects. One is tempted, from such evidence as this, to suggest that morale "begins at the top" and is in some way transmitted through the management structure down to the very coalfaces where the men work; further analysis of the records shows beyond doubt that junior managers tend to pass on the quality of treatment that they themselves get at the hands of their superiors.

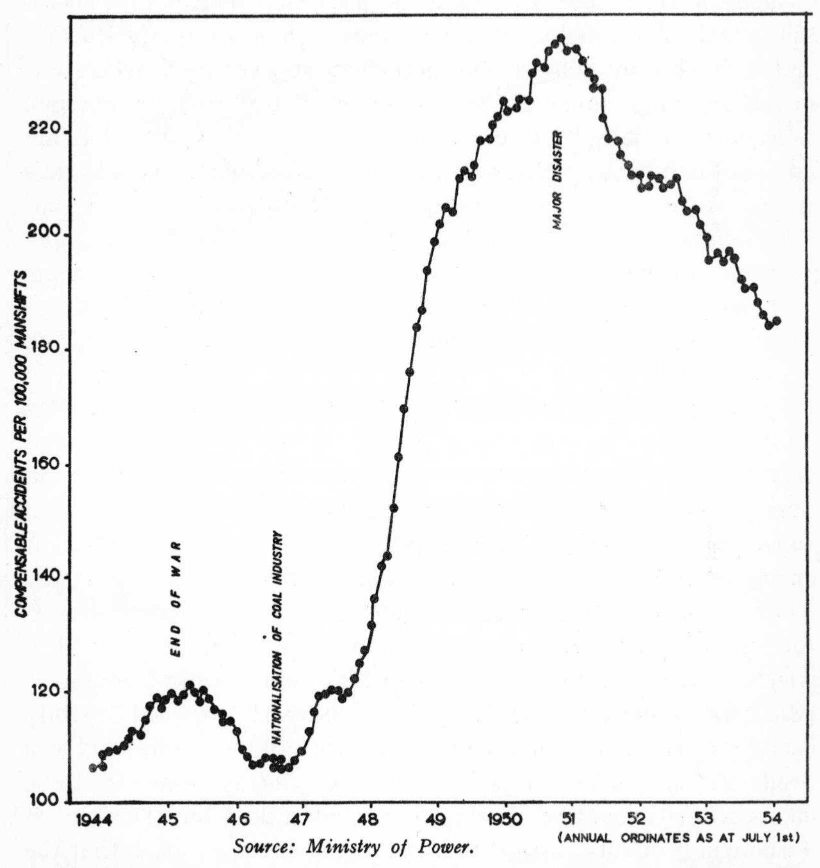

Source: Ministry of Power.

Fig. V. Twelve-monthly moving averages of accident rates at 4 adjacent pits.

No less striking is the story of Fig. V. This records the average accident rate over the years 1944—1954 at a group of four adjacent mines, of which three were very large. Following a major disaster at one of them there was an entire reorganization of the management and administrative structure; the result of this is clearly apparent in the accident rate, for the disaster occurred at the very peak of the accident curve. It is apparent also in the output per manshift, which has increased by over 25 % since the reorganization. Both of these illustrations suggest other factors on which both morale and productive efficiency depend.

We need, if we are to understand the nature of industrial morale —and there is no task more imperative awaiting us today— some new concepts. It is not enough to believe that the elementary tricks of analysis that have been used in this essay—correlation coefficients, classification by size and supervision, tests of significance and so forth—are going to do more than suggest to us where our search for enlightenment should be directed. But abstractions such as leadership, delegation, power, incentives and so forth, that are used so liberally by writers on management subjects need, if they are to be of any use, to be more accurately defined and, in particular, to be related *inter se*. We need not only a general theory of management but a clearer definition of what, in the physical environments of the mine or the department store, it is that management believes itself to be, what the workpeople think it is, and what a detached observer from outside actually sees it doing. We need frames of reference in which such miscellaneous abstractions as "pride in the job", "status in the eyes of mates", and "a fair day's work for a fair day's pay" all have a necessary and sufficient part. We need concepts about communications through administrative networks, that will enable us to deal with lost, mutilated or misdirected instructions or reports; we need to relate these probabilities of confusion at any point in the network to what else may happen to be passing through that point (a busy man may misread a message); we need to establish whether whatever is passing through that point should be doing so (what was making the man so busy?); above all, we need to study exactly what the organization is doing or should be doing, and as a result to suggest how this is most economically done. In these observational excursions we shall learn a great deal, but the simplest lesson will probably be this: that men have an expectation that the boss for whom they work will give them the best conditions he can and let them get on with that work. In so far as that expectation is not met, their morale will suffer, and since, when managers and supervisors are either overloaded or caught up in a snare of functional complexity, they will not know the men's troubles, the morale will suffer most readily in the biggest unit. It may be as simple as that.

References

1. *Influence of Plant Size on Industrial Relations*, Princeton University Press, 1955. p. 53.
2. *Size and Morale*, London: Acton Society Trust, 1953.
3. Exodus, 18.13.
4. Aristotle, *Ethics*, Bk. IX c X para. 2.
5. Aristotle, *Politics*, Bk. VII c IV para. 11. (trans. Barker).
6. Aristotle, *Politics*, Bk. VII c IV para. 13. (trans. Barker).
7. *Cambridge Ancient History*, Cambridge University Press, 1927. Vol. V, p. 15.
8. Rostovtzev, M. I., *Social and Economic History of Rome*, Oxford University Press, 1926. p. 169.
9. Rostovtzev, M. I., *Social and Economic History of the Hellenistic World*, Oxford University Press, 1941. Vol. I, p. 413; Vol. II, p. 898; Vol. III, p. 1549.
10. *Cambridge Ancient History*, Cambridge University Press, 1934. Vol. X, pp. 391-395.
11. Lipson, E., *Economic History of England*, London: Black, 1949. Vol. I, pp. 469-477.
12. Galloway, R. L., *Annals of Coal Mining*, London: Colliery Guardian Company, 1898. p. 199.
13. Nef, J. U., *Rise of the British Coal Industry*, London: Routledge & Kegan Paul, 1932. Vol. II, p. 140.
14. Defoe, D., *Tour through Britain*, London: J. M. Dent. Vol. III, p. 67.
15. Mantoux, P., *Industrial Revolution in the Eighteenth Century*, London: Jonathan Cape, 1928. p. 198.
16. Hutton, W., *History of Derby*, London: J. Nichols, 1791. p. 160
17. Mantoux, P., *op. cit.* p. 232.
18. Urwick, L., *ed.*, *Golden Book of Management*, London: Newman Neame, 1956 p.l.
19. Mantoux, P., *op. cit.* p. 343.
20. Halévy, E., *History of the English People in the 19th Century*, London: Benn, 1950. Vol. III, p. 272.
21. Mumford, L., *Technics and Civilisation*, London: Routledge & Kegan Paul, 1934. p. 173.
22. Ure, Andrew, *The Philosophy of Manufactures*, London: Charles Knight, 1835. p. 368.
23. *Report of the Minutes of Evidence taken before the Select Committee on the State of Children Employed in the Manufactories of the United Kingdom.* Ordered by the House of Commons, 1816. p. 167.
24. *Catechism of a New View of Society*, letter in a London newspaper, 1817.
25. Roll, Erich, *An Early Experiment in Industrial Organisation*, London: Longmans, 1930.
26. Clapham, Sir J. H., *Work and Wages*. In *Early Victorian England* 1830–1865; ed. by G. M. Young. Oxford University Press, 1934. Vol. I, p. 55.
27. Booth, C., *Life and Labour of the People in London*, London: Macmillan, 1903. Second Series, Vol. II, part II, chap. ii, p. 105.
28. Booth, C., *op. cit.*, Vol. III, part I, chap. v, pp. 67–80.
29. Booth, C., *op. cit.*, Vol. V, part II, chap.iv, pp. 106–110.
30. Booth, C., *op. cit.*, Vol. V, part II, chap. xii, p. 302.
31. Booth, C., *op. cit.*, Final Vol., part IV, Conclusion. p. 213.
32. Crosland, C. A. R., *The Future of Socialism*, London: Jonathan Cape, 1956.
33. Beacham, A., *Economics of Industrial Organisation*, London: Pitman, 1948 p. 58.
34. Smith, Sir R. V., *The Task of Modern Industry*, London: Federation of British Industries, 1955. p. 7.

35. Franks, Sir Oliver S., *Central Planning and Control in War and Peace,* London: Longmans, 1947. p. 28.
36. Board of Trade, *Census of Distribution and Other Services,* Vol. II, London: H. M. S. O. , 1950.
37. Coal: *Report of Coal Mining Productivity Team,* London: Anglo-American Council on Productivity, 1951. para. 74.
38. Walker, C. R. and Richardson, F. L. W., *Human Relations in an Expanding Company,* Yale University Labor and Management Center, 1948.

CHAPTER 8

THE FUNCTION OF MANAGEMENT

E. WIGHT BAKKE

Sterling Professor of Economics, Yale University

The first and most important function of management is to think. Thinking produces the objectives for action. Thinking produces the policies which are supposed to govern action in the interest of achieving those objectives. Thinking produces the basic ideas and attitudes which become the guide lines and measuring rods for policies. Thinking produces the standards, the expectancies, and the fears by reference to which performance is evaluated.

If this managerial function is well performed, the techniques managers use have some chance of achieving their objectives. If this function is poorly performed, success of the techniques must depend on luck and not on sound analysis, plans, and administration.

In no field of operations is this more true than in the management of the men upon whom managers must ultimately depend for carrying out the operational plans and decisions that they make. Behind every decision managers make about the organization and relations of men at work, in other words, behind their decisions about "human relations" in their plants, are major premises, ideas, and basic attitudes which suggest to them the kinds of policies, decisions, and actions which are appropriate in the face of a given problem. These are the working assumptions on which action is based.

It is my conviction, which I share with a large number of managers whose paths have crossed mine, that the foundation function upon which all others rest is the maintenance of the quality of these assumptions which guide their activity. It is not that the other functions are unimportant, or "will take care of themselves." It is simply that managing by and of human beings is, in the first instance, a "thinking" job.

It is for this reason that I have chosen to discuss the "human relations" function of management in terms of the basic premises, ideas, and attitudes, that is the assumptions, which I have observed many managers using in Europe and America as a foundation for their decisions and actions in this area.

The assumptions which are of particular importance can be classified into seven groups. They are assumptions concerning:

1. What human relations policy and practice really mean.
2. The basis for human motivation and morale.
3. The nature of organization.
4. The relation between technical, organizational, and human factors.
5. The role of others than policy and decision makers in the problem-solving process.
6. The possibilities and dangers of extended participation of subordinates in administrative functions.
7. The beyond-the-plant significance of human relations practices in business and industry.

The generalizations made in this chapter concerning these assumptions are based on observations made since the War in seven European countries[1] and in America. Although these observations were extensive I cannot claim that the "sample" was adequate, and even when it is implied that an idea is "widely held", this should not be taken as implying "universal", "typical", or even "average". Moreover, while comments on or criticism of these assumptions have been suggested by research I have done or am acquainted with, they have also been made by some managers in these countries, indeed by some in *all* the countries visited. It is thus desirable to make it absolutely clear that the generalizations in this chapter are presented not as a criticism *of* managers but as a basis for self-examination and evaluation *by* managers of their own concepts and as a basis for thinking about whether their own ideas are an adequate basis for their practice in the field of human relations.

The Meaning of Human Relations Policy and Practice

What strikes me, as I think back over these post-war experiences and over 25 years of research and consultation, is the futility of discussing management's function in the field of human relations until we come to a better and more common concept of what the "field" of activity is with which the "function" concerns itself. The character of the practice must inevitably be adapted to the concept of the character of the field and the consequent nature of the problems the practice must solve.

It is possible that every idea expressed about the "field" is an important and useful ingredient in the total concept, and that the ideas are inadequate only because they are not related to, and integrated with, each other. But the variety of ideas about the field is a bit overwhelming to one who would try to define a clear-cut and practical managerial function related to human relations. Here, for example, are some of them:

1. Managing like a human being, a man with a heart.
2. Following Christian principles, especially the Golden Rule.
3. Having respect for the dignity of man.
4. Applying in industry the principles of political democracy.
5. Using diplomacy instead of authority to get people to do what you want them to do.
6. Using the psychological approach.
7. Decentralization of authority and responsibility.
8. Two-way communications.
9. Setting up good working conditions and security-and-happiness-producing facilities and benefits both inside and outside the plant.
10. Developing mutual confidence, trust, and loyalty.

I have no doubt that all of these ideas are related to the practice of human relations, and that, if sincerely and intelligently applied, they could produce better human relations. But what *is* "human relations"; what is the THING to which these methods are related? What are the "better human relations" which these methods are to produce? For notice they are *methods* for reaching a goal, not the goal itself. It is no more possible to define the *goal* of better human relations by reference to techniques, than to define "health" as the employment of the best modern methods of medical practice and personal hygiene.

Let me present a concept of human relations for which I have found support from some of the most thoughtful of managers in Europe and America.

The basic and central ingredient in this concept is that the *focus and objective of management's function in the area of human relations is* PRODUCTIVE WORK. It is upon the results of productive work that the economic position and contribution to the community of the firm rest. It is not enough to produce light hearts and happy faces. Without productive work the shutters must soon be put up. It is in doing productive work that the employees of the firm at all levels must find the main source of personal development and satisfaction. This does not mean that there are not other factors that make or break a firm, or that contribute to or subtract from the growth and sense of wellbeing of employees. It is simply that productive work is the heart of the matter, the *sine qua non* which impinges on the functions of every last member of the team, executives, middle management, foremen, workers, and trade union officers and stewards.

The next ingredient in this concept is that PEOPLE *are the most important resource* for organizing and doing this productive work. Even in the most automatically mechanized of factories or offices, it is the decisions and behavior of people which weave the other basic resources of materials, money, and machines, of ideas, and of nature together into a productively working whole. Even a manager completely lacking in humanitarian concerns and tendencies (I have never known one) neglects at his peril the fact that people are his most essential and important productive resource.

The third ingredient in this concept is that *people require* MOTIVATION *to do productive work for other people and institutions.* They may have to be motivated to do productive work for themselves also. But there is no question about the work they do which produces products or services that were someone else's idea, from the sale and distribution of which someone else or some institution gets the proceeds and then decides how much of the proceeds or credit employees get for their contributing effort. Motivation is required.

The fourth ingredient in this concept is that *the primary determinant of motivation is the degree of opportunity offered to people for* SELF-ACTUALIZATION AND REALIZATION both in doing the productive work, in their relations with the other people with whom they are associated in the doing, and in the receipt of other rewards which they consider consistent with the effort expended.

It should be obvious that the productive work assigned to an individual in a particular company, the relationships with his colleagues there, and the rewards he gets for his work from that company are not the sole resources he has at his disposal for self-realization. It is not intended to suggest that a company assume the whole load. Indeed the emphasis at this point is not upon the "obligation imposed upon" but upon the "opportunity offered to", a company in view of this basic interest in and drive toward self-realization on the part of all its people. At this point we begin to approach the fundamental idea which suggests the character of the practices necessary in order to produce the THING we are interested in, better human relations.

The fifth ingredient in this concept is that the INTERESTS OF THE COMPANY, AS WELL AS OF THE INDIVIDUAL, *must be served by organizational arrangements designed to give the maximum possible opportunity for significant participation and self-expression to the individual.* The individual, of course, benefits from the greater opportunity for self-development through productive work and the heightened faith in himself which comes from involvement in significant affairs. The company gains from the application of a wider range of the capacities of its personnel to the productive work and from the motivational power of the experience of a larger degree of self-realization.

The remaining sections of this chapter discuss ideas which are basic to the implementation of this point. We can well stress at the very beginning, however, that no practice of human relations which benefitted *either* the company *or* the individual at the expense of the other, would meet the standards of the concept we are here developing. The objective of any sound human relations practice is the *simultaneous and mutual advancement of the basic welfare of both the company and the individual.*

The final ingredient in this concept is *that motivation becomes negative unless it is based on* MUTUAL RESPECT *of the motivator and the one motivated for each other.* Any indication that "motivation" is in reality "manipulation" will reverse the intended effects. There is also a good deal of evidence to support the probability that the manager who tries to motivate individuals in ways which are "unjust" to the firm's interests or which discriminate unfairly on a personal basis among individual members of the work group loses the respect even of the individuals he attempts to motivate. Loss of respect weakens his power to motivate.

We may now draw together these ingredients and relate them to a definition of human relations practice and policy which will be assumed in the sections which follow. When used in this chapter, the phrase "human relations policy and practice" will mean:

The policy and practice of a company designed to *integrate* the objectives, needs, interests, and activities of the people at all levels in the organization, *both as agents for the company and as persons.*

Specifically this means the policy and practice of the agents of the company designed:

1. To contribute to the development and maintenance among people, at all levels, of *relationships at work* which are useful and satisfying both to the company and to the individuals involved.
2. To discover, develop, and give greater opportunity for expression to, *the capacities and talents of people* at all levels in the company, toward the end that the needs both of the company and of the individuals concerned shall be met.
3. To supply the *facilities and rewards for work* to people at all levels in the company which they consider just and which the firm considers possible and appropriate in view of the effort expended in, and the contribution made through, productive work.

To put the matter more briefly: The policy and practice of human relations is concerned with the *integration* of the objectives and interests of the company and its people through the maintenance and development of:

1. Productive and satisfying relations at work.
2. Opportunity for self-realization through maximum development and utilization of human capacities.
3. Appropriate, possible, and just rewards for productive work.

The Basis for Human Motivation and Morale

One hears a good deal in Europe about the difference between the "old style" and the "new style" managers. The chief differentiation between the two would appear to be their methods for getting people to work, their ways of motivation. The old style are described as men who *imposed* their will on people, the new style as those who *elicit* or *encourage* the willingness of people to do what they, the managers, want them to do. The first depended on their *power to compel* performance, the second on their ability to develop a *morale* which leads to performance.

I have never met in my travels any managers who admitted to being of the "old" school. Every one associated himself with the "new" school and emphasized the necessity under present day conditions (such as full employment and the improved economic, educational, and social status of everyone except those in the top-tax brackets) of understanding the "secrets" of motivation and morale. But their explanation of these secrets sounded very much like those which I suspect were made by the "old" style managers, with one exception. The exception is that today's managers appear to believe that diplomacy is a more successful method than a display of authority.

Three examples of "secrets" of this sort can be named. First, motivation and morale are primarily matters of how much a man is paid and the economic security provided him by the person or firm for which he works. Second, motivation and morale are primarily the product of the success or failure of people as individuals. Third, motivation and morale are produced primarily by what a company does to or for its people.

I doubt if anyone with experience in managing other people and their activities would quarrel with these assumptions as indicators of important factors which are at the root of the degree of motivation and morale one can create in people whose activities must be governed in the interests of a firm or a person for whom these people work. But the results of research and the experience of many managers raise some question as to whether paying exclusive attention to such factors is an adequate guide to the motivation and morale which lead to productive work.

Consider the matter of economic rewards. One cannot imagine that a company which failed to maintain a standard of wages and economic security for its employees equal to or better than those maintained by the majority of firms in the community would get very far in preserving the kinds of relations with employees that lead to satisfactorily productive work. Yet every survey and research conducted in order to find out what workers and management desire from their work discloses that workers rate wages as less important than a number of other psychological and social rewards of work.

One suspects that this would not have been true in 1900 when the bare struggle to provide a minimum of food, clothing and shelter occupied a worker, and many in management, during their working hours, which incidentally, were a large proportion of those they did not spend sleeping. But we are trying to motivate men, not in 1900, but in 1957. And the failure to take into account in the shop community, the newly emphasized cravings for recognition, social status, participation as a significant part of a group, the doing of meaningful work, equal and just treatment from superiors, etc., is a failure to consider factors of motivation, for the lack of which no differential wage above the "going" rate most firms can afford to pay is a compensation. Such producers of motivation and morale cannot be supplied from the payroll office. They are the accompaniments of organization and leadership directed toward creating satisfying jobs, job relations, and the opportunities for self-development and expression.

The assumption that men are motivated as individuals and that their morale is proportional to their individual success or failure is based on a volume of commonsense and experience, and on a mass of scientific evidence that cannot be gainsaid. But as interpreted by many managers, the assumption can lead to misdirected efforts. A series of research efforts in industrial and business organizations, since the famous Hawthorne experiments, has underscored the importance of the impact of *group* standards, compulsions, and associations on the individual's conception of himself. There is no conflict between reality and this assumption if it is kept in mind that the individual who is being motivated may identify himself with a group or groups, that he may picture himself, even predominantly, as a "group man," that he absorbs into his "individual" personality the norms and habits of the group, and that loyalty and service to the group's interests supplement, and at times may supplant, loyalty and service to what another might consider to be his "selfish" interests. It is more important to some people to be an accepted and significant member of "a winning team" than to succeed as an individual, especially if that success weakens the solidarity of, and their acceptance by, the team.

This sense that one is not merely an "individual" man but a "group" man is not a result of welfare state economics or of the influence of trade unions or of any so-called "cause" of the "decline of self-reliance." It is an inevitable product of experience which has rewarded mutual aid and group solidarity more than it has rewarded winning out over the other fellow as the way of gaining individual success and satisfaction.

As one looks up the occupational and social pyramid, he finds the number increasing who have been rewarded for "standing out from" rather than "standing in with" the group. It is to be expected that they, on the basis of successful attempts to stand out from and win out over their fellows, should consider that motivation consists of providing the individual with opportunities to do that. Their diagnosis is correct, as far as *their own* motivation is concerned.

The diagnosis breaks down, however, when applied universally to workers whose "wisdom of experience" leads to a different conclusion. The bewilderment of many employers is understandable when a worker with the opportunity to make twice as much on piece rates responds to that incentive system by pacing his production to a group-agreed-upon quota instead of earning "twice as much." So is his amazement when a worker prefers to remain at the bench instead of taking the "opportunity" to become a foreman. So is his appraisal of the worker as stupid who continues on strike and loses wages which he cannot possibly make up for years to come with the 10¢ increase in pay he is presumably striking for. But his bewilderment, amazement, and appraisal are based on the assumption that what motivates him, the employer, is "normal" and what motivates others is "abnormal."

These worker responses are no mystery to one who is aware of the importance of the maintenance of group status and group ties in the motivation and morale of workers.

The projection by a manager to subordinates of his own standards of personal success in calculating the basis for activities which motivate and build morale among these subordinates is bound to lead to disappointing results. The source of the disappointment lies, however, not in the stupidity or "irrationality" of his subordinates, but in the manager's failure to acquire, accept, and take realistic account of the facts with which motivating and morale building activities must deal. The role of the group, and of relationships to and identification with the group, as a factor in individual motivation and morale, is an essential ingredient in the assumptions management needs in order to operate wisely and effectively in the area of human relations.

The third assumption concerning motivation and morale also has a large grain of truth in it. Motivation and morale, it is said, are the product of what a company does *to* or *for* its employees.

Observing the reaction of workers over the years to employers who paid men as little as possible, who were apparently unconcerned about safety and work conditions, who provided men with no security beyond the day's pay, who made no provision for sickness, unemployment, old age, etc., many managers have said, "What kind of morale can you expect from that kind of treatment? A company has the responsibility to do more for its employees than to buy their labor when it can use it, and forget them the rest of the time. It has to have a program of human relations that gives men a security and source of satisfaction beyond the wages for a day's work."

Observing the reaction of workers to the autocratic boss, many managers have said, "What can you expect from the modern worker if you subject him only to compulsion and discipline? It's the old question of the donkey, the stick, and the carrot. You get more results from holding a carrot in front of a donkey than by applying a stick to his back. Why should human beings be different?"

The conception just outlined of the bases of motivation and morale lies behind the most common first response of managers in Europe and America to the question, "What can a company do to raise the morale of workers and their supervisors?" Here are the most frequent answers given by European managers.[2]

1. Better suggestion programs to tap the employees' suggestions for increased productivity.
2. More thorough training programs to make people more effective.
3. Better communication programs to communicate management's real feelings directly to the workers.
4. Better working conditions such as buildings, layout, lighting, etc.
5. Health facilities and benefits.
6. Social services, social workers, nursery school, etc. to help alleviate problems at home.
7. Clean and pleasant restaurants, locker rooms, washrooms, recreational rooms, etc.
8. Better wage systems.
9. Bonuses, profit sharing, loans, stock ownership, etc.
10. Adequate housing for employees.
11. Emphasis on reward rather than penalty.

An important addition to these ideas of what many managers think will improve human relations, and hence morale, is concerned with teaching supervisors and managers "how to treat people like human beings," "how to give orders and correct mistakes politely and with consideration," "how to create good tone in the shop," "how to be a friendly boss," "how to transform discipline into positive encouragement," etc.

It has not been infrequent in the past 25 years that men in America who have been appointed by companies to "clean up a bad human relations situation" have discussed their new job with me before they set to work. In almost every case they come with a proposed program, a major part of which consists of the introduction of such techniques as those named above. The agenda of management conferences in America, and the journals for managers, are plentifully supplied with articles on "How we improved human relations by introducing . . ." and then follows an account of a particular company's version of one or more of these techniques.

No one can consider this list of ideas concerning human relations practices without recognizing that they grow from an increasing and genuine sense of responsibility felt by managers as to what a company should do *for* its employees or *to* its employees. Nor can the testimony of many managements who have tried such techniques be neglected, namely that such human relations practices have resulted in heightened motivation and morale, that they have "paid off" in more peaceful relations and "a good attitude" among the employees.

It is not my purpose to discount either the importance or effectiveness of such practices. But there is growing evidence both from research and the testimony of thoughtful managers that these things are not *the* causes of high motivation and morale, and that under certain circumstances they may actually be negative influences. The evidence appears to suggest that motivation and morale hinge first of all on *what the company does with its employees* and *what the employee is in a position to do for himself*, not on *what the company does for him*. Or perhaps it would be better to say that what the company does to or for the worker acts positively to produce motivation and morale to the extent that what the employee can do with the company and for himself provides satisfactory possibilities for self-realization.

Let me pose several questions about the introduction and administration of these techniques which will indicate what is meant by the difference between what a company does *to* or *for* its employees at all levels on the one hand, and what it does *with* the employees and what these employees do *for* themselves, on the other.

1. Were the techniques introduced at the suggestion of employees themselves, as well as on the initiative of higher management?

2. Do these techniques constitute what the employees think is most important in order that they may have improved chances for self-realization in connection with their work and associations in the plant, or do they consider these things substitutes for other arrangements which, in their experience, are more fundamental?

3. Have the employees, who presumably benefit from these techniques, a significant voice in planning and administering them?

4. Are these techniques, which are mostly outside the work process experience, even if planned and administered as suggested, accompanied by the opportunity for employees to help plan and control the work process itself to the full extent that this can be permitted in view of the need for centralized coordination and control of performance of particular jobs in the work process?

5. Are these techniques merely a supplement to a basic management policy of employee participation, one which makes use of mental as well as physical and technical skills of employees, or are they considered by the employees, along with wages, as the price top management is willing to pay employees for submitting without question to complete exclusion from any kind of action, except doing what they are told to do?

6. Are these techniques considered by top managements as "gifts" out of *their* generosity and based on *their* conception of what is good for the employees and for which the employees should be grateful, or are they considered facilities made possible by the proceeds from the productive work of *all* participants in the operation of the organization?

These are serious questions. They do not raise doubts about the value of the techniques themselves. They merely suggest that as related to the requirements for motivation and high morale, techniques are not likely to be effective unless introduced and administered on the principle that they meet the *mutual needs* of employees and top management, that they are the products of, and made possible by, the *mutual efforts* of all concerned, and that they are *expressions of a sincere and basic managerial philosophy and responsibility which gives increasing emphasis to self-development and realization of all partners in the enterprise.*

THE NATURE OF ORGANIZATION

It is self-evident that all human contacts within a company take place within a framework of organization. Even the narrowest concept of human relations, that of the relations of one employee to another, implies that the behavior which brings them into contact is consistent or inconsistent with an overall system of organized activities which constitutes the productive work process of a company. One does not talk long with managers or other employees about problems of human contacts in a company without realizing that the nature and quality of these problems is always to some degree dependent on the way the activities of people are organized. The department chiefs don't cooperate; each thinks of his department as a kingdom unto itself. People disagree as to where their authority leaves off and the other fellow's begins. One man is angry because his work is held up until another man does his job. People are dissatisfied because they don't receive information about what others are doing which is of major importance to what they are doing. The foreman is frustrated because his subordinate goes directly to higher authority to get a problem settled. People who have complaints to make never get a positive and quick answer. People don't follow orders or don't get work done on time. Two foremen are always quarrelling over the use of a particular crane or other equipment.

Such problems may be rooted in factors which stem from either or both words in the phrase "human relations." They may arise from the fact that the *human* units, that is the people, lack qualities needed. Or they may arise from the fact that the *relations* are so organized that the most capable of persons could not carry on the contacts satisfactorily under such poor organizational arrangements. In most cases both types of factor are probably responsible. Our present concern is with the *organization* of relations between people, and with the concept of organization which guides most managers in working on that angle of the problem.

One gains the impression from talking with most managers about "organization" that their concept has two basic elements (a) the content of functions for persons holding a certain title, and (b) the person from which authority to carry out these functions is obtained and to whom the one possessing the function is accountable. In other words organization is conceived of as an *organization of functions into positions, and of lines of authority between the positions*. The resulting concept can be, and frequently is, diagrammed as the typical organizational chart thus:

Chart A. Organization of Function and Authority

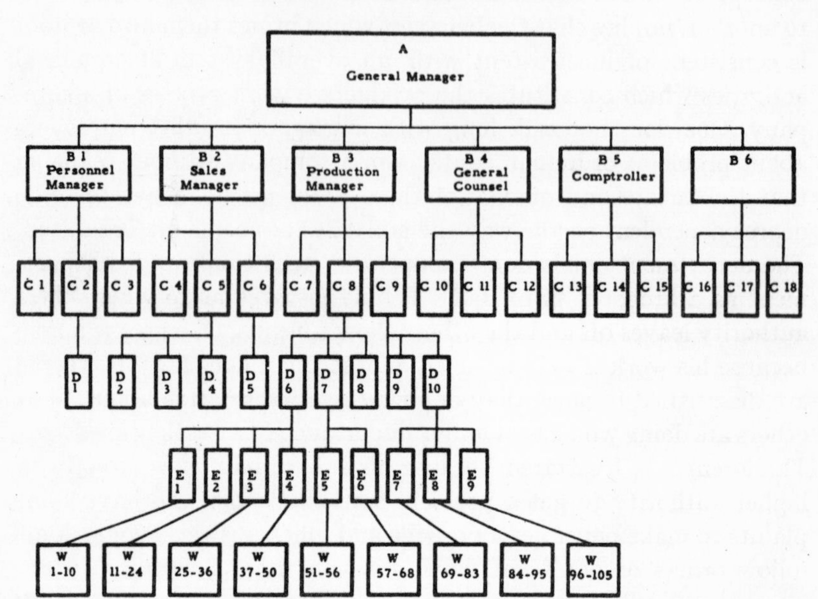

Frequently a supplement is added to such an organizational chart in the form of a set of functional specifications for each of the boxes or positions, thus: "B3 Production Manager. It shall be the function of the Production Manager to: a . . ., b . . ., c . . ., etc." These responsibilities are usually defined in very general terms, and each general responsibility is understood to contain a large number of specific tasks which could be represented as a^1, a^2, a^3, etc.

This concept of organization is certainly useful for solving many problems including a number which could be labelled "human relations" problems, such as conflicts over who is to do what and who is accountable to whom. It is a concept which stresses:

a. *Organization of the division of work* and
b. *Organization of authority to supervise and control work.*

Careful analysis of a large number of human relations problems indicates, however, the need for an additional ingredient in the concept, which can be labelled:

c. *Organization as the process of work*

if one is to have a framework representing organizational reality which is an adequate tool for diagnosing the relevance of these problems to the functioning of the whole organization.

It is chiefly in connection with contacts arising from the organization of the *process of work* that human relations problems occur. A chart representing this concept of organization would picture each major step or task performed, let us say, from the time an order was obtained from a customer to the time the payment for the order was deposited in the company's bank. Each box in such a diagram would contain the number of the position performing a task and a symbol indicating the major task in that position's function which has to be performed before the next step in the work process can be performed by someone else. Work processes carried on by people in one department, say personnel or legal, would "feed in" at various steps into the process being carried on by people in another department, say production. The process, as carried on primarily by people in one department, includes steps performed by people from other departments as well, steps which *must* be taken by the latter before those in the first department can continue with their work. Along the path of the process people of different status levels find themselves related to each other, following each other, and performing a task to which that performed by the person of a different (either higher *or* lower) status level is a necessary prelude. Some steps, a staff conference, for example, involve participation of several people in making a common decision.

A section of such an organization of work process might, for example, look like the diagram below. The top symbol in each box indicates the position whose task is involved, and the bottom symbol indicates the particular task in the function of that position which is being performed.

It may be objected that such a concept of organization as the process of work is very complicated. To this objection there are several answers.

a. The concept, and the chart representing it, is no more complicated than reality itself. Indeed, it reflects reality if carefully drawn.

b. It is less complicating to have an accurate picture or map of an involved number of tasks which must be coordinated in order to achieve productive work than not to have such a picture or map.

c. It is this reality of the successive steps in the work process, and the human contacts essential to performing them, which participants in a company experience. It is from that experience that most problems in human relations arise. The concept of organization used to diagnose such problems arising from experience must be consistent with that experience.

d. The chart is no more complicated than charts representing the dynamic processes of the human body which a doctor must master in order to deal adequately with the human "organization."

Chart B. Portion of Organization as Process of Work

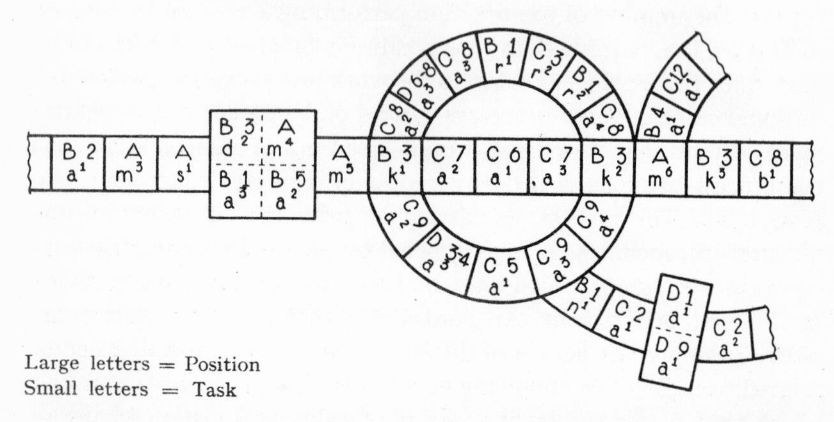

Large letters = Position
Small letters = Task

It is desirable to recognize that the traditional simple concepts of organization (and the rough sketches* representing the concepts) may betray us into thinking that the administration of the human relations within an organization is simpler than it really is. Simplicity in a concept is an advantage only if it reflects reality. The concept of human relations we discussed above focuses the function of management on the relations of people in productive work, and on the realization both of company and individual objectives through cooperation in productive work. Decisions about carrying on that function are poorly served by a concept of organization which does not have as its essential ingredient *the organized process of the productive work itself.* That process is what an organization is all about, its reason for being. The other aspects of organized activities, like communications, direction and supervision, paying and disciplining people, training, maintenance of plant, keeping records, etc., are merely helper activities to this fundamental one.

* For instance, see Chart A.

All of them, including the definition and allocation of positions and functions and the establishing and maintaining of lines of accountability and authority, have as their only legitimate objective the *servicing* of that flow of productive work, and the maintaining of the kinds of human relations in the performance of that work which get the job done.

It should be clear, therefore, that the essential ingredient of a basic concept of organization which can be used to isolate accurately the organizational factors in human relations problems must be an accurate and comprehensive diagram of the successive and interrelated steps in the flow of work. The importance of this basic ingredient will become clearer in the discussion of the next assumption which lies behind many so-called human relations practices.

Relation of Technical, Organizational, and Human Factors

The quality of human relations is affected, most managers would agree, by a wide range of factors. It is, of course, affected by the kind of people who must work together, their ability to get along with their fellows, their attitudes towards work, the company, and each other. It is affected by the division of labor, responsibilities, and authority, and by the arrangements for cooperative effort, and by the planning of all operations which are carried out. It is affected by the physical conditions of work, the plant layout, the nature of the technical equipment, and the technical processes with which people must associate themselves. Human, organizational, and technical factors are all involved. The assumption made by management discussed in this section is *not*, therefore, "Only human weaknesses lie at the root of human relations problems." We do not find among managers any lack of intellectual acceptance of the generalization, "Human *and* organizational *and* technical factors, all are involved in producing human relations problems."

Nevertheless when one contemplates what management *does* about these factors in most companies, it is difficult to escape the conclusion that they *assume* these factors to operate in isolation from each other instead of in a state of mutual interdependence. There is a tendency, for instance, to turn over to internal or external organizational "specialists" the problems of reorganization. There is a tendency to count on the industrial or rationalization "engineer" to propose and carry through technological improvements. There is a tendency to turn over to the "personnel man" the human problems in plant operations.

I have attended company conferences in which these specialists proposed changes in their special "fields", and have listened to the evaluation and decision-making of management with respect to these proposals. I have read articles in trade journals about the problems in each of these "fields", by both specialists and general management. I have attended conferences on problems in these fields. I have attended management training courses in which these individual fields were the topic of discussion. On occasion the possible consequences of a change, say in the field of rationalization, for the character of organizational arrangements or for the morale of and cooperation among workers, foremen, and engineers were mentioned. But this seldom led to any serious attempt to modify the nature of the rationalization proposals in order to avoid the possible consequences for the other areas of managerial concern. The same can be said for proposals with respect to reorganization and its impact on the technological and human interests involved; or about proposals for personnel practices and their impact on, or consistency with, the organizational and technological structure and needs of the company. The assumption appeared to be that these separate fields of endeavor could be carried on by reference to "principles of operation" which were germane only to the field itself. The assumption appeared to be that the "life principle" of a company's total activities consisted of a *summation* of principles of separate and distinct aspects of the company's activities.

On the basis of research with which I am familiar, it would appear that this assumption inadequately reflects reality, and that the word *summation* ought to be changed to *interdependence and integration.*

It is not necessary to refer to research, however, to recognize that the totality of factors characterizing the arrangements for, the instruments and personnel for, and the doing of, productive work are so closely tied together in a steady state of interdependence, that a modification, of whatever nature, in any of these areas starts a *chain reaction* which spreads throughout all the areas. The wisdom of experience of any observant and thoughtful manager will bring him to the same conclusion. It only is necessary to make this assumption the *working assumption* of managerial endeavor.

What would this mean in practice? It would mean that when a

development is planned in one area, say technology, the full range of factors, not only technical and engineering, but organizational and human, would be surveyed and analyzed for their probable effect on the development, and that dealing with these factors would be considered as an integral part of the technological development itself. It would mean that when a problem in reorganization of functions or departments was being considered, plans would be drawn not only in line with traditional concepts of "good organizational structure and administrative procedure," but in the light of the specific technological demands of this company, and of the particular kinds of personal and social circumstances characterizing the relations of people in this company. It would mean that personnel practices would be initiated and carried out not merely in accordance with the principles of individual and group psychology, but in the knowledge of the impact on human behavior of technological and organizational facilities and arrangements and the reciprocal impact of human attitudes and behavior on the effectiveness of these facilities and arrangements.

Beyond the internal activities of the company, this idea of the interdependence of the factors has significant implications for the type of university, business, and technical school education, and for the kind of on-the-job training which these "specialists" in these individual areas require.

The Role of Others than Policy and Decision Makers in The Problem-Solving Process

"Many human problems in carrying on productive work focus on the relations between those who manage and those who are managed. The art of management consists of getting others to want to do what you have decided you want them to do." Implicit in that statement from a European employer is a traditional assumption about the role of management which has a significant bearing on management's ability to establish effective human relations.

This assumption, widely held among managers in America and Europe, is as follows: Major problem-solving in an organization begins at the top when top management becomes aware of a problem. They then (1) study and analyze the factors involved; (2) determine the goals to be reached; (3) outline their policy; (4) decide what is to be done, in what way, at what time, and by whom; (5) mobilize the resources needed; (6) motivate those who are to do the tasks; and (7) coordinate, supervise, and control their work so that top management's policy and decisions are effectuated. That assumption certainly reflects what is normally done (and probably must be done) in order to carry through productive operations effectively. It implies that major problem-solving is done by those managers who make policy and decisions and then control the work of others (middle management, foremen, workers) in such a way that the policy and decisions are implemented as the top managers intended.

Without challenging this assumption as such, I would like to point out two ways in which others than the top management group *make* the *actual* policy and decisions which characterize a company's operations.

In the first place, the way the "implementers" perform their assigned tasks can modify (and even nullify) a formulated and announced policy or decision just as effectively as can top management before the policy or decision is formulated. It will be recognized, of course, that everyone involved in "making" and "implementing" a policy or in operating a decision participates in the problem-solving process. It is my point, however, that every one of these people participates in *making* the *effective decision* itself which goes on the company's record, that is, the decision the company has to live with.

Top management *decides*, let us say, to produce 100 units for delivery by May 10th. The people involved in implementing that decision produce only 80 units by May 20th in spite of all top management's efforts at motivation, coordination, supervision and control. Which is the real "company" decision, 100 units by May 10th, or 80 units by May 20th? And who made that decision? The correction implied in this point of view is that top management cannot *decide*; it can only "suggest and urge and try to enforce" what are really *proposals*. Company *decisions* are "made" by every participant in the operational processes set in motion by top management's proposals.

But this is not all. Unless top management is able to keep completely secret the problem it is working on, it is not the only body which is thinking about it. At the same time as the first four steps in problem-solving named above are being taken, subordinates are doing, informally, the same thing. Let us say it is common knowledge that the company faces a major need to carry out certain steps in rationalizing its equipment and methods. While top management is (1) carrying on its study and analysis, (2) determining what goals *of theirs* are involved, (3) getting more clearly in mind what *their* policy should be, and (4) deciding what *they* should do, others among middle management, foremen, and workers are going through the same steps with respect to the bearing of the problem on *their* interests. When top management, therefore, comes to step 5, that is, implementing *their* decision, which they have come to on the basis of *their* preparatory steps, they find that "decisions" of other participants in the company about who "ought to" do what, and how, have been made. It is possible that these parallel preparatory steps taken by all who are aware of the problem have led to decisions identical with those of top management as to what, where, when, how, and by whom something is to be done. Since all have proceeded, however, on the basis of different interests and with the help of different kinds of information, this happy identity is hardly to be expected.

To sum up, all involved in the implementation of a top management "decision" determine what the "company" version of that decision is going to be, that is participate effectively in *making* the actual company decision; and in any case they also carry out, on their own, the same steps preparatory to making a decision about what they would do if they were in command. It would, therefore, appear reasonable for top management, in making major decisions which affect the vital interests of their subordinates, to involve these subordinates, as much as possible, through genuine and effective consultation, in the steps preparatory to, as well as following, the actual decision.

"Consultative management" is no bed of roses and certainly no panacea for human relations problems between management and the managed. There are testimonies from managerial experience as to both successes and failures. But much evidence from psychological and social science research as well as from many outstanding practical experiments indicates that such a practice is based on a sound principle derived from the nature of human beings and their management in the doing of productive work.

The principle I have in mind is that self-realization in our culture is intimately bound up with the degree to which people are able to participate, under intelligent and rational leadership, and the degree to which they have an effective voice, in determining the rules and conditions under which, and the plans according to which, they live and work. Life and work within a company are no exceptions to the general rule. Self-realization is a realization of, and opportunity to give expression to, *all* of man's capacities including his thinking and planning and self-regulating abilities.

It is at this point that we come upon an assumption widely *acted on* by managers in America and Europe which is a major obstacle to experimentation in the area of consultative management. That assumption is that such mental activities as goal-setting, planning, coordination, self-motivation, and control in the solving of problems in industry are the appropriate function chiefly, if not exclusively, of those who occupy the higher positions in management. (I may add that most professors and scientists I know appear to make the same assumption if they think about the matter at all.)

This assumption, if used as a basis for practice, makes management disinclined to experiment with organizational arrangements which involve *all* employees in the processes, such as planning and administration, which would give men the opportunity to utilize the most human of human qualities, the ability to think. "You're not paid to think, just do what you are told" is an expression of this assumption which no manager I have met would admit to employing. But after talking with many of the foremen and workers who work for these managers, I am certain that these managers give their subordinates the impression that this is their attitude.

I know of no study of the human resources and relations in industry in America or the European countries I have visited which does not indicate such an assumption as extremely damaging to the establishing of effective human relations which are satisfying and rewarding alike to the participants in industrial enterprise and to the enterprise for which they work.

It is not necessary to deny that, on the whole, competition for and promotion to the higher managerial positions operates to bring to the top those best equipped with the mental capacities required by those positions, in order to question the adequacy of this assumption about who actually does, or should do, the thinking in an organization. The question I would raise has nothing to do with the relative degree of such capacities possessed by top managers, middle managers, foremen, and workers. The question I would raise is whether *all* positions, particularly those occupied by workers, foremen, and those on the lower levels of management, do not necessarily require a greater amount of goal-setting, planning, co-ordination, self-motivation and control, in other words, a greater mental activity, than is ordinarily supposed.

Such a question involves no assumption as to the "higher" or "lower" mental capacity of any one, whatever his place in the industrial hierarchy. It does imply that, in the productive work engaged in jointly by many people, there is *no* task performed by human beings which does not demand the peculiarly human processes of goal-setting, planning, coordination, self-motivation, and control from its performers, and hence the degree of mental abilities proportionate to that task.

Let us take, for example, the typical mental activity of planning. Whenever management can implement a decision by turning a task over to a machine *which that manager himself operates*, he can do all the "planning" for the machine. But if he turns the task of operating the machine over to another person, he cannot do all the "planning" for either the machine or that person. It is not seldom, as a matter of fact, that the thinking and planning of the one to whom the task is delegated is required to correct the inadequacy of the planning done and instructions given by the one who assigns the task. *And the sum total of all the planning done by every last individual engaged in a company's productive work is what constitutes the company's planning activities brought to bear upon the doing of the job the company is established to do.*

One could represent the fact that every participant in the company has planning to do, and at the same time that the scope of the planning is broader and more comprehensive as we go up the hierarchy of positions, by the following diagram in which the length of the line represents the scope of problems falling within the area of planning responsibility of those at several positional levels in the company.

————————————	General Manager's planning
——————————	Department Heads' ,,
————————	General Foremen's ,,
————	Foremen's ,,
—	Workers' ,,

Now if we connect the ends of the lines we have a figure which could represent a "wedge of planning" to be driven into the doing of a job associated with the company's operations thus:

Chart C. The Planning Wedge

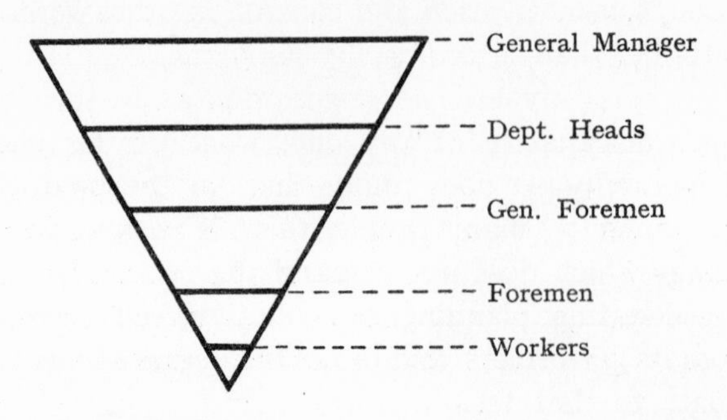

It is not only true that all individuals plan. It is also true that the plans they make and the circumstances, problems, and human tendencies which cause them to plan as they do are vital data for the planning activities of those above them in the supervisory hierarchy. As already indicated, it is frequently true that planning of "implementers" is necessary to correct, for practical implementation, the plans of the "planners." If then the assumption that the mental capacities required for planning are limited chiefly to those occupying the higher positions in management expresses itself in an organizational arrangement whereby the company "planners" include say only those at the general foreman's level and above, the consequences are clear. We have an organizational planning wedge to be driven into operating problems which lacks a point. It is a blunt instrument thus:

Chart D. Planning Wedge Without Foremen and Workers

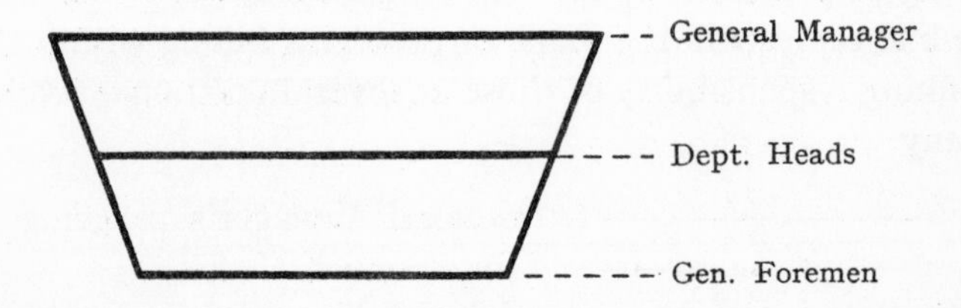

It requires only common sense mechanics to see that the amount of force or power that needs to be applied to the top of such a wedge will be proportional to the bluntness of the wedge; or to suggest that an alternative to the application of more force or power from above, is the sharpening of the wedge at the bottom.

The Possibilities and Dangers of Participation

We have already suggested that the interests both of individuals and of the company as a whole are served by an involvement of *all* concerned in the exploratory and planning stages in the solution of major operating problems. The possibility and probability that this is so can be illustrated by reference to a concept resulting from research in a number of going organizations which has occupied my attention for the past decade or so. I label that concept, "The Fusion Process." It is a model of the way in which the interests, objectives, needs, and behavior of the organization (in this case a company) and the individual are integrated or "fused."

The essential content of this model suggests that there are two processes taking place *simultaneously* whenever an organization and an individual are in contact with each other, the "socializing" and the "personalizing" processes.

By the socializing process is meant the efforts made by the formal agents of the organization and the informal groups of people in the organization to mould the individual, as it were, in the image of the organization and the group respectively, as an aid to the "self-realization" of the organization and the group. This is done by attempting to orient the individual toward the objectives and interests of the organization and the group and to influence him to "identify" himself with them. This is done by assigning to him a formal and informal position and expecting and requiring him to behave in the manner considered appropriate to these positions by the responsible leaders and planners of the organization and the group.

By the personalizing process is meant the efforts of the individual to mould the organization and group in his own image as an aid to *his* self-realization. This is done by his attempts to "orient" the agents of the formal organization and the members of the informal groups toward his own objectives and interests and to influence them to "identify" themselves with these. It is done by attempting to get these people to recognize and accept his personal standing and to behave in a way which gives him the chance to engage in the conduct he believes necessary for self-realization.

Since both these processes take place simultaneously, and since they involve behavior of persons directed toward each other, each trying to modify the behavior of the other, neither process is, or can be, completely successful. The actual result with which the formal organization and the informal group on the one hand, and the individual on the other, must live is the "fused" product of both processes.

The concept may be represented by the diagram below in which the triangles represent the scope and focus of *each* process and in which the overlapping parts of the triangles represent the actual fused product of *both* processes which determines the character of the human resource which is available to the organization.

Chart E. The Fusion Process

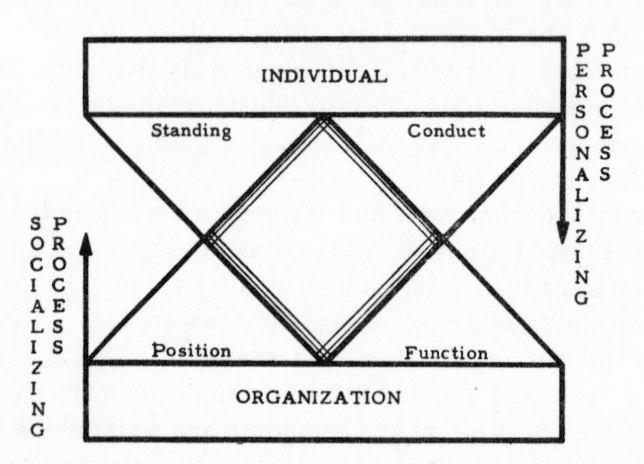

It should now be clear why the provision of organizational opportunities for self-realization on the part of the individual, that is to say opportunities for him to give maximum expression to basic human capacities such as thinking, planning, self-regulation, etc., is important not only to the individual but to the organization and group of which he is a member.

If, for instance, the formal organization attempts *solely* by stronger demands, more detailed and limited task assignment, more authoritarian order enforcement, and heavier discipline to strengthen the socializing process, the attempt is likely to erect stronger barriers to the self-realization efforts of the individual. The fused product, with which the company must live, then resembles the overlapping portions of the triangles as diagrammed below.

Likewise, if the individual attempts *solely* to strengthen the personalizing process by stronger insistence that his personal rights be recognized, that others conform to his ideas and behavior, and

Chart F. Fusion When Socializing Process is Dominant

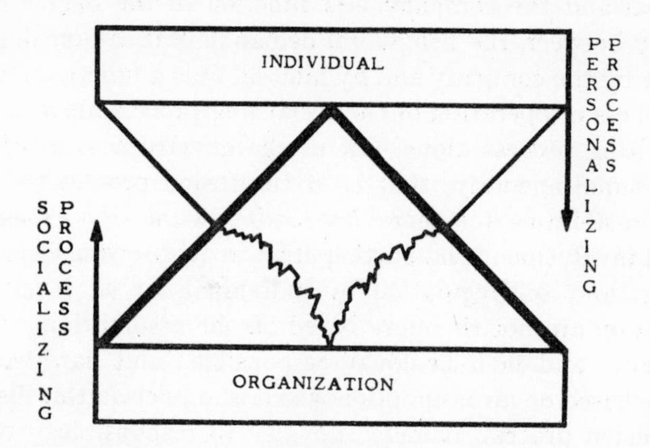

that the organization and its people put his interests always in the forefront and rely solely on his wisdom, the attempt is likely to erect stronger barriers to the "self-realization" of the company, that is, to the socializing process. In that case the fused product with which both the individual and the company must live resembles the overlapping portions of the triangles as diagrammed below.

Chart G. Fusion When Personalizing Process is Dominant

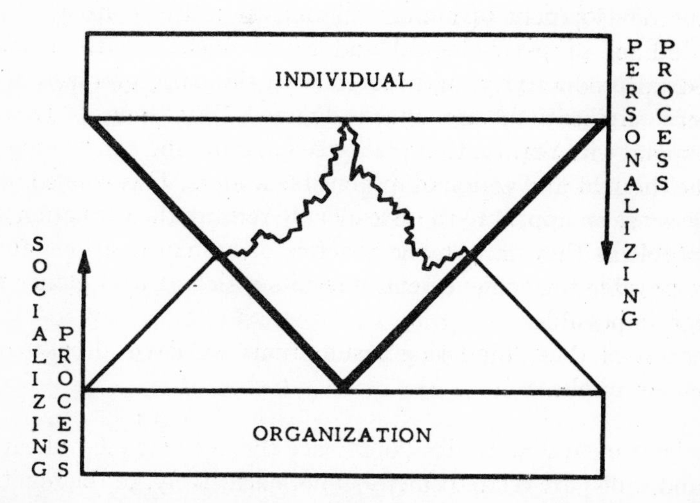

It is not merely the human individual's personality that suffers from such a one-way emphasis. The possibilities for the development of an effective human unit in the productive work of the organization is harmed also. The maximum benefit for *both* the individual and the company is a function of the degree of compatibility between the behavioral demands imposed on the individual *both* by the company and by himself. It is a function not of the effectiveness of operation of the socializing process alone, or of the personalizing process alone, but of the effectiveness of operation of both simultaneously, that is of the fusion process.[3]

The possibilities for more productive work in increased and enlarged involvement and participation in goal-setting exploration, planning, and self-regulation by individuals at *all* levels in the organization are not therefore based on the assumption, "be good to the guy, and he'll be loyal, responsible, and hard-working." They are based on an assumption which is implicit in this discussion of the fusion process, namely "Loyalty to, responsibility towards, and hard work for an organization, are in proportion to, and a by-product of, significant and self-realizing participation in the productive work of that organization."

What then is it that prevents companies in America and Europe from making wider and more imaginative experiments in ways of achieving this result? Limitations on space permit me merely to list the ideas and assumptions which raise obstacles to such experiments. These assumptions may correspond to reality. If they do, the hope for the development of human relations practices consistent with the findings of psychological and social science, with increased industrial productivity, and indeed with the basic premises of our western civilization, are much dimmed. But even if they do correspond with reality, that reality is dynamic, and can be modified by the thought and action of responsible leaders. This whole book is in one sense an appeal to those leaders to rethink their functions and the problems they face in the practice of human relations and to make possible the achievement of results which at first glance may appear impossible.

Certain of these hindering assumptions we have already mentioned or implied:

1. That mental activities (and hence the need for mental capacities and skills) are related chiefly, if not exclusively, to the functions of those who occupy the higher positions in management.

2. That those below the person making the judgment are almost exclusively interested in the pay check which they then can spend

in self-realization pursuits when they are *finished* with their work.

3. That the lower in the hierarchy of positions in a company one goes, the more inclined are the occupants of those positions to want someone else to plan for them and tell them what to do, or at least to be satisfied with that arrangement.

Beyond these assumptions are those that represent very genuine anxieties of management about the dangers to be encountered if they were to increase and expand the participation of people at all levels in the thinking, planning, and regulating operations of the company:

1. That any move in this direction is a move toward anarchy.

2. That such moves imperil the degree of authority needed by management in order to meet their responsibilities, and incidentally experience "self-realization" for themselves.

3. That such moves will undermine discipline.

4. That trade unions will "take advantage" of such moves to increase their encroachment on affairs which are the appropriate sole concern of management. This is a particularly vivid fear in countries in which the Communist influence in the labor movement is strong.

5. That such moves, in some intangible fashion, strengthen the social democratic political forces with which a substantial number of managers find themselves out of sympathy and a regulating instrument which they would prefer to see weakened.

Both groups of assumptions undoubtedly influence the behavior of management, whatever their degree of approximation to a real state of affairs. The assumptions themselves, as well as any degree of reality at their root, are serious obstacles to the development of better human relations in industry.

The stakes involved in that development, however, are so high for individuals, for companies, and for the whole economy and society, that the assumptions offer a challenge and an opportunity to industrial leadership rather than a fixed and binding set of restrictions on thought and action. Nothing is so fixed and eternal in the area of human relationships that it cannot be more completely and accurately understood, that it cannot be modified by intelligent and purposeful action of imaginative, inventive, and skillful people.

Conception of the Wider Significance of Human Relations

The final assumption widely held among managers in Europe and America is pregnant with hope for the future. It is the conviction that no company lives unto itself and that what is done about human relations in the plant has a vital significance for the triumph or defeat of democratic ideals and faith in the larger society. A part of this conviction is tinged with anxiety, as we have already seen in the section above. But beyond these anxieties are insights of a most positive nature. There is a widespread recognition that the life within industry and business must ultimately be consistent with and strengthen the ideals and faith upon which the whole way of life of our western world rests, the ideals of maximum possible development of, and freedom of self-determination for, all individuals; the faith that that nation is strongest which puts its trust in the wisdom, inventiveness, and energy of *all* its people. There is a clear awareness that the eight hours a day spent at productive work produce expectancies, abilities, habits and values in people which must inevitably find expression in, and make their impact felt in, the relations men have in the larger community. There is a widespread understanding of the fact that in a business and industrial civilization the pattern of life within business and industrial organizations sets the tone and determines to a large extent the pattern of life of the whole civilization.

The degree of certainty and conviction with which these assumptions are held varies, of course. But they are seldom lacking among the influential ideas by reference to which managers in Europe and America chart their present course and formulate their conception of their role and try to understand the nature of the responsibility for leadership which rests upon them. The deepening and the broadening of these convictions can but strengthen the sound foundations upon which rests the function of management in the development of more satisfying and productive human relations among all the participants in industrial and business life.

Summary

We have been concerned in this chapter on management's human relations function, not with the evaluation of techniques, but with the discussion of ideas and assumptions on the basis of which management itself may evaluate techniques it employs in carrying out its function. It may be useful, in conclusion, to bring together pairs of these assumptions in two parallel columns. In the left-hand column are those which, in my judgment, provide an inadequate foundation for the improvement of human relations practice. In the right-hand column is a corresponding assumption which I believe to be more adequate. Assumptions in both columns, however, are held and stoutly defended by successful and thoughtful managers in both America and Europe. The lists are presented, therefore, in order that each manager may be stimulated to clarify his own ideas about the subject and compare the results of his thinking with the conclusions reached by other managers.

1. Human relations policy and practice is concerned with devices which compensate the employees for the frustrations and burdens inevitably associated with the doing of productive work with and for other people.	1. Human relations policy and practice is concerned primarily with the organization of work and the relations among people doing it in such a way that the work and relations themselves are productive and satisfying and the main foundation for self-realization on the part of both the employee and the company.
2. Motivation and morale are a function of the adequacy and justice of economic rewards and security provided for the employee.	2. Motivation and morale are a function of the degree to which the economic, social and psychological rewards of productive work and relationships experienced in doing it are adequate to provide the employee with the experience of self-realization.
3. Motivation and morale are a function of the success of people as individuals in comparison with the achievement of their fellows, in other words, of the degree to which the individual *stands out from* the group.	3. Motivation and morale are a function of the degree to which one's individual success is consistent with the standards and welfare of the group, is accepted and respected by the members of the group, in other words, of the degree to which the individual *stands in with* the group.
4. Motivation and morale are a result of what a company, or its management, does *to* or *for* its employees.	4. Motivation and morale are a result of what a company or its management does *with* its employees, and of what they are enabled to do *for* themselves.
5. The basic ingredient in the concept of "organization" is the allocation made of functions to posi-	5. The basic ingredient in the concept or "organization" is the arrangement of successive steps in

tions and the lines of authority and accountability relating the persons occupying these positions to each other.	the flow of productive work. The allocation of functions and authority to positions is a helper process whose only legitimate objective is to *serve* the organization conceived of as the flow of productive work.
6. The technical, organizational, and human factors in productive work can be analyzed and dealt with by specialists by the use of engineering, administrative, and personnel principles of operation respectively, which are germane to the factors in each individual area.	6. The technical, organizational, and human factors in productive work are mutually interdependent so that a modification of one type of factor starts a chain reaction which ultimately makes its impact felt on factors in all areas. The factors cannot then be dealt with on the basis of principles of operation germane to one field alone.
7. Problem-solving in a company is carried on most effectively when higher management carries through the exploratory, analytical, and planning work, comes to a decision, and *then*, through purposeful and reasonable leadership, mobilizes, motivates, coordinates, and controls the "implementers" in doing the job. This arrangement is desired by and satisfactory to most people.	7. Problem-solving in a company is carried on most effectively when the "implementers" as well as higher management participate in the exploratory, analytical, and planning work to the extent of their abilities and then are self-motivated and controlled in implementing plans and reaching objectives they themselves have helped to formulate. This arrangement is desired by and is satisfactory to a substantial number of people.
8. The "planners" in a company are appropriately those at the general foreman level and above, and the planning activities *can be* effectively carried through by these people.	8. The "planners" in a company are in fact every single participant in the flow of productive work, the planning activities *are* carried through by all of them, and their activities are essential to the whole of the company's planning.
9. Decisions in a company are *made* by management and carried out by implementers.	9. Decisions in a company are *proposed* by management, and *made* by every one whose activity and work is involved in carrying out the proposals.
10. Self-realization for employees in the productive work and work relations of a company is a consequence of intelligent and rational leadership.	10. Self-realization for employees in a company, in our culture, is intimately associated with the degree to which people are able to participate, under intelligent and rational leadership, and have an effective voice, in determining the rules and conditions under which, and

	the plans according to which, they live and work.
11. The mental capacities required for planning, self-motivation and control are possessed chiefly, if not exclusively, by those occupying the higher positions in a company.	11. The mental capacities required for planning, self-motivation and control, with respect to the task assigned, are possessed by all participants in the productive work of a company.
12. The development of productive and loyal employees is proportional to the degree to which the company is able to get its people to identify their objectives, interests, needs, and behavior with the company's objectives, interests, needs, and behavior expectancies. In other words, it is proportional to the effectiveness of operation of the socializing process, the objective of which is "self-realization" for the company.	12. The development of productive and loyal employees is proportional to the degree of compatibility between the objectives, needs, and interests of, and the behavior demanded by the company *and* the individual employees. In other words, it is proportional to the effectiveness and integration of the simultaneous operation of the socializing and the personalizing process, or, more simply, the "fusion" process, the objective of which is the simultaneous self-realization of the company *and* its individual employees.
13. There are a number of dangerous consequences of the attempt to involve people at all levels in the company in planning, self-motivation and control, and in other processes through which a greater degree of self-realization is possible. Among these dangers may be named: that the authority and disciplinary powers of mangement may be undermined, and that trade union and political social democratic forces will take advantage of the situation to increase their encroachment on and regulation of the decisions and activities of management.	13. There are a number of difficulties incidental to the attempt to involve people at all levels in the company in planning, self-motivation and control. These difficulties are not dangers whose realization is inevitably assured, but challenges to managerial skill and thought. The obtaining of advantages while at the same time avoiding disadvantages is no new task for management. It is an essential ingredient in their function and experience.
14. The consequences of human relations practices in industry are of concern to the company involved and to its people.	14. The consequences of human relations practices in industry are of concern, not only to the company and its people, but to the community and the whole society.
15. The responsibility of managers is to manage in the best interests of those who obtain their income from the company, and of those who buy the company's goods or services.	15. The responsibility of managers is so to manage in the best interests of those who obtain their income, goods, or services from the company that the welfare of the whole society will be served.

References

1. These visits were made during the summer of 1954 as Advance Agent for European Productivity Angency, Project 178, "Diagnosis of Human Relations Policy and Practice". The purpose of the visits was to discuss with leaders in industry, labor, and research their ideas and problems in the area of human relations so that the program of the E. P. A. team, which was to follow, could be geared to the actual conditions in each oountry. The first question I asked was, "When you pick out a company which you say has 'good' and one which has 'bad' human relations, what are you thinking about which distinguishes one from the other?" For twelve months following, a team composed of Chris Argyris and A. B. Cummins held seminars with management, labor, educational, and research groups in these countries trying to help these leaders of thought and practice diagnose their human relations problems. I have kept closely in touch with their results. In the summer of 1955 I was acting as a consultant to three management training institutes in the field of human relations in Norway. Some of the conclusions set forth in this chapter were more briefly stated originally in a Report made to the Norwegian Productivity Institute in October 1955. The permission of the Institute to restate and elaborate those conclusions is gratefully acknowledged.

2. This statement is based on the work of Chris Argyris and A. B. Cummins in connection with E. P. A. Project 178.

3. A more elaborate discussion of the fusion process will be found in E. Wight Bakke, *The Fusion Process*, Yale Labor and Management Center, New Haven, Connecticut 1953.

INDEX